# Late Achievers

# LATE ACHIEVERS
## Famous People Who Succeeded Late in Life

Mary Ellen Snodgrass

1992
## LIBRARIES UNLIMITED, INC.
Englewood, Colorado

LIBRARIES UNLIMITED, INC.
P.O. Box 6633
Englewood, CO 80155-6633

---

**Library of Congress Cataloging-in-Publication Data**

Snodgrass, Mary Ellen.
    Late achievers : famous people who succeeded late in life / Mary
Ellen Snodgrass.
        x, 286p. 17x25cm.
    Includes bibliographical references.
    ISBN 0-87287-937-2
    1. Celebrities--Biography.  2. Middle aged persons--Biography.
3. Aged--Biography.  4. Biography--20th century.  5. Success.
I. Title.
CT120.S59  1992
920.02--dc20                                                      91-32136
                                                                      CIP

*For Della Coulter, my friend*

# Contents

# Introduction

Achievers, whatever the obstacle that holds them back, manage to find a way to surmount these obstacles. Some, like Grandma Moses and Colonel Sanders, wait a long time to start, then they keep moving ahead to the end of their days. Others, like Norman Cousins, Kurt Hahn, James Beard, Vaclav Havel, Cardinal Newman, Dr. Peter Mark Roget, and Ronald Reagan, know success early in life, but encounter reasons to adopt a different route later in their careers. A few, like Mary Kay Ash, Shirley Temple Black, and Wally Amos, have little choice but to try something new when their first choices turn sour.

Among the names in this lineup of forty late achievers are well-known people—Julia Child, Erma Bombeck, Colonel Sanders, Ethel Waters, and Dr. Albert Schweitzer. Some are famous in a particular sphere of interest: Jean Auel is known to readers of contemporary fiction, Madeleine Kunin to the citizens of Vermont, and Irene Hunt and Laura Ingalls Wilder to librarians and teachers of young readers. One, George Dempster, is recognized mainly through the name of his invention, the Dempster Dumpster. Likewise, Sam Walton's Wal-Mart is better-known than he is, and the ubiquitous Cliffs Notes are widely recognized, though founder Cliff Hillegass is not.

Not all achievers gain widespread acclaim. The names of a sprinkling, such as G. Gordon Liddy and Carry Nation, carry a distinctly negative ring. One, Bill Wilson, founder of Alcoholics Anonymous, deliberately chose the anonymity of Bill W. Similarly, Dr. Ruth Westheimer answers to the truncated name of Dr. Ruth. Another handful—Corrie ten Boom, John Newton, Clara Hale, Sarah Walker, and Dorothy Day—are scarcely recognizable to most people today.

In every case, the subjects in this work are people whose lives followed a late rising spiral. They took on new challenges in their thirties, their forties, even their sixties and seventies. Their good deeds and claims to fame cover a span of endeavors, from making a home for AIDS babies to creating wholesome soil, from writing about a childhood on the American prairie to election as president of Poland. For Sir Francis Chichester, achievement was the intensely personal challenge of sailing around the world; for Billy Sunday, it was saving souls; for L. Frank Baum, it was entertaining children with stories of a whimsical fictional land called Oz.

Whatever the success—teaching rescue methods, publishing study aids for classroom use, speaking on public radio, baking chocolate chip cookies, merchandising hamburgers, teaching business people how to protect their companies from industrial espionage, or encouraging American cooks to enjoy the recipes that their ancestors created—these people deserve study for their late achievements. From them, others can learn to apply faith, will, self-confidence, and perseverance. By examining the life of a middle-aged watchmaker who opened her home to persecuted Jews, women can take pride in a lone female's indomitable courage. By following the metamorphosis of a St. Louis washerwoman into the first African-American female millionaire, minorities can learn hope and belief in innate talents. And by studying the change of heart in a hedonistic English slaver, anyone can derive faith that human faults are correctable.

# Wally Amos

Success seems to fit Wally Amos as naturally as jeans, as comfortably as moccasins. Laid-back and loving his chocolate chip cookie business, he appears to have reached his stride. But, in truth, this is Amos's second climb toward financial security. The first time brought only frustration, unhappiness, and a false sense of self. To feel welcome at the top, he had to tumble to the bottom and accept a fair amount of bruises before he could appreciate success.

When he was young, Amos maintained unrealistic goals dependent on temporal, glitzy rewards, particularly alcohol, flashy clothes, popularity, and passing affairs with women. Then his house of cards collapsed, leaving him with a more attainable ambition and the skills and drive to cinch it. Following a series of career turn-arounds and two divorces, he found peace in his most recent incarnation, as "Famous Amos," cookie baker for the jet set.

## Hards Knocks and Ambition

Wallace Amos, Jr., son of Wallace, Sr., and Ruby Amos, was born July 1, 1936, at the tail end of the Depression when times were still tenuous. He grew up in a small two-room house in the black section of Tallahassee, Florida's state capital. His father worked as a laborer at a gas plant; his mother as a maid. From early childhood, Wally got little overt affection from his serious-minded parents, a fact which plagued his later relations with his own family. For spoiling he turned to his Grandma Hawkins. Her death during his childhood left him craving the love she provided—the kind with no strings attached.

Amos remembers his father, a poorly educated man, as distant, but concerned for his son's welfare. Known as "Mr. Wallace" to neighborhood children, he escorted Wally for monthly haircuts and was as good a parent as he was able. A tight-fisted and somewhat forbidding man, Wallace Amos shared little in common with his wife, but they agreed that their son had to be disciplined.

Like most southern children, Amos internalized two controlling strictures— courtesy and religion. Although both his parents ascribed to the work ethic as well as the belief that dancing and too much fun were sinful, it was Mama who applied the stick and enforced the rules. In later years Amos observed: "I don't think I would be the person I am today if she had not been so strict and so committed to [discipline]. I'm also certain that my daily adherence to Ruby's commands was responsible for my discovery that there is more than a little of Ruby Amos in me."[1]

Ruby and Wallace Amos steered their son toward a religious calling in hopes that he would one day be a preacher. For four years, Wally Amos walked the four miles to Lincoln Elementary-High School, where he displayed a talent for singing. Then, to improve on the opportunities offered to most blacks, he was enrolled in a parochial school nearer home where he got more attention and a better education.

A go-getter from the age of ten, he built a shoeshine box and opened his first business, later followed by a stint as carrier for the *Tallahassee Democrat*. Of his early life, Amos remembers his growing interest in business with pride: "I have always been an achiever. I've done well in all my jobs, whether I was shining shoes or baking cookies."[2] He also recalls the down side of ambition, the fact that he looked upon money as the sole proof of success.

## Life in the Big City

When divorce shattered the Amos family unit in 1948, Wally and his mother moved to Orlando, Florida. Within a month, the boy, armed with a box lunch and his shoeshine kit, moved again, this time boarding the *Silver Meteor* for Pennsylvania Station and his Aunt Della Bryant's one-bedroom apartment in the Washington Heights section of New York City, which she shared with Uncle Fred and Aunt Lillie. The move may have earned Amos a million dollars, for it was Aunt Della's cookies that inspired his chocolate chip cookie business.

At first, city life was a painful wrench from the familiarity of Tallahassee and southern ways. Amos was ridiculed for carrying his shoeshine box and later was bilked of his money by street thugs, once at knifepoint. His Aunt Della retrieved him from the police station, where she found him in tears, more from humiliation than fear. Meanwhile, at Edwin W. Stitt Junior High School he had accustomed himself to an integrated class with Jews, Orientals, Puerto Ricans, Italians, and Irish. And his progress with girls required more courage than it had back home in Tallahassee.

Still sparked by the entrepreneurial spirit, Amos tried several jobs. Shining shoes was a humbling task. Delivering newspapers, groceries, and blocks of ice was too difficult and paid too little. He briefly attempted to reestablish himself at his father's home in Tallahassee, until terse words from Ruby returned him promptly to Aunt Della. He enrolled in the New York City Food Trades Vocational High School with thoughts of becoming a cook. Later, Wally reunited with his mother, who moved north to Harlem with his Grandmother Julia and found a job as a live-in maid in Forest Hills, Long Island. The job was welcome for financial reasons, but worried Ruby because it parted her from Wally.

## On His Own

Amos found work at the Essex House Hotel. During on-the-job training, he learned how to manage foods. But without Ruby's firm hand, he wasted after-school time at Manny's Pool Room. Because of the school's racial favoritism toward whites, he became disillusioned and joined the Air Force in 1953 to earn a diploma and learn a trade all in one step. After basic training in Geneva, New York, Amos was shipped to Biloxi, Mississippi, where he studied radar and radio equipment in hopes of becoming a television repairman.

From Mississippi, Amos was sent to Honolulu. Before shipping out, he took a Greyhound home and rode through Mobile, Alabama. Reacquainting himself with the racist South, he abandoned his order at a station cafe rather than accept it at the back door, where non-whites were served. Yet, even though Amos rejected segregation and its attendant humiliation, he also spurned militance, which was becoming more common at that time.

## Becoming a Man

Honolulu brought good times and a sporty white convertible. But his immaturity surfaced frequently in the form of traffic tickets, a run-in with the Air Police, two court-martials, and a short stint in the stockade for refusing to observe his penalty. Another demon began to take hold during a temporary assignment to Guam. With time on his hands, little excitement, and easy money from gambling, Amos drank heavily.

Back in New York after his tour of duty, he poured himself into studies at the Collegiate Secretarial Institute, learning shorthand, typing, business law, English, accounting, banking, and bookkeeping. He left school without achieving a diploma so that he could move into a tempting position as stock clerk at Saks Fifth Avenue. On his own at last, he married Maria La Forey in 1958, moved in with Ruby, and fathered a son, Michael Anthony, the next year, followed by Gregory two years later. Soon he and Maria had their own apartment in the Bronx, and Wally was looking forward to a future as buyer for Saks.

Amos's rise reached a familiar stopping point—the glass ceiling, through which he could see advancement, but could not reach it. After a request for a $5.00 raise resulted in a turndown, he quit Saks. He tossed around the idea of working on a garbage truck, driving a cab, or selling insurance and securities, then in 1961 settled in as a secretary with the William Morris Agency. After only one year in their new music department, he rose to the position of agent for various rock and roll groups. For this feat he called himself the "Jackie Robinson of the theatrical agency business," after the first black pioneer to break into major league baseball.[3] Eventually he felt confident enough to freelance as a manager.

## The Career Treadmill

Because Amos was a driven, goal-oriented man, he began placing his family second to his job. Not surprisingly, his first marriage failed. Unfazed, he acted the playboy role for two years before marrying singer Shirlee Ellis in 1966. After the birth of his third son, Shawn, Amos headed for Los Angeles, intent on connecting with a West Coast star and boosting his prominence as manager. He joined John Levy's firm and immersed himself in the pretentious, shallow side of the Beverly Hills lifestyle. As part of his job, he made recording studios and night spots his evening and weekend haunts and continued chasing women, to the detriment of his second marriage, which ended the same way as the first.

Clients came and went without doing much for Amos's career. When his ambitions soured in its fourteenth year, he found himself in a pickle, out of cash, owing $1,250 in back taxes to Uncle Sam, and casting about for new clients. At this lull in his prospects, he gave up the dream: "I finally realized that the big star I was waiting for might never come. Or it could be ten years down the road, and I would have wasted ten years of my life."[4] To shore up his ego, he returned to Hawaii on vacation to enjoy some of the magic of his service days.

Back home in Los Angeles, he searched for leads to a new career. To stave off depression, he began baking cookies. Through a few top-secret recipe enhancements, he developed Aunt Della's original cookie into a unique flavor sensation. At the urging of a friend, Amos began searching for financing. Local banks and the Small Business Administration took no interest in his project, but Helen Reddy, Helen's husband, Herb Alpert, and Marvin Gaye liked his idea enough to invest. Friend B. J. Gilmore, who nicknamed him Famous Amos, provided the company name. Utilizing as much public hoopla as he could garner, he issued formal invitations, hired a parking attendant, and opened his first cookie store Sunday, March 9, 1975, on the corner of Formosa Avenue and Sunset Boulevard.

## A New Career

The prologue of Amos's autobiography, *The Famous Amos Story*, describes opening-day enthusiasm in typical California style: "Happy feet left their Rollses, VWs, Benzes, and Hondas in the care of young men in red jackets and then stormed the red carpet leading up to the entrance of the shop as though they had found the trail leading to Oz."[5] Guests entered, signed the guest register, and sampled the refreshments, consisting of champagne, milk, and cookies. To the sounds of a West Indian steel drum band, a Dixieland jazz group, and pulsing dancers, 2,500 customers responded to Wally's wish that they have a "very brown day." By closing time, Amos—bolstered with support from his mother and sons, ex-wife Shirlee, Los Angeles Mayor Tom Bradley, and his friend, Chuck Fly—knew he had a winner.

On the dedicatory page of his book, Amos paid tribute to the people who pushed him along toward the cookie-baking hall of fame. His mother merited top billing. Ruth Wakefield, of Whitman, Massachusetts, got credit as the American cook who founded the chocolate chip cookie. She is followed by Aunt Della, the woman who brought Wally and the cookie together. Finally he named Chuck Casell, a friend who helped launch the business.

What Amos omitted in the dedication were the numerous small details he had to work out before he could get rolling. Most serious was the escalation from baking for friends to baking for the masses. Then came the need for a 60-quart mixing bowl and restaurant-sized containers of pecans rather than dinky cans from the grocery store. At the suggestion of a veteran salesman, Amos made a wise move in buying only top-quality ingredients. From attention to these minor details came a premium cookie and a generous dollop of satisfaction.

## Wally Amos in Triumph

Praise rolled in from the quarter where Amos least expected it—satisfied chocolate chip cookie fans. And the world began beating a path to his door. News of his entrepreneurial achievement appeared in *Time, Forbes,* the *New York Times,* and other nationwide magazines and newspapers. He got wholesale orders from gourmet grocery stores, Macy's and Bloomingdale's. Outlets sprang up in Studio City, Tarzana, and Tucson. An old friend from Tallahassee began wholesaling tins of cookies by the case in Florida.

Using his considerable talents as a promotion specialist, Amos dressed in a brown jumpsuit embroidered on the back with a large cookie. He made deliveries in his yellow Volkswagen Rabbit, complete with oversized cookie on the hood. Other promotional items, such as T-shirts and posters, helped sell his wares. In no time, Amos had to arrange for an East Coast bakery to handle the New York-based orders. To dramatize the opening, he placed a cookie on a satin pillow, elevated it on a pedestal, and invited the press.

Problems cropped up, some requiring consultation. Amos, accustomed to flying by the seat of his pants, called in more experienced business heads. Once, he battled a zoning board for permission to operate a bakery. After tedious niggling, a councilman cut through the babble with a sensible statement: "Here's a man talking about bringing income into the community, employment, and a reputable name. He's even going to make the area smell good. What are we arguing about?"[6] With that build-up, Wally got the go-ahead to open his bakery.

## Growing into Success

On July 1, 1979, Wally Amos, after a long courtship, married his third wife, former TWA flight attendant and fabric painter Christine Harris. He moved his baking operation to Hawaii and settled into a life's work that suited him. His store, which produced an exclusively Hawaiian cookie laced with macadamia nuts, was a hit from the first day, with lines forming at the door for his renowned product. During this same period he rediscovered his former religious faith. No longer driven to reach beyond his grasp, he gave up frenetic ways and moved with the business flow.

Amos, in an introspective mood, commented on the irony of his search for excellence: "For years, I was trying to make things happen and suddenly, when I stopped trying to control everything, when all I wanted to do was make an excellent chocolate chip cookie and have some fun doing it, my whole life turned around."[7]

Located in Lanakai on the island of Oahu, Hawaii, in 1977, Amos enjoyed using all the skills he had gained over a lifetime. Because of his ties with Macy's, he participated in their Thanksgiving Day Parade, which brought the name Famous Amos into the homes of a nationwide television audience. After losing the Bloomingdale's account, he established an account with Neiman Marcus with outlets in Dallas, Houston, and Atlanta and did even better.

More money and more notoriety enabled Amos to indulge in outreach projects. He helped St. Elmo's Village, a ghetto of Los Angeles. He also took part in Macy's Christmas party for underprivileged children. Later, he participated in Black History Week at the Hollypark Library in Hawthorne, California, which impelled him toward involvement with Literacy Volunteers of America. Ultimately he was named national chairman of the effort to boost reading skills.

Wally Amos feels at home in the limelight. He described his new persona in positive terms: "I was also Famous Amos, the kazoo-blowing, happy-go-lucky greeter of the Friends of The Cookie, a role I enjoy playing. No matter how sophisticated the situation, people see me as *fun* and want to have fun with me."[8] He combined cooking and business skills with fourteen years in the talent management business to produce a genuine superstar—himself, baker of cookies.

## Notes

[1] Wally Amos. *The Famous Amos Story: The Face That Launched a Thousand Chips.* New York: Doubleday, 1983, 6.

[2] Carol Colman. *Late Bloomers.* New York: Macmillan, 1985, 55.

[3] Colman, 56.

[4] Colman, 57.

[5] Amos, 1.

[6] Amos, 157.

[7] Colman, 57-58.

[8] Amos, 166.

## Sources

Amos, Wally. *The Famous Amos Story: The Face That Launched a Thousand Chips.* New York: Doubleday, 1983.

Buchalter, Gail. "Happier Cookie," *Forbes*, March 10, 1986, 176-177.

Colman, Carol. *Late Bloomers.* New York: Macmillan, 1985.

"Famous Amos' Dynamite Double-Chocolate Desserts," *Redbook*, February 1989, 11-15.

"Turning Points in the Lives of Self-Made Millionaires," *Ebony*, May 1983, 53-55.

# Mary Kay Ash

Whipping adversity is a special talent. For Mary Kay Ash, once divorced and twice a widow, hard times came in 1963, when she was forced out of a thriving sales job by males envious of her success. Undaunted by bitterness and loss of esteem, she sat at the kitchen table and worked out her frustrations by outlining on yellow legal pads her view of the ideal company. Then the answer came to her. She could supplant her former job by starting her own beauty business.

Turning her list into a plan for the perfect direct sales firm, Mary Kay Ash launched Mary Kay Cosmetics, a model of American entrepreneurial achievement employing more high-salaried women than any other company in the United States. For these achievements she won the Horatio Alger Award in 1978 and the Gold Plate Award from the American Academy of Achievement in 1980. A recipient of the Cosmetic Career Woman of the Year and the Direct Selling Hall of Fame award, she is listed in *Who's Who of American Women*. In addition, in 1979 she was the subject of a "60 Minutes" profile and was named one of America's top corporate women by *Business Week*.

## "You Can Do It!"

Although coy about her age, Ash, a petite, jovial, conservatively dressed blonde, admits to having been born Mary Kathlyn Wagner in Hot Wells, Texas, the child of Edward Alexander and Lula Vember Hastings Wagner. From her early memories, she recalls having to tend her father, who suffered from tuberculosis. Her mother, sole breadwinner, managed a Houston restaurant, but manifested her belief that her seven-year-old daughter could succeed on her own. Through many personal sacrifices and a positive spirit, she bolstered Mary Kay into a frame of mind that never lost hold of the magic words, "You can do it!"

Mary Kay married a local radio star when she was seventeen. Because there was little money for college tuition, she attended the University of Houston, in hopes of establishing a medical career, only from 1942 to 1943. She juggled motherhood, Stanley parties, and studying, but found her multiple roles too exhausting. As her mother warned her, she couldn't chase two rabbits and catch either one. The saying proved prophetic.

An unforeseen snag forced Ash to jump in the driver's seat to direct her life. During his service in World War II, her husband left her to raise three children, a daughter, Marylyn, and two sons, Ben and Richard. Upon his return, he gave up on the marriage, abandoning his wife at a serious ebb in her life.

But Mary Kay's inborn pragmatism took over. She rejected any notion that a career ten or twelve years down the road was viable. In place of her medical dream, she substituted direct sales, for which she had a decided knack. Both before and after her husband left, from 1939 to 1952, she took a typical route for a woman with no education and sold Stanley Home products. To enlist her children's support, she involved them in filling orders, making deliveries, and sorting and counting the proceeds, which she poured out on the living room carpet.

## A Will to Compete

Quickly Mary Kay was infected with the competitive spirit and rose in the Stanley company. She served as manager of the company in Houston until a fireball female, Mary Crowley, recruited her to work for the World Gift Company, a home accessories firm in Dallas. For the next eleven years, she excelled as national director until interoffice rivalry forced her out in 1963.

At a low in her business career, Mary Kay established her own multi-million dollar cosmetic business, basing her storefront startup on $5,000, nine salespeople, and a single product—a skin lotion formulated by a Texas hide tanner whose tanning potions made hands soft. To cut expenses, she bottled the concoction in her own bathroom. The original label read "Beauty By Mary Kay."

## A Solution for Texas Skin Problems

The beginning of such a venture is appropriately set in the desert of the southwestern United States, where skin suffers the daily assaults of wind, dryness, and heat. Mary Kay, knowing the struggle of most women to find cosmetics to nurture damaged skin, decided to initiate her customers into a full campaign of cleaning, moisturizing, and making up the face. Her approach paid off. Women were eager to try something better than surface coloration. Not only was she selling beauty in a bottle—she was teaching the purchaser the rudiments of skin care.

During the development stages of her new business, Mary Kay's second husband, who superintended the firm, died of a heart attack. Mary Kay considered throwing in the towel, but against her accountant's and attorney's advice, opted to make the most of her investment. Despite limited skills and business training, she took her husband's place. She talked over the prospects with her children, then lured her twenty-year-old son Richard from his job at Prudential, offering him a considerable cut in pay to take the role of administrator.

At first, Mary Kay feared that she was expecting too much of so young a man. Then she reminded herself that God never fails to provide opportunity. With Richard's assistance and a loan from her other son Ben, Mary Kay opened on schedule—one month after her husband's funeral. Later, when Mary Kay Cosmetics appeared on the New York Stock Exchange, Richard was one of the youngest presidents of the companies listed there.

## Starting Out Small

From her first headquarters in a storefront in Dallas's Exchange Park, Mary Kay dispensed rapid facials, even drying the masque with an electric fan. She enticed customers by displaying and styling wigs, which were a popular gimmick in the mid-1960s. Gradually, she phased out her wig sales and zeroed in on cosmetics, which proved her best bet. In one month, sales rose by $20,000.

At the end of the first year, Mary Kay, along with her sons and daughter, had expanded to 200 on-site employees and had moved to new offices on Majesty Drive, enlarging their square footage from 500 to 5,000. Her sales force mushroomed to 100,000. The uniqueness of Mary Kay's acumen hinged on her worldwide recruitment of those thousands of saleswomen or "beauty consultants." They sold her products door-to-door, at parties and gatherings—wherever there were interested women. As Mary Kay words her objectives: "God first, family second, career third.... All my life, I've found that's a satisfying way to live. I don't understand how it works, but it does."[1]

A believer in Dr. Norman Vincent Peale's power of positive thinking and student of the organizational wizardry of evangelist Oral Roberts, Mary Kay touts no particular religious denomination, but she respects the role that God has played in her life. Her book, *Mary Kay on People Management*, claims that the Golden Rule works as effectively in the office as in any other aspect of life. Her nonthreatening brand of capitalism replaced profit and loss with another P and L: people and love. Her style in motivational gimmicks appeals to other business leaders, notably the president of J. C. Penney, who advised his managers to read her book.

## Faith in Women

Dismayed by "men only" favoritism and double-dealing in her early business years, Mary Kay supports economic equality for women and offers a business climate free from sex discrimination and the underhanded methods she ascribes to male-dominated organizations. She jokes, "The idea that 'You're in the wrong body' is for the birds."[2] At her annual conclaves, which dispense a mix of inspiration, training, motivation and recognition, she emphasizes looking on the bright side.

Membership in Mary Kay's work force, composed in the mid-1980s of more than 200,000 women with virtually no business training or experience, offers a chance at self-direction, a concept which appeals to housewives whose children are leaving the nest. Her devoted workers, who crowd the podium at her public appearances and photograph her while she gardens, often use her as a personal role model.

Mary Kay consultants, extending into twelve foreign countries, command around two percent of the cosmetic market. They respond to her mothering, even visit her home and deluge her with letters asking for advice about personal matters. "You would think I'm Ann Landers," she quipped.[3] To spur them on to greater sales, Mary Kay is known—and, at times, lampooned—for handing out pins, buttons, badges, jewelry, shopping sprees, fur coats, and pink Cadillacs as tokens of her appreciation for work well done. "I call the pink Cadillacs 'trophies on wheels'," she comments, "because if I gave them money as a reward, they'd just turn around and spend it on their families. That's the way women are. They're too practical."[4]

## The Mary Kay Reward System

One of her most famous symbols—a jeweled bumblebee pin based on one given to her by her husband—is Mary Kay's favorite representation of womanly strengths. In her biography, *Mary Kay*, she describes feminine toughness via the model of the flightless bumblebee, which is theoretically incapable of flying with its weak wings and heavy body. Mary Kay chortles that the bumblebee flies anyway because it isn't bothered by doubts. Women, she insists, feel the same way about obstacles.

Another motivator, similar to one she knew during her Stanley years, is the Golden Goblet Award. These goblets, followed by a tray and pitcher, serve as a carrot-and-stick incentive to reward women who thrill to a challenge and who love to be recognized for their accomplishments. In these contests, Mary Kay rewards all initiative rather than organizes contests in which a few win and the rest lose. Her instincts have proved her right.

Mary Kay also practices what she preaches about beauty. Never hesitating to make a joke at her own expense, she confesses that she used to go to bed looking like Elizabeth Taylor and wake up more like Charles de Gaulle. To please her husband, Mel, she began working at beauty with a twenty-seven minute makeup regimen each morning and evening. Her devotion to the ritual paid off by keeping Mary Kay younger-looking than women half her age.

## Putting Her Philosophy into Words

Part of Mary Kay's zingy, joyous approach to selling is her ability to develop catch phrases. From the beginning, she has taught representatives to sell cosmetics the same way they would eat an elephant—a bite at a time. Other one-liners such as "A friendly, productive environment begins with you" and "Let people know you appreciate them,"[5] helped her to impart her philosophy without tedious instructions. However trite and humble, these minuscule homilies, along with sensible advice about juggling busy schedules and, when finances allow it, hiring a housekeeper to make it all possible, quickly boosted her saleswomen toward individual achievement. Many topped their husbands' salaries and made it to her Millionaires' Club.

A satisfied workaholic and firecracker saleswoman in her own right, Mary Kay declares that women, who are not by nature self-starters, must learn to believe in themselves. Without making excuses, she acknowledges that some would-be beauty consultants "didn't realize the four-letter word W-O-R-K."[6] But the ones who develop a positive attitude never let her down.

## Mary Kay versus Feminists

To the dismay of feminists, Mary Kay maintains her belief in women's subservience to men. Even though she encourages women to battle for top billing in the sales department, she still maintains that women must return home, cook and clean, tend homefires, and bolster the male ego. She champions self-supporting women, but at heart never shrugs off the persona of hausfrau. To whip all dragons, the Mary Kay representative must compete in three arenas—wife, mother, and saleswoman.

To utilize femininity to the limit, Mary Kay encourages her staff to dress with extra care, emphasizes softness and traditional beauty, and encourages taste and grooming over assertiveness. Her faith in the dynamism of women, however, does not preclude a desire to make them more beautiful. She insists that the beauty treatments and cosmetics are beneficial: "If you make a woman pretty on the outside, suddenly she has more self-confidence and shine and more poise than she would have without that little lift that cosmetics give her."[7]

To the credit of her representatives, Mary Kay Cosmetics has found its way into Canada, Guam, Puerto Rico, Australia, Argentina and other countries. The appeal of her products and her approach also extends to many male converts and to the elderly as well. To spare them embarrassment in using skin care lotions from pink containers, Mary Kay designed Mr. K, a skin care line aimed at men.

## The Personal Touch

Part of the success of Mary Kay's personalized selling is its improvement on the way people buy facial care products. Rather than purchase untried cosmetics in a store, or worse, sit at a department store counter and be made up while people walk by and gawk, Mary Kay's customers receive a one-on-one tryout at home in natural light and with appropriate training. To top the home sales methods of Avon, her closest competitor, Mary Kay encourages her representatives to keep enough stock on hand to make the sale and deliver the goods on the spot.

Not all of Mary Kay's experiences have been positive. Doctors diagnosed her as suffering from rheumatoid arthritis. In 1980, she withdrew from work for seven weeks while her husband, Mel Ash, succumbed to cancer. She refused up to the end to be separated from him. After his death, with typical courage, she swallowed grief and appeared at a sales meeting, inspiring her devoted followers by her selflessness.

In 1985, Mary Kay Cosmetics went private after a buy-back worth $315 million; her younger son, Richard Rogers, assumed the role of president. Mary Kay's purpose in establishing herself more firmly at the helm was to free funds for greater recruitment incentives so that she can challenge Avon for the lead in the direct-sales cosmetics market. Her worth has been estimated at over $100 million. Still, she has no doubts that Mary Kay Cosmetics, just like Dupont Chemicals, will survive her eventual retirement.

As indicated by her reevaluation on the issue of animal testing for cosmetic products, Mary Kay remains sensitive to the marketplace. She donated funds to Johns Hopkins University in hopes of evolving a testing method using tissue samples instead of live animals. Her activism in support of better health care for women has led to a directorship for the Wadley Institute of Molecular Medicine and an honorary position as chairwoman of the Texas Breast Screening Project for the American Cancer Society.

A grandmother and great-grandmother herself, she relaxes by painting, a hobby inspired by Grandma Moses. Two knee replacements have slowed down her usual break-neck speed, but the bubbly guru of cosmetics still leads seminars. Insisting that high-heeled pumps add to her authority, she ignores doctor's orders and forges ahead, confident in the future of her company.

## Notes

[1] Linda Thomson. "The Messiah of Makeup Spreads Cosmetic Credo," *Madison Capital Times*, Madison, Wisc., October 19, 1985, n.p.

[2] Pat Baldwin. "No Time to Quit," *Dallas Times Herald*, July 9, 1989, n.p.

[3] Baldwin, n.p.

[4] Linda Helser. "Mary Kay Puts a New Face on Enterprise," *The Arizona Republic*. n.d., n.p.

[5] Thomson, n.p.

[6] Abby Karp. "Optimism Reigns at Mary Kay," *Baltimore Sun*, April 13, 1987, n.p.

[7] Thomson, n.p.

## Sources

Anderson, John, and Valerie Wright. "Mary Kay Ash, Dallas, 1971," *Texas Monthly*, August, 1989, 146-148.

Ash, Mary Kay. "How to Play Boss: From Mary Kay's People Management," *Cosmopolitan*, August 1985, 84-86.

_____. "Management: Becoming a Good Follow-Through Person," *Working Woman*, December 1984, 29-31.

_____. *Mary Kay: The Success Story of America's Most Dynamic Businesswoman.* New York: Harper & Row, 1987.

Baldwin, Pat. "No Time to Quit," *Dallas Times Herald*, July 9, 1989.

Chan, Mei-Mei. "Mary Kay Ash," *Chicago Tribune*, July 18, 1986.

Donovan, Jennifer Boeth. "Thanksgiving at Mary Kay's," *Woman's Day*, November 24, 1987, 185-188.

Helser, Linda. "Mary Kay Puts a New Face on Enterprise," *Arizona Republic*, n.d., n.p.

Karp, Abby. "Optimism Reigns at Mary Kay," *Baltimore Sun*, April 13, 1987, n.p.

"The Mary Kay Guide to Beauty: Discovering Your Special Look," *Publishers Weekly*, August 19, 1983, 65-66.

Rubenstein, Carie. "Lifelines of the Rich and Famous," *Money*, Fall 1988, 132-134.

Stuttaford, Genevieve. "Tender Power," *Publishers Weekly*, December 23, 1988, 72-73.

Thomson, Linda. "The Messiah of Makeup Spreads Cosmetic Credo," *Madison Capital Times*, Madison, Wisc., October 19, 1985, n.p.

# Jean Marie Auel

For at least one success story, an MBA degree led to a challenging career far from the office. A self-proclaimed "closet" poet and contributor to *From Oregon with Love*, a poetry anthology, Jean Auel moved on to fiction. After raising a family of five and working at a technical firm for ten years, she completed a master's degree, then turned an intriguing idea for a short story into a monumental first novel and the controlling motif of a five-volume saga.

On her first venture, Auel tried to write a story of a woman who stood out from the rest of society because of her innate differences. The story evolved into *The Clan of the Cave Bear* (1980), an adventure novel depicting a stone-age woman in ice-age Crimea. The saga quickly developed not only into a bestseller, but also a movie, translations into eighteen languages, and the beginning of a bestselling series. The Auel family earned enough money for Jean's husband to quit and serve as her business manager.

Jean Auel's fiction-writing success was no flash in the pan. A painstaking researcher, she studied all angles of her historical fiction, delineating the finer points of Neanderthal society amid a natural setting rife with clan conflict, cultural upheaval, natural disasters, daily confrontations wth bears and bison, sexual awakening, and the burgeoning of romance. The surprising fact to the publishing world was that fiction about cave dwellers could rivet the attention of the reading public to the point of obsession. Jean Auel interested her readers and kept them coming back for more as later installments in the story of heroine Ayla appeared on the stands.

## Moving toward Business

Jean Marie Auel, born on February 18, 1936, in Chicago, Illinois, is the daughter of homemaker Martha Wirtanen and Neil S. Untinen, a painter and home decorator of Finnish-American descent. She married her high school sweetheart, electronics operations planner Ray B. Auel, on March 19, 1954. Before they were twenty-five, the couple produced five children—Rae Ann, Karen, Lenore, Kendall, and Marshall.

Auel, who worked while her husband attended school on the GI bill, lived in an unpretentious one-story home in Portland. She briefly attended Portland State

University and accepted a lackluster career as a keypunch operator at Tektronix, Inc., in Beaverton, Oregon, from 1965 to 1966. The work was woefully unsuited to her considerable imaginative talents. In a description of her boredom and frustration she said, "I was quietly exploding inside."[1]

In the tumultuous 1960s, Auel tuned in to feminist consciousness-raising philosophy, particularly the challenge of Betty Friedan's *The Feminine Mystique*. Tying in with the image of the career-conscious, self-actualizing woman, Auel passed a competitive exam and advanced to circuit board designer, a post she held from 1966 to 1973. Then she worked a year as a technical writer and two years as a credit manager. During this period she wrote brochures and pamphlets for the firm, but no fiction.

Without receiving a bachelor's degree, Auel entered night classes at the University of Portland and studied physics and calculus with the aim of becoming a physicist. Reality set in with her awareness that "you don't get to be a physicist taking one or two night courses a semester."[2] She changed her major to business administration and received an MBA in 1976 at the same time that husband Ray was receiving his own degree. Along the way, she joined Mensa, a group created for people with high IQ's.

With her three girls enrolled in college and her two sons in high school, Auel found herself with a steady job by day but empty hours on her hands at night. To fill the void, she began writing the Earth's Children series. Even though she was a lifetime reader with more than the average background knowledge, she discovered a paucity of information about the Pleistocene Era, commonly known as the Ice Age, which occurred two million years before the modern era. In general, she needed to know about weaponry, burial customs, and musical instruments as well as the lay of the land and biological data.

## Hitting the Books

Auel began her saga with an outline hastily penned at her kitchen table. To fill in the chinks in her knowledge, she started with *Encyclopaedia Britannica* and quickly advanced to shelves of scientific books from the library covering climatology, anatomy, anthropology, and archeology. As she perused them, she jotted down copious notes. The extent and depth of her research made her realize that she had enough data to tell Ayla's story in novel form. As she described her method: "I picked out those notes, pulled them together and, in probably half an hour, did a page outline as a sort of overview to point the direction. Then I sat down at the typewriter and started to type, telling the story to myself."[3]

When asked why she chose prehistory as a setting for her first literary attempts, Auel replied that she had no more interest in that era than in any other. At the age of forty, while between jobs, she went with the flow of her imagination, adapting a story about a one-eyed amputee into the character of Creb, the shaman. Then the gap in her education opened wide, admitting the realization that she knew little about early humanity, not even when people discovered fire.

After six months of twelve- to sixteen-hour days at the keyboard, she compiled a huge manuscript of around 450,000 words and spawned an obsession with prehistory that evolved into the Earth's Children series. Frequently working at night, her most productive time, Auel wrote over six- to eight-hour stretches, interspersed with hikes in the woods and reading sessions.

As she drew back from her first draft to assess its worth, Auel perceived that she had mastered the details, but lacked skill with fiction. Her work did not come alive on the page. Rather than invest time in creative writing courses, she checked out more books from the library. She later credited Leon Surmelian's *Techniques of Fiction Writing: Measure and Madness* with crystallizing her understanding of plot, character, and point of view.

## Ice-Age Superwoman

From its inception, Auel's story of Ayla the ice-age woman struck the fancy of feminists. Long wearied of Superman- and Rambo-type heroes, they found in Ayla a lithe, intuitive, creative, and intelligent heroine. Blessed with the ability and will to survive as well as with the long-legged beauty of her screen embodiment, Daryl Hannah, Ayla became a kind of cult figure to modern readers, most of whom are female.

After Ayla's family dies in an earthquake, she exists alone. A Cro-Magnon child, she is adopted by a Neanderthal clan of hunter-gatherers and exists on the fringe of their charity as they pick their way across the steppes north of the Black Sea. Auel lightens Ayla's burden by creating Iza, a gentle foster mother, and Creb, the wise sage who teaches Ayla how to practice ice-age medicine.

Auel endows Ayla with the moxie to fight back against a repressive society that rescues her, then forbids her to tackle male-only skills, notably hunting. Her rejection of Neanderthal values and her refusal to submit to sexual and psychological tyranny result in her physical and spiritual rape. A pariah from the clan, Ayla, labeled ugly and malformed, makes her way alone, minus her child, and ultimately teams up with a horse and a lion.

Eventually, Ayla meets a man, Jondalar, who is like her, tall, blonde, and blue-eyed. With his assistance, she allies with other Cro-Magnon people who cultivate Ayla's talents. Among her own kind at last, she blossoms in an unlikely number of directions, including cooking, medicine, inventions, weaponry, language, athletics, and sewing.

## Researching Prehistory

A lifetime reader with such diverse interests as palm reading, cooking, and poetry, Auel had more than an inkling of the elements of good fiction. She was equally familiar with nonfiction, especially those works which detailed the evolution of stone tool technology. Borrowing from anthropological texts, she searched for more fact on the everyday life of people who hunted and gathered.

Like other women in social fields, she deduced that the current view of prehistory is male-dominated. Because male researchers have rarely approached the question of lifestyle from the female perspective, there is a dearth of information about how women and children functioned in the clan, how food was cooked, and how people managed daily matters of hygiene.

To overcome these gaping holes, Auel ventured into surmise. To explain how Neanderthals communicated, she hypothesized that they were capable of telepathy. With equal confidence, she explained the evolution of female fertility rites and the purpose of cave painting. Staunchly faithful to her material, she proclaimed, "These people were not the Flintstones. Their lives were incredibly rich."[4]

To prove her point, she delved into diverse elements of their lives, especially sexual relations. This physical thrust, plus an emphasis on evolution, met opposition by Moral Majority censors in a small Texas town. Her reply to them was fair and honest: "...there is no human activity that is not valid for the novelist to explore, to write about."[5] In Jean Auel's view, sexuality must remain a major concern of a book that details the rise in status of a lone outcast female.

## Critical Appraisal

From the beginning, critics zeroed in on Auel's chief skill—the ability to absorb and utilize minute details about Cro-Magnon and Neanderthal life and to apply them to a simple, but stirring girl-meets-boy situation. The authenticity of detail, the appropriateness of the main characters' response to each other, and the human struggle against the elements all ring true.

In answer to an interviewer's question about a typical day for cave people, Auel replied that Cro-Magnon people spent from two to three hours each day "doing the things necessary for survival—obtaining food, clothing, and shelter. The rest of the time was spent in leisure activities, such as story-telling, making things for pleasure, and causing trouble for each other, because that's what makes life interesting."[6] She concluded that women participated in hunting and gathering and that the clan as a whole enjoyed group projects.

In order to explain why Neanderthals gave way to Cro-Magnon successors, Auel had to let imagination supply the missing facts. What anthropologists and historians had not explained, she surmised to be a difference in mental focus. Whereas Neanderthal culture harked to the past achievements of the race, Cro-Magnon people, more nearly like modern humans, looked to the future and made a greater attempt to adapt. It is this forward-looking drive that gives Ayla her special quality—and which, ironically, isolates her from the Neanderthals who denigrate her individualism and despise her intrusion on their accepted ways.

## Encountering Success

At first, Auel had difficulty connecting with a willing publisher. After five rejections, she joined forces with Jean Naggar, an agent whom she met at a writers' conference. Together, they approached Crown Publishers, which offered an unheard-of $130,000 contract, a genuine coup for a first-time novelist. Not only did Auel's *Clan of the Cave Bear* reach the best-seller list within four weeks; it also became the basis for a 1986 Warner Brothers film by the same name, for which John Sayles provided the screenplay. The movie version gave the reader a vivid notion of how the blonde protagonist moves about the banks of the Danube, which constitute her world. However, the movie's end result proved none too pleasing to the author, who filed a suit against Warner Brothers, claiming that the company owed her more than $40,000 for the movie rights and that they failed to receive her stamp of approval before filming.

In subsequent works, including *The Valley of the Horses* (1984), *The Mammoth Hunters* (1985), *The Plains of Passage* (1990), and the remaining volumes planned for the saga, the setting shifts among known Cro-Magnon digs. Heroine Ayla migrates to Dordogne in southwest France, where she eventually dies. To give these works the mark of authenticity, Auel visited France's famed Lascaux caves in the Pyrenees between France and Spain, where prehistoric dwellings are inscribed with ritualistic drawings of animals and hunters.

The extra work must have been worth the effort. *The Valley of the Horses* remained on the best-seller list for nearly a year. *The Mammoth Hunters*, the third installment of the six-part series, reached best-seller status before its official release. *The Plains of Passage* hit the markets at a dead run, netting Auel a $25 million advance from Crown Publishers for it and two more installments.

To promote the series, Auel undertook a two-month tour of eighteen cities. To be at her best for her fans, she tackled a 500-calorie-per-day diet and slimmed down. Likewise, she spruced her appearance with adjustments to hair and makeup. But the irrepressible wit needed no refinements, as interviewers were quick to learn; Auel bandied words with the best of them.

## A Gentle Obsession

Jean Auel's success is evident from the pleasure she derives from all things primitive. At her kitchen table, she displays obsidian cutting stones, a hand-softened leather pouch, and a fork made out of an antler. These items recall her week-long survival courses at Oregon's Malheur Field Station. During this trail-blazing segment of her research, she even spent the night in a snow cave on Mt. Hood. In her new house in Arch Cape, Oregon, atop a cliff overlooking the craggy coastline of Oregon, Auel displays a copy of a cave drawing depicting a prehistoric horse. In honor of her central character, her Volkswagen Dasher sports a license plate graced with a single word—Ayla.

In the interest of authenticity, Auel also practiced stone-age techniques, from lighting fires to making arrowheads and weaving baskets, from trapping small animals to gathering roots and tubers for food and medicine. She braved the Pacific Northwest woods armed only with knife and blanket. In the early 1980s, she made a three-week jaunt to prehistoric caves in Europe and Russia to study her settings firsthand.

Auel's expertise has resulted in invitations to hobnob with experts on pre-history at such prestigious locations as the Smithsonian Institution and the Center for Early Man Studies at the University of Portland. She stated the purpose of her works in an interview for *People* magazine: "I want people to understand that our ancestors were not a bunch of savage, groping animals. I'm trying to show the diversity and complexity of Ice Age man. These men aren't that different from your sons or your college roommates."[7]

## Window on Success

Today Auel is a member of Authors Guild, Authors League of America, National Women's Forum, PEN, the Oregon Writers Colony, and the Willamette Writers Club. After publication of the first novel in 1980, she won an award from the Pacific Northwest Booksellers Association, the Vicki Penziner Matson award, and a Friends of Literature commendation, along with a nomination for best first novel from the American Book Awards. For subsequent installments of her series she received a Golden Plate award, an American Academy of Achievement award, and honorary doctorates from the universities of Portland and Maine and Mt. Vernon College. As she puts it, the rewards have been worth the effort: "I'm living every writer's fantasy."[8]

When pinned down to future plans, Jean Auel recalls that her original outline indicated at least six books in her first series. From there, she estimates there will be an unlimited supply of ideas to keep her busy. "I'm going to keep on writing," she concludes. "I guess if I live to be a hundred and fifty, maybe I'll be able to do all the writing I want to do."[9]

## Notes

[1] Jack Fincher. "Author Jean Auel Makes Literary Hay by Thinking Like a Neanderthal," *People*, November 10, 1980, 97.

[2] "Sweet Savage Love," *Newsweek*, November 18, 1985, 101.

[3] *Contemporary Authors*, New Revision Series, Volume 21. Detroit: Gale Research, 1976, 31.

[4] Thomas Hopkins. "I'm Living Every Writer's Fantasy," *Macleans*, October 6, 1980, 65.

[5] *Contemporary Authors*, 33.

[6] Mary-Ann Bendell. "Cosmo Talks to Jean Auel," *Cosmopolitan*, April 1986, 146.

[7] Andrea Chambers. "A Mammoth First Printing Makes Jean Auel's New Epic an Instant Best-Seller," *People*, December 16, 1985, 114.

[8] Hopkins, 64.

[9] *Contemporary Authors*, 33.

## Sources

Bendell, Mary-Ann. "Cosmo Talks to Jean Auel," *Cosmopolitan*, April 1986, 146-148.

Chambers, Andrea. "A Mammoth First Printing Makes Jean Auel's New Epic an Instant Best-Seller," *People*, December 16, 1985, 113-115.

*Contemporary Authors*, New Revision Series, Volume 21. Detroit: Gale Research.

*Contemporary Literary Criticism*, Volume 31. Detroit: Gale Research, 1985.

Fincher, Jack. "Author Jean Auel Makes Literary Hay by Thinking Like a Neanderthal," *People*, November 10, 1980, 96-98.

Hopkins, Thomas. "I'm Living Every Writer's Fantasy," *Macleans*, October 6, 1980, 64-65.

Hornblower, Margot. "Queen of the Ice Age Romance," *Time*, October 22, 1990, 88.

"Sweet Savage Love," *Newsweek*, November 18, 1985, 100-101.

Van Gelder, Lindsy. "Speculative Fiction: From the Immense Past to the Immense Future," *Ms.*, March 1986, 64-70.

# L. Frank Baum

To at least one late achiever, finding a satisfying career was like coming home. For Frank Baum, midwestern chicken farmer, actor, traveling salesman, and newspaper columnist and editor, supporting a wife and four sons proved difficult. As one venture after another caved in, leaving him with the bitter taste of defeat, he searched for a stable career, one suited to his particular set of strengths and values. By chance, he found it in his own backyard. While telling stories to his children, he conceived an idea for a children's book that was destined to become a classic.

The success of *The Wonderful Wizard of Oz* has continued for nearly a century. Perhaps its current reception among readers and movie lovers would surprise even Frank Baum. As he himself mused in a letter to his sister about his lifelong yearning to write a novel: "Now that I am getting old my first book is written to amuse children. For, aside from my evident inability to do anything great, I have learned to regard fame as a will-o'-the-wisp ... but to please a child is a sweet and lovely thing that warms one's heart."[1]

## A Sheltered Childhood

Baum was from early times an appreciator of juvenile literature. He admired the masters—Aesop, Hans Christian Andersen, the brothers Grimm, and Lewis Carroll, as well as Mother Goose. Born Lyman Frank Baum in Chittenango, New York, on May 15, 1856, he was the seventh of the nine children of Cynthia Stanton and Benjamin Ward Baum, an oil tycoon and theater owner. His early years were spent at Rose Lawn, a Victorian mansion surrounded by expanses of grass and flowers, graveled paths, and shady verandas.

Though tall, wiry, and endowed with bursts of imaginative energy, Baum suffered from a heart condition. Consequently, his childhood was sheltered and idyllic, filled with time to dream, but lacking rough and tumble activity. He studied at home under private tutors and immersed himself in nineteenth-century novels, poetry, and drama.

To shake young Frank from lethargy and an over-developed flair for make-believe, his mother enrolled him in Peekskill Military Academy. The experience was disastrous. Lockstep regimentation and physical demands resulted in a heart attack. Even though Baum recovered physically, his memories of heavy-handed discipline colored many of his later writings.

At fifteen, Baum fell in love with the printing trade and badgered his father to buy him a small press. Young Frank and brother Harry published their own newspaper, *The Rose Lawn Home Journal*, and filled it with poems, stories, and information about stamp collecting. Two years later, Frank developed the journal into a professional-looking pamphlet, *Baum's Complete Stamp Dealers Directory*.

## From Printing to the Stage

About this time, Baum's interests blossomed in another direction. Influenced by his aunt, actress Katherine Grayson, he alternately assumed the stage names of George Brooks and Louis F. Baum and toured New York with a Shakespearian company. To steer him toward a more socially acceptable means of earning a living, his father encouraged him to settle into full-time sales for the family business, but Baum maintained his interest in the theater and achieved both success and satisfaction.

From his fascination with drama Baum moved into serious journalism and wrote for a Pennsylvania paper, *The New Era*. He tried his hand at theater management and even formed a company to perform his original melodrama, *The Maid of Arran*. Set in a sentimentalized Ireland, the production pleased audiences, although his later plays never measured up to its initial success.

At twenty-six, Baum married Maud Gage, daughter of a notable feminist, Matilda Joslyn Gage. The Baum family was often uprooted by tenuous finances, yet this lopsided union of strong-minded wife and impractical, visionary husband produced happy years and four sons. Baum seemed oblivious to Maud's occasional reorganization of his helter-skelter financial dealings and put his trust in her ability to manage not only the boys but himself as well. As evidence of his contentment, he dedicated *The Wonderful Wizard of Oz* to Maud, whom he called his "good friend and comrade."[2]

## The World of Business

At thirty, Baum abandoned his creative leanings and entered a commercial phase. He settled in Syracuse and joined his father's business, representing an axle lubricant known as Baum's Castorine. Within two years, however, he fell prey to the pioneer spirit and migrated to Aberdeen, South Dakota, to become an entrepreneur and variety store owner. However, his emporium, Baum's Bazaar, fell on hard times. During the family's struggle to stay afloat, Baum developed other interests, including management of a local baseball team, storytelling for his own sons as well as neighborhood children, and amateur photography. Yet, ineptitude for business ended his hopes for success on the American frontier. He sold Baum's Bazaar and moved on.

Luck put Baum in contact with John Drake, who asked him to edit *The Dakota Pioneer*. Baum accepted the challenge. At his new post, he tickled the fancy of his readers with a column written from the point of view of a fictional landlady named Mrs. Bilkins. Through her comments, he characterized midwestern concerns, inventions, changes in lifestyle, and other topics of the day along with a generous dollop of banter.

In his editorials, he tackled more serious problems and made a noticeable impact on attitudes toward woman's suffrage, the plight of farmers, and spiritualism, which was the hobby of both Maud and her mother. Unfortunately, the exodus of people from South Dakota weakened his readership despite the popularity of his writing. In 1891, Baum resigned with the comment: "I decided the sheriff wanted the paper more than I did."[3] Baum moved to Chicago and worked first as a reporter for the *Evening Post*, then as a traveling china and glassware salesman for Pitkin and Brooks.

## Becoming a Writer

During this period, Baum struggled for balance. His income stabilized as he became more skillful at selling, but the job kept him far from home. To compensate, Baum spent leisure time telling stories to the young of the community. It was this series of impromptu narratives that evolved into Baum's first children's literature. In 1896, at the prompting of his nagging mother-in-law, he promoted "Adventures in Phunniland" and "Tales from Mother Goose" to a publishing house, but only the second half of the project came to fruition.

Because selling from town to town was taxing Baum's weak heart, he was pleased to develop writing, a more sedentary profession, as a source of income. He produced a trade periodical for window trimmers in 1897; by 1900 he developed his successful magazine, *Show Window*, into *The Art of Decorating Dry Goods Windows and Interiors*. From this promising start, Baum diversified to books of verse, one of which he typeset and produced on his own. Teaming up with illustrator William Wallace Denslow, who produced a steady flow of work for Rand McNally & Company, Baum published *Father Goose, His Book*, which became a best-seller by 1899, and followed with *The Songs of Father Goose, A New Wonderland, The Army Alphabet*, and *The Navy Alphabet*.

By this point in his career, Baum had earned respect as a major producer of whimsical, nonviolent fiction for children. Freed from his former weight of debt, overtaxed heart, and worry, Baum and his family enjoyed a bit of luxury, including the purchase of a summer cottage on Lake Michigan which he dubbed "The Sign of the Goose." He built oak furniture and carried out a theme of painted, cut-out geese modeled on his works.

Baum's masterpiece, about a mystical city which he named for a reference volume marked o-z, emerged from a long period of incubation. Halting a storytelling session, he began writing down a fairy tale that had been flitting through his mind. Entitled "The Emerald City," the modernistic fairy tale took shape, yet required much additional thought and work.

Of his slapdash method, Baum wrote to his publisher, "When I get at a thing of that sort I live with it day by day, jotting down on odd slips of paper the various ideas that occur and in this way getting my material together.... I must rewrite it, stringing the incidents into consecutive order, elaborating the characters, etc."[4] He estimated that the story would require from six to eight weeks honing.

## The Road to Oz

In their contracts, Baum and Denslow received equal royalties for their creation, which was slated for publication in 1900. The publisher rejected the proposed title, so Baum toyed with *From Kansas to Fairyland*, *The Fairyland of Oz*, and *The Land of Oz* before settling on *The Wonderful Wizard of Oz*. Positive of success, he wrote to his brother Harry about the book and predicted sales of 250,000. Still Baum quavered: "But the queer, unreliable Public has not yet spoken. I only need one hit this year to make my position secure, and three of these books seem fitted for public approval. But there—who knows anything!"[5]

Baum sent the first copy to Harry. It contained 124 illustrations, one-fifth of which were in three colors and the rest in two colors. In addition to its graphic artistry, a major strength of this and other of Baum's books was his ability to comprehend and explain technical processes. In the climactic unveiling of the Wizard, Dorothy demands to know how he managed to appear as the Great Head. He leads the way to a chamber in the rear of the Throne Room, points out the papier maché mask with its painted features and explains that it hung from the ceiling on a wire. The Great Oz stood behind a screen and pulled a cord to move the eyes and mouth.

"But how about the voice?" she enquired.

"Oh, I am a ventriloquist," said the little man, "and I can throw the sound of my voice wherever I wish; so that you thought it was coming out of the Head."[6]

The Wizard continues his engaging narrative to Dorothy by explaining how he gave up ventriloquism and became a balloonist. His ventures in the clouds carried him far away from his native Omaha and landed him in Oz, where an adoring populace made him their great Wizard.

## And On to Fame

Reviewers of this fantasy raved about it, some guaranteeing Frank Baum a place among the great writers of children's literature. *Dial* and other critical magazines compared Baum's style to that of Lewis Carroll. *The Bookseller and Latest Literature* predicted that the story should appeal to children and adults as well. The most significant applause came from *The New York Times*, which delineated the difference between nineteenth-century children's literature and that of a new, invigorating generation of books, as represented by the works of Kate Greenaway and Frank Baum. For nearly a century, critics continued to praise Baum for his control of character, flow of imagination, depth of humor, and narrative control.

*The Wonderful Wizard of Oz*, which has sold 5 million copies, remains one of the top fifteen books in the twentieth century. It has influenced movies, recordings, radio plays, puppet shows, musical comedies, toys, games, clothing, and art prints. Baum's fans number such notables as Ray Bradbury, Shirley Jackson, Gore Vidal, and William Styron.

*Kindergarten Magazine* commented that, even though Dorothy's companions are farfetched, through Baum's creative pen and Denslow's skillful brush, the story seems quite real. The article concludes that "delightful humor and rare philosophy are found on every page" and that "no child but will have a warm corner in his heart for the really thoughtful Scarecrow, the truly tender Tin Woodman, the fearless Cowardly Lion."[7] Other reviewers concentrated on William Denslow's art work, some even awarding a major share of praise to the illustrator and tossing lesser scraps to the writer.

To his credit, Baum never verbalized discontent with his collaborator's success. Yet, his silence leaves a question mark in biographers' minds. Much later in their relationship, Baum distanced himself from Denslow. By 1901, he had reached an impasse and commented, "Having learned my lesson from my unfortunate experiences with Denslow, I will never permit another artist to have an interest in the drawings he makes of my described characters, if I ever can help it."[8] The two parted for good over a proposed musical based on *The Wizard of Oz*, for which Denslow demanded a share of royalties for dramatizing even though his part in the production was costume design.

Of his own career, Baum clearly states his mission in a quotation taken from the *Grand Rapids Herald* of 1907, promising to write children's literature to amuse and divert children, particularly the sick, and to keep children occupied during bad weather. As Baum envisioned his mission, its importance overshadowed the writing of adult novels, which seldom last a year in print. In comparison, children's literature remains constant, he said, "since children are always the same kind of little folks with the same needs to satisfy."[9]

## Making Some Improvements

Indeed, Baum rescued children's literature from the pomposity of the previous century. Avoiding imitation of his forerunners, he instinctively appealed to the tastes of young people by stressing lively, comic dialogue devoid of didacticism or sentimentality. In his introduction, he stated his belief that modern children prefer entertainment rather than terror. He concluded, "Having this thought in mind, the story in 'The Wonderful Wizard of Oz' was written solely to pleasure children of today. It aspires to being a modernized fairy tale, in which the wonderment and joy are retained and the heart-aches and nightmares are left out."[10]

Once launched in the direction of books for children, Frank Baum continued churning out fantasy and delight with *The Life and Adventures of Santa Claus, Dot and Tot of Merryland, The Master Key*, and *The Woggle-Bug Book*. With a financially promising cushion of manuscripts behind him, Baum and his wife bought a home named Ozcot in Hollywood, California, and toured northern Africa and Europe.

From his travel experiences Baum planned to write a new children's series. The books never materialized; instead, Baum developed an interest in the fledgling film industry, a new direction for his talents. He toured with filmed versions of his works in 1908 and, dressed in white frock coat and trousers, lectured to admiring audiences. The cost of the entourage, including orchestra and projectionist, ate up profits. By 1911, Baum, who went bankrupt, was forced to scale down his lifestyle.

Late in life, Baum turned to homey pleasures, especially gardening. Content among his blossoms, he penned children's stories in longhand on plain white sheets fastened to his clipboard. He worked up each manuscript on the typewriter, speeding along in two-fingered fashion as he edited his original text. His friends remember him in old age as good-looking, gentle, affable, but a bit reserved. He enjoyed conversation and was a good listener. His letter-writing tended toward answers to youthful fans rather than correspondence with his contemporaries.

Gradually, Baum's heart and gall bladder caused him more pain and deprived him of jaunts about the garden. Even in ill health, he never gave up writing children's stories. Baum died at Ozcot in the spring of 1919.

His popular series of Oz books continued, with additional stories written by Ruth Plumly Thompson. Because of the ingrown nature of the industry, in the 1920s Baum slipped from popularity. Book publishers touted their own wares at the expense of the classics; Baum's books were seldom lauded or reviewed. He himself had been unconcerned with critics and relied more on his intuitive sense of what children wanted to read rather than what impressed critics.

Shortly before his death, in a letter to his son Frank, a doughboy in World War I, Baum grew philosophical. He said, "In life nothing adverse lasts very long. And it is true that as years pass, and we look back on something which, at the time, seemed unbelievably discouraging and unfair, we come to realize, after all, God was at all times on our side."[11]

## Notes

[1] Daniel P. Mannix. "The Father of the Wizard of Oz," *American Heritage*, December 1964, 36.

[2] L. Frank Baum. *The Annotated Wizard of Oz*. Introduction by Michael Patrick Hearn. New York: Schocken Books, 1983, 88.

[3] Mannix, 41.

[4] Hearn, 27.

[5] Hearn, 30.

[6] Baum, 265.

[7] Hearn, 33-34.

[8] Hearn, 42.

[9] Hearn, 26.

[10] Hearn, 85.

[11] Hearn, 65.

## Sources

Baum, Frank. *The Annotated Wizard of Oz.* Introduction by Michael Patrick Hearn. New York: Schocken Books, 1983.

Baum, Frank J. "Why the Wizard of Oz Keeps on Selling," *Writer's Digest,* December 1952.

Baum, Frank Joslyn, and Russell P. MacFall. *To Please a Child: A Biography of L. Frank Baum, Royal Historian of Oz.* Chicago: Reilly & Lee Co., 1961.

Bewley, Marius. *Masks and Mirrors.* New York: Atheneum, 1970.

Brotman, Jordan. "A Late Wanderer in Oz," *Only Connect.* Sheila Egoff, ed. New York: Oxford University Press, 1969.

Erisman, Fred. "L. Frank Baum and the Progressive Dilemma," *American Quarterly,* Fall 1968.

Ford, Alla T., and Dick Martin. *The Musical Fantasies of L. Frank Baum.* Chicago: The Wizard Press, 1958.

Gardner, Martin, and Russel B. Nye. *The Wizard of Oz and Who He Was.* East Lansing: Michigan State University Press, 1957.

Kopp, Sheldon. "The Wizard Behind the Couch," *Psychology Today,* March 1970.

Lanes, Selma G. *Down the Rabbit Hole.* New York: Atheneum, 1971.

Littlefield, Henry M. "The Wizard of Oz: Parable on Populism," *American Quarterly*, Spring 1964.

Manguel, Alberto, and Gianni Guadalupi. *The Dictionary of Imaginary Places.* New York: Harcourt Brace Jovanovich, 1987.

Mannix, Daniel P. "The Father of the Wizard of Oz," *American Heritage*, December 1964, 36-47.

Prentice, Ann E. "Have You Been to See the Wizard?" *The Top of the News.* American Library Association, November 1, 1970.

Seymour, Ralph Fletcher. *Some Went This Way.* Chicago: Privately printed, 1945.

Snow, Jack. *Who's Who in Oz.* Chicago: Reilly & Lee, 1954.

Starrett, Vincent. "The Wizard of Oz," *Best Loved Books of the Twentieth Century.* New York: Bantam, 1955.

Wagenknecht, Edward. "The Yellow Brick Road," *As Far As Yesterday.* Norman, Oklahoma: University of Oklahoma Press, 1968.

# James Beard

The way to late achievement does not always lead straight ahead. Sometimes it takes side roads. For James Andrews Beard, notable American cook and eclectic gourmand, success came after a series of false starts and unforeseen opportunities. What began as a singing and stage career diverted to radio broadcasts and then to the kitchen and notoriety as a television cook. By middle age, Beard was on the way to becoming the nation's expert on foods and cooking. He established a specialty in outdoor barbecuing and for fifty years continued perusing domestic and foreign tables for something new to whet the American palate.

A jolly, well-padded figure often compared to Buddha and Santa Claus, Beard stood well over six feet in height. His good-natured smile, twinkly green eyes, and bald pate were his trademarks and often decorated the front covers of his twenty-four books. A bachelor with a flair for taking notes on tasty menus whenever food pleased his fancy, he lived part of his adult life in a tiny New York flat. There he cooked in a minuscule kitchen and treated friends and colleagues to his one-of-a-kind gourmet treats. Because he gave generously of himself and his talents, he was always surrounded by friends and acquaintances, cooks, restaurateurs, and theater buffs, whether in Portland, Oregon, New York, Catalonia, London, or Paris.

Keen on theater productions from his high school days, Beard was famous for combining food with drama. Often, his main dish was an eye-catching salad or flaky, cream-filled dessert rather than a more mundane entrée. Whatever the draw, he delighted guests with well-rehearsed recipes made from the finest of ingredients. In his words, "Like theater, offering food to people is a matter of showmanship, and no matter how simple the performance, until you do it well, with love and originality, you have a flop on your hands."[1]

Beard's writing continued to influence diversity, adventure, and flair in American kitchens after his death. His books were reissued, and there were several excellent biographies, including Evans Jones's *Epicurean Delight* and Barbara Kafka's *The James Beard Celebration*. In Beard's memory, Peter Kump and other friends and colleagues established the James Beard Foundation in Beard's Greenwich Village townhouse. The purpose of the foundation is to underwrite workshops, parties, dinners, demonstrations, and exhibits of food art. In addition, the group hopes to offer scholarships to promising students.

# The Makings of a Cook

James Beard was a native of Portland, Oregon. Born May 5, 1903, to Jonathan A. Beard, who worked in the Portland shipyards as an assistant appraiser, and Mary Elizabeth Jones Beard, who owned and managed the Gladstone Hotel, James was an only child. He attended public schools in Portland, graduated from Washington High School, then went on to Reed College and the University of Washington.

From his strong-willed and independent English mother, Beard learned from babyhood to develop his taste for food, particularly foreign cuisine. The family enjoyed the services of a Chinese cook and a wide array of imported and home-grown foods. Beard accompanied his mother on regular trips to the public market in Portland's Yamhill Street, and adopted her shopping and canning techniques.

In later years, Beard spoke fondly of the fish stews, apple desserts, and other Oregon specialties that pleased him in childhood. One of his favorites was a simple cream-and-butter-based clam chowder, which he ate when he was sick. As an adult he imitated it from memory. He once commented, "I cooked fairly seriously by the time I was 14 or 15. I never really learned. I had a funny feeling that I could take something I ate and reproduce it—like a musician with music."[2]

The Beard family admired the whole spectrum of gourmet foods. They frequently went to dine at the best eating establishments in San Francisco, balancing this elegant fare with simpler meals on annual trips to their Pacific beach house at Gearhart, 18 miles south of the Columbia River. Consequently, James was exposed to both upscale restaurant dining and less formal picnicking and outdoor cookery by his discerning, eclectic parents.

At Gearhart, he reveled in picking huckleberries and strawberries. His family introduced him to crabs, clams, and oysters, as well as salmon and crawfish, often roasted over an open fire on the beach. The experience of watching his mother cook for friends over blazing driftwood led to his later triumphs in outdoor cookery.

## Cultivating His Talents

From early times, James Beard also demonstrated vocal skill. His parents, as adept in music as in fine foods, groomed their son for a professional career until a throat infection ruined his voice. He then opted for a stage career. Participation in high school and college drama groups strengthened his sense of stage presence. He entered Pittsburgh's Carnegie Institute of Technology for dramatics training and acted in theatrical presentations.

Journeys outside the United States became standard fare for Beard. En route to England aboard the English freighter *Highland Heather* in 1922, he visited St. Thomas in the West Indies and delved into island produce sold by islanders at local markets. When he arrived in England later that year, he met Helen Dircks, who initiated him into the theater district and the wide selection of restaurants in

Soho, which served everything from Indian to Chinese to Mexican to Moroccan cuisine. From there he continued his immersion in world food culture with his first trip to Paris.

One of his fondest memories was of European outdoor food and flower stalls. A believer in fresh produce for both nutrition and taste, he nurtured a tactile sense that he later passed on to protégés. The joy of selecting his own fruits, vegetables, and fish became a mainstay of his love affair with food. Later in his career, he passed along useful tricks in his numerous food articles as a means of helping timid shoppers overcome their fears of selecting the best in fresh produce.

## A Mixed Career

In the 1920s, Beard found satisfying work on the American stage. He played in *Cyrano de Bergerac* and *Othello* at New York's Hampden's Theatre. But roles did not come easily to a man six foot four and weighing nearly 300 pounds. In San Francisco he found more suitable pickings—in radio drama and food commercials. At the age of thirty, still interested in food preparation, he taught cooking in private homes in Portland as a part of Agnes Crowther's decorating service. Along with designing a modern and efficient kitchen, she offered international cuisine and wine selection, compliments of James Beard.

In his mid-thirties, Beard migrated to New York and cast about for an outlet for his unusual blend of talents. At first, he did some in-house cooking for friends, but found no permanent position that appealed to him. In 1938, he accepted a post as teacher of history, French, and English in a New Jersey country day school.

That same year he joined with William Rhode in a catering service, Hors d'Oeuvre, Inc. The business, which originated on Manhattan's East 66th Street, worked its way up from small party foods to salads, entrées, and showstopper desserts. From his initial success, Beard published *Hors d'Oeuvres and Canapés* (1940). The book sparked an unhealthy competition with his partner and led to the dissolution of the company.

## Military Life and Beyond

Though he was thirty-seven at the beginning of World War II, Beard joined the army air corps in September 1942 and served first at Fort Dix, New Jersey, then in Miami and Pawling, New York, where he studied cryptography. He had nurtured hopes of learning hotel management with the Quartermaster Corps, but instead spent his wartime service decoding messages for the Pentagon. Discouraged, he took the option offered to soldiers over thirty-eight years of age and left the army in March 1943. The remainder of that year, he worked on a dairy and truck farm in Reading, Pennsylvania.

In late 1943, Beard became part of the explosion of interest in world cuisine when he joined the United Seamen's Service and directed recreational clubs in Puerto Rico, Rio de Janeiro, Marseilles, Cristobal, and Naples. At each location, he organized the kitchen and serving facilities. During this period, he published *Fowl and Game Cookery* (1944). He returned to the United States with a stronger reputation among gourmets.

## Gaining Respect

By his late forties, James Beard was well known in the cooking world. Until 1948 he served as cooking demonstrator on *Elsie Presents*, a televised food program sponsored by Borden milk products. He published *The Fireside Cookbook* (1949) and lectured to various women's clubs, hobby shows, food festivals, and benefits in the United States and Canada, often with the sponsorship of suppliers such as the wine industry and kitchen equipment companies. He also pioneered the concept of consulting for major restaurants, such as New York's Four Seasons, and the live television cooking demonstration, which was later refined and popularized by such on-screen personalities as Julia Child and the Galloping Gourmet.

During this phase of his evolution as food guru, Beard candidly debunked the haughty, froufrou cookery that passed for European cuisine in the decade following World War II. More honest than others in his field, he decried pretense, particularly multi-course meals served with the best of china, silver, and crystal. In place of these snobbish displays, he urged food lovers to broaden their horizons and to prepare simple menus with flair and sensitivity.

As mentor to notable imitators, he encouraged adventure, good taste, and honesty, but not at the expense of subtlety and dramatic appeal. To Beard, eating was a multi-sense experience, pleasing to eye, nose, touch, and taste. The simplest of foods received his complete attention to detail, from the selection of cooking equipment to temperature, spices, and presentation.

With the introduction of his cooking school in 1955, Beard opened an experimental kitchen, first in New York's Lexington Hotel and three years later on the premises of *McCall's* magazine. He found a permanent home for his school in a four-story building in Greenwich Village in 1959. From the kitchen's semicircular work island, he offered courses to amateur cooks interested in international cuisine, party cookery, baking, and buffets as well as basic information about breads, crêpes, soufflés, sauces, and omelets. One of his key lessons involved having his students taste raw ingredients, and then sample the same items cooked by a variety of methods and in contrasting sauces. He ended each session with sampling and analysis of his students' creations.

## New Horizons

Beard added to his broad base of information with frequent journeys to interesting places. He roamed out-of-the-way parts of Europe, where he sampled traditional regional cuisine. His critiques of post-war European restaurants noted an increasing erosion of quality because of the influx of the tourist trade, which placed too great a demand on discriminating kitchens. He gave his highest marks to his favorite, L'Auberge de Père Bise.

Beard's steady barrage of cooking manuals includes *Paris Cuisine* (1952), *James Beard's Fish Cookery* (1954), *The Complete Book of Barbecue and Rotisserie Cooking* (1954), *The Complete Cookbook for Entertaining* (1954), *The Complete Book of Outdoor Cookery* (1955), *How to Eat Better for Less Money* (1956), *Jim Beard's New Barbecue Cookbook* (1958), *James Beard's Treasury of Outdoor Cooking* (1960), *American Cooking* (1972), and *Beard on Pasta* (1983). One book, *The James Beard Cookbook* (1958), was a best-seller in paperback and is today considered an American classic. In addition, he wrote a monthly column for *House and Garden* and produced frequent articles for *Woman's Day*, *Harper's Bazaar*, and *Vogue*.

## Late Achievements

Until his death on January 23, 1985, from a heart attack brought on by a kidney infection, James Beard, a lover of fun and gossip, remained active and enthusiastic about his hobbies and interests. He dressed in bold colors and distinctive plaids. He decorated his home with oriental robes, antique wine glasses, and other food paraphernalia. For recreation, he swam, talked to friends on the telephone, collected records and tapes, attended plays and operas, and continued developing his skills in cooking, even when he dined alone.

Proud of his designation as an epicurean and the dean of American food, Beard encouraged classes for children so that they could become the next generation of great cooks. He also maintained close ties with great chefs of Europe and America. He touted culinary liberation and fostered an American cuisine based on fresh ingredients from local markets.

Beard believed that America's contribution to world eating lay more in ingredients than in recipes. In an article for *U.S. News and World Report*, he commented that beans, corn, nuts, and strawberries are uniquely American. He concluded that the "discovery of America changed the diet of the world."[3] And it was Beard who introduced Americans to their own cuisine by reviving farm and working-class fare such as scrapple, tongue, tripe, fried tomatoes, and Indian pudding.

## A Flexible Philosophy

Beard kept up his career well into his seventies and eighties. He adapted to changes in taste and style, particularly the move toward lighter menus with less fat, calories, salt, and deep-fat frying, and dependence on food processing and microwaving to shorten cooking time. He recognized that more people were studying their ethnic heritage and sampling foodstuffs and recipes that tied them to ongoing traditions. In answer to questions about food prejudices, he credited inflexible palates to early home training. His understanding of the American point of view helped him develop a philosophy that segued neatly into trends, not only in eating, but also in gardening and raising unusual foods for the table. As George Lang, owner of New York's Cafe des Artistes, summarized, "To oversimplify matters, [Beard] was the person who almost single-handedly transformed America's eating habits from salt and pepper and ketchup on the table to much more complex pleasures."[4]

## Notes

[1] Mary MacVean. "Dean of American Food Heats Up Gossip," *Hickory Daily Record*, December 1, 1990, 8C.

[2] MacVean, 8C.

[3] "Discovery of America Changed the Diet of the World," *U.S. News & World Report*, June 13, 1983, 64.

[4] MacVean, 8C.

## Sources

Beard, James. *Delights and Prejudices*. New York: Atheneum, 1964.

*Current Biography*. Detroit: Gale Research, 1964, 1985.

"Discovery of America Changed the Diet of the World," *U.S. News & World Report*, June 13, 1983, 64.

"Having Trouble with Your Weight? Consider These Eleven Who Eat for a Living," *People Weekly*, October 27, 1980, 22-28.

Jacobs, Jay. "James Beard, an American Icon," *Gourmet*, February 1984, 26-39.

"James Beard," *Newsweek*, February 4, 1985, 75.

"James Beard, Emperor of Epicures," *People Weekly*, September 28, 1981, 65-67.

MacVean, Mary. "Dean of American Food Heats Up Gossip," *Hickory Daily Record*, December 1, 1990, 8C.

Sheraton, Mimi. "America's Grand Pooh-Bah of Food: James Beard," *Time*, February 4, 1985, 81.

Weiss, Patricia. "Beard's Castle," *New York*, July 5, 1982, 72-74.

"What's to Come in American Cuisine," *House & Garden*, February 1981, 151-153.

# Shirley Temple Black

The satisfactions of an early success do not always last into adulthood. In some cases, the need to navigate the shoals of career choice recurs late in life. For Shirley Temple Black, the screen career that made her America's dimpled, apple-cheeked darling waned with time, changes in public taste, and the arrival of puberty, leaving her open for new challenges. For a time, she devoted her talents to rearing a family. Eventually, she saw a need for citizen concern and involved herself heavily in national politics. Tapped by President Richard Nixon, she served as representative to the twenty-fourth United Nations General Assembly at the age of forty-one. In 1974, at the urging of President Gerald Ford, she became United States ambassador to Ghana.

Then followed activism in ecology groups and more public service jobs: chief of White House protocol, delegate to a conference on African refugee problems, and member of a United Nations group studying the law of the seas. Her involvement in worthy projects expanded to the U.N. Conference on Human Environment, President's Council on Environmental Quality, and U.S. Commission for UNESCO. For Shirley Temple Black, an interest in third world countries developed into a consuming passion. At one point, she explained her concern for human needs with typical candor: "If you hear someone scream, you shouldn't close the drapes. You should help. You've got to try."[1]

## An Early Start

A native of Santa Monica, California, Shirley Temple, born on April 23, 1928, was the third child of bank manager Francis George and Gertrude Krieger Temple. At that time, the family, including twelve-year-old George, Jr., and seven-year-old Jack, lived in an unassuming single-story stucco house. Her mother, who was eager to have a girl, claimed to have influenced her daughter's future by associating with music, art, and nature during her third pregnancy. Her regimen paid off. At birth, Shirley was plump, good-natured, and blessed with a clear advantage—curly blond hair.

In early childhood, Shirley studied tap dance at Ethel Meglin's Hollywood dance studio for children, where Charles Lamont, a talent scout for Educational

Studios, discovered her at age three. Pushing aside the more importunate candidates, he pointed out his choice: "I'll take the one under the piano."[2] From the beginning, Gertrude Temple, who served as mentor, disciplinarian, and friend, accompanied her child to all engagements.

A year later, Shirley edged out 200 other candidates and won her first movie role in *Stand Up and Cheer.* By 1934, she and her mother together were earning $1,250 a week, in a time when much of the country worried about survival. Within two years, the sum rose to $3,500. Even her father netted a promotion to branch bank manager. From the earnings of their much-exploited child, the Temple family bought a bigger house, this time in Brentwood.

Because Shirley launched an acting career with Twentieth Century-Fox Studios that same year, her parents denied her ordinary classrooms and hired private tutors. After her appeal peaked in 1939, they allowed her to enroll in the Westlake School for Girls, from which she graduated in 1945. The level-headedness of her parents helped protect Shirley from arrogance and conceit. Her mother reminded her that people did not really love her, but that her movies brought audiences a fleeting moment of happiness. Her employer, showman Darryl F. Zanuck, however, underscored her value to the screen: "Her films didn't make Shirley; she made them."[3]

In a pragmatic evaluation of her early stardom, Black writes in her autobiography, *Child Star,* about how the studio weighed two possibilities: "...first, was my public film image an extension of myself or one created by the industry; and second, did my popularity stem from acting, dancing, or singing, and in what combination? The answers involved not only artistic judgment but finance.... It was just that simple. Art had little to do with it."[4]

During the height of her fame, the studio housed Shirley in a private four-room bungalow on a half-acre lot with picket fence, gate, birdhouse, rabbit hutch, and rope swing. They insured their biggest money-maker through Lloyd's of London. She began her screen appearances in the Baby Burlesk series and advanced to her first starring role in 1934 with *Little Miss Marker.* Among her memorable films are *Rebecca of Sunnybrook Farm, Baby Take a Bow, Bright Eyes, Curly Top, Poor Little Rich Girl, The Blue Bird, The Little Princess, Wee Willie Winkie,* and *The Little Colonel.* In her adolescent years, she continued to draw audiences, but the success of *Since You Went Away, Kiss and Tell,* and *The Bachelor and the Bobby-Soxer* was decidedly lessened by Shirley's loss of her angelic babyhood charm.

In her salad days, dressed in patent leather Mary Janes, sailor suit, gloves, and fifty-five perky blond sausage curls topped with matching ribbon, Shirley was everybody's sweetheart—poised, cheery, mischievous, and cherubic. Far from perfect, she was just the right mix of doll baby and hoyden, Kewpie doll and minx. To ordinary movie fans, who mobbed her at the circus and on a visit to a department store Santa Claus, she was the rainbow that promised an end to the Depression. To little girls, she was the epitome of what they should strive to be. As one admirer describes her, "For nearly six years she managed to make time stand still, as she miraculously maintained a balance between adorable child and vamping coquette. She was the all-American child."[5] An international sensation in movies, public appearances, and the press, the petite starlet counted among her admirers such names as Albert Einstein, J. Edgar Hoover, and Franklin D. and Eleanor Roosevelt.

## Tapping to the Top

Not only was Shirley Temple the image of little-girl sweetness, she was a powerhouse of talent. She could imitate headliners of her day, such as Fred Astaire and Ginger Rogers. Even more to the tastes of her admirers, she could top the antics of veteran tap dancer Bill "Bojangles" Robinson. She held her own with the cream of co-stars James Dunn, Randolph Scott, Joseph Cotten, Cary Grant, Buddy Ebsen, and Ronald Reagan. The fact that she could keep audiences coming to a series of movies that each resembled the other in weepy story lines and out-of-the-fire solutions is a tribute to her personal charm. Even today, she ends her resume with a claim to forty major motion pictures and fifty major television productions.

Shirley Temple's film career came to an abrupt end in the late 1940s. The studio continued to comb through hordes of would-be Shirleys for the one-in-a-million replacement. They banked first on Sybil Jason, then Gigi Perreau and a string of others, but never came close to a windfall like Shirley. During this same period, her late-teen marriage to soldier-turned-actor John Agar crumbled. She ruefully commented about her headlong rush into matrimony: "I wanted marriage more than a career because you can get awfully lonesome with your scrapbooks."[6] By the time of her divorce, Shirley testified that she had been on the brink of suicide.

Early in 1950, Shirley, the mother of one daughter, Susan, vacationed in Hawaii and rested up from the public embroilment over her divorce. There she met a handsome surfer and graduate of Stanford and Harvard, Charles Alden Black, scion of a prominent and wealthy family and specialist in marine industries. In mid-December that same year, they married and settled first in Bel Air, then in Bethesda, Maryland, for the duration of the Korean War, and finally in a Tudor brick and stucco house in a sylvan, hilly suburb 30 miles south of San Francisco. By cesarean section, Shirley bore two more children, Lori and Charles, Jr., coming close to death from complications resulting in pneumonia.

Yet, even after three pregnancies and her share of heartbreak, Shirley retained the bubbly, round-cheeked face that she bore in childhood, so anonymity has always been out of the question. To her credit, however, she did not duck her admirers; rather, she turned her notoriety into a major asset. Still, with some discomfort, she points to bruises and pinches and remarks, "Any star can be devoured by human adoration, sparkle by sparkle."[7]

## Ambassador Black

In the next decade, Black took a keen interest in activism and charities, particularly the National Wildlife Federation and the National Multiple Sclerosis Society. In 1967, she ran unsuccessfully for the U.S. House of Representatives against Pete McCloskey, who demeaned her campaign with references to her Hollywood stardom. Press releases belittled her with inane remarks about being a "former child." She found it necessary to remind her challengers that everyone at some time was a child.

Even though her original nomination as a U.S. ambassador was also treated lightly in the press, Black ignored the flak and poured herself into her mission, becoming an outspoken opponent of apartheid. One colleague recalls that the U.N. General Assembly was on the verge of laughter upon her introduction, almost as though they expected "a little towhead to come in singing the 'Good Ship Lollipop.' Their incredulity turned to respect fast."[8]

While representing U.S. interests in Ghana, she earned a reputation for caring and cemented strong bonds of friendship and trust between her country and black Africa. Of her interest in Africa, she remarks, "I'm particularly pleased with my friendship with the developing countries. They're much more interesting to me than the super powers."[9] Undergirding her success were the sixteen-hour days and meticulous background study she devoted to each responsibility.

Even a mastectomy at the age of forty-four failed to deter Black's enthusiasm. Immediately after she regained consciousness, she helped distribute the mass of flowers from well-wishers. Her acknowledgement to the press of a successful bout with breast cancer was a forthright message to other victims, whom she claimed as sisters. She noted that victims of breast cancer needed to reach out and sustain one another through the shared ordeal. Her empathy resulted in a deluge of over 50,000 letters.

## Continued Successes

In the spring of 1989, President George Bush met little resistance to his nomination of Shirley as ambassador to Czechoslovakia. To questions posed by the Foreign Relations Committee, Senator Patrick Moynihan remarked: "It is such a great pleasure to have before the committee an experienced diplomat and a person with a very special capacity for the task she is about to undertake."[10] At age sixty-one, she had much to offer the world of diplomacy. Well-groomed and poised, she greeted guests and dignitaries with suitable courtesy and control, knowing when to remain firm and when to break into a wide vivacious smile.

The ambassadorship was a fitting tribute, for in 1968 Shirley had been stranded in a Prague hotel during the Russian invasion that led to Czechoslovakia's loss of democracy. That day, her appointment with Alexander Dubcek was unceremoniously cancelled. Representing the International Federation of Multiple Sclerosis Society at the time, she found herself a virtual prisoner in her hotel room as tight-jawed troops lined city streets and tanks rumbled past. As she candidly comments, "Nothing can crush freedom like a tank."[11]

Over twenty years later, immediately after her nomination, Shirley and Charles enrolled in a Czech language course. Her quick ear won her points with Czech President Husak as she listed her credentials for him in his native tongue. Likewise, she was not hesitant to voice her support of human rights, which was a major issue during Czechoslovakia's ousting of twenty-one years of communist domination.

Ambassador Black credited the Czechs with skillful handling of their orderly switch from communism. With the knowledge of an insider, she states that Czechs can take pride in their "velvet revolution."[12] Because of her facility with people and difficult political situations, her name has surfaced as a potential nominee for the vice-presidency or a cabinet post.

## Moppet No More

Name recognition has been useful to Black. She asserts, "Shirley Temple opens doors for Shirley Temple Black."[13] As she makes the connection between little Shirley and Ambassador Black, she comments: "Sometimes I feel like the oldest living American. That little girl has ... been a big advantage, *but she's not me*."[14] Even though her moppet years were filled with organdy dresses and starchy hairbows, she had a tough side. She was a tomboy at heart, carrying a slingshot in her little purse and longing to be the first female G-man.

Today, Black, a firm but soft-spoken rebel, maintains her allegiance to the Republican party, yet refuses to be categorized by narrow conservative platforms or labels. A union member in the Screen Actors' Guild from childhood, she refused to cross picket lines at age six. She supports AIDS research programs, advocates help for homeless people, and favors the Equal Rights Amendment and the pro-choice position, both strong feminist stands.

In her autobiography, *Child Star*, which Black dedicated to her mother, she broaches painful subjects from her past, particularly sexual harassment and an assault by a lecherous movie magnate, and, without sensationalizing either issue, puts them behind her. A shocking fact to many fans is the shrinkage of her $3 million in earnings, which dwindled to $89,000 through a series of bad financial moves, myriad expenses, and "loans" to people who never bothered to pay her back. With a noticeable touch of cynicism, the author commented, "Baby bountiful from childhood, she purchased clothing, a parade of automobiles, every dog bone, golf ball and diamond for seventeen years.... One human theme pulsed loud and clear: Keep dancing, kid, or the rickety cardhouse collapses."[15]

A believer in living in the present, Black states firmly, "The happiest moment is now."[16] She retains her porcelain complexion, erect carriage, and bright eyes, but has moved on from the past and accepted maturity and the challenge to make herself useful. Her Woodlands, California, home features memorabilia from her diplomatic career alongside her Oscar; she often dresses in Ghanaian garments and mentions with pride her role as honorary tribal chieftain. For a time, she volunteered as a receptionist at a clinic for handicapped children. Her children make her proud, especially Susan Black Falaschi, a successful journalist and science fiction writer and mother of Shirley's granddaughter, Teresa. Charles, Jr., works for the Department of Commerce in Washington, D.C.; Lori, two years his junior, is a photographer and new wave musician.

Black continues to manage 400 fan letters per month, although, without a secretary, she cannot reply to each. Her memories of the past are pleasant since to her, her childhood, with all the glitz and adulation, was normal. If pressed to give advice to other aspiring stage mothers, she draws on her knowledge of many wretched child stars and urges the questioner to let the child do whatever brings happiness.

## The Right Stuff

Part of Black's success is self-discipline, learned on movie sets and stages from the age of three. The rest stems from pragmatism, which steadies her progress. Charles Black, her most outspoken fan, openly speaks his pride in Shirley's strengths: "You won't find a chink in her armor." He summarizes more eloquently the traits that make his wife unusual: "She's an admirable character who's been a powerful source of happiness and good for the human race since she was three years old. Her whole life has been spent in various types of public service, either by entertaining people or by serving them."[17]

## Notes

[1] Joseph N. Bell. "Shirley Temple: Her Movies, Her Life," *Good Housekeeping*, February 1981, 191.

[2] Bell, 185.

[3] Bell, 185.

[4] Shirley Temple Black. *Child Star*. New York: McGraw-Hill, 1988, 164.

[5] Doug McClelland. "Child Star," *Asbury Park Press*, January 8, 1989, n.p.

[6] Bell, 189.

[7] Heidi Yorkshire. "Shirley Temple Black Sets the Record Straight," *McCall's*, March 1989, 88.

[8] Penelope Rowlands. "Shirley Temple Black," *Palo Alto* (California) *Peninsula Times-Tribune*, June 1, 1986, n.p.

[9] Rowlands, n.p.

[10] Vivian Cadden. "Return to Prague," *McCall's*, April 1990, 63.

[11] Cadden, 66.

[12] Cadden, 66.

[13] Cadden, 64.

[14] Bell, 114.

[15] Yorkshire, 93.

[16] Rowlands, n.p.

[17] Rowlands, n.p.

## Sources

Bell, Joseph N. "Shirley Temple: Her Movies, Her Life," *Good Housekeeping*, February 1981, 114-115, 185-190.

Black, Shirley Temple. *Child Star.* New York: McGraw-Hill, 1988.

Cadden, Vivian. "Return to Prague," *McCall's*, April 1990, 60-66.

"Happy Birthday, Shirley Temple Black!" *McCall's*, April 1982, 58.

"The Joys of Being a Grandmother," *McCall's*, December 1983, 102-108.

McClelland, Doug. "Child Star," *Asbury Park Press*, January 8, 1989, n.p.

"Mutiny on the Lollipop," *Time*, October 31, 1988, 59.

Rowlands, Penelope. "Shirley Temple Black," *Palo Alto* (California) *Peninsula Times-Tribune*, June 1, 1986, n.p.

"Shirley Offers Diplomatic Advice," *Newsweek*, December 7, 1981, 178-180.

Yorkshire, Heidi. "Shirley Temple Black Sets the Record Straight," *McCall's*, March 1989, 88-94.

# Erma Bombeck

For many people, finding a satisfying late career is a matter of refining an earlier one. Such a refiner is Erma Bombeck, a perennial kitchen humorist and laundry room wit since the late 1960s. A gladsome, open-faced woman with light brown hair, green eyes, and short stature, she caricatures her middle-age paunch, but never allows it to get the better of her. She once summarized her appearance with typical sauciness: "I am the quietest person at the party. I position myself at the chip dip and don't leave all night. The whole thrust of my existence is that I'm ordinary."[1]

As her fans attest, Erma Bombeck is far from ordinary. She not only creates hilarious family vignettes for a syndicated column, but also makes regular television appearances and writes witty features for popular magazines. Her funny, often piquant turns of phrase suggest a down-to-earth humorist who understands firsthand that middle-class American life is fraught with tribulations, some of which make ripe pickings for an enterprising funnywoman.

## Midwestern Beginnings

Erma Louise Bombeck is a product of midwestern America. Born in Dayton, Ohio, on February 21, 1927, to Cassius Edwin and Erma Fiste, she was an only child. Her mother was a housewife until Cassius, a crane operator for the city of Dayton, died of a stroke on June 4, 1936. In *Family: The Ties That Bind ... and Gag!*, Erma reflects on the loss of the man who "never did anything," but adds in the next breath, "I didn't know his leaving would hurt so much."[2]

Times were difficult for a single woman with a child to raise. Erma describes her mother as "raised in an orphanage, married at fourteen, and widowed at twenty-five, left with two children and a fourth-grade education."[3] Erma recalls how creditors arrived the day after the funeral and repossessed the car, furniture, and icebox. Her mother moved the family into Erma's grandmother's house, found work making rubber strips for General Motors' car doors at the Leland Electric factory, and met and subsequently married Tom Harris, a fellow worker.

For Erma, there were necessary adaptations. She felt isolated among her friends as the only child whose mother worked. She chafed at the idea of having a stepfather and a half-sister, Thelma. Later, however, Erma came to appreciate her stepfather, who demonstrated his love by keeping her in line and being there when she needed a replacement parent.

## In Training for the Future

An ambitious student from the age of thirteen, Erma attended Patterson Vocational High School. On her own she studied humor with an eye toward writing. To hone her skills, she read James Thurber, Robert Benchley, and Max Schulman. During hands-on training, she served as secretary to the *Dayton Journal-Herald*. Then in 1944 she graduated from school and took a job as the newspaper's copy girl, the low woman on the journalistic totem pole. She quipped about her skill as a reporter: "I was terrible at straight items. When I wrote obituaries, my mother said the only thing I ever got them to do was die in alphabetical order."[4]

After a year in full-time newspaper work, Erma enrolled at the University of Dayton, where she majored in English. She wrote witty articles for the university newspaper and literary magazine. To pay tuition, she handled public relations for the YMCA, wrote a column for a department store newsletter, and edited a small newspaper. She returned to the *Journal-Herald* in 1949 after completing her BA and began learning the trade of newspaper writing, from obituaries and radio listings to white sales, crime, and household hints, the latter a part of her post as feature writer for the women's page.

## Marriage and a Family

The summer after graduation, Erma followed the course of honor for women of her generation: she married sports reporter William Lawrence "Bill" Bombeck on August 13. She continued her journalistic career until the adoption of Betsy, her first child, four years later. Within five more years she gave birth to two sons, Andy and Matthew. Until the 1960s, she remained anonymous in her role as wife, mother, and homemaker in a housing development in Centerville, Ohio.

Motherhood was an awakening for Bombeck. In *Family: The Ties That Bind ... and Gag!*, she allowed herself an honest, unfunny reflection of her matriarchal role: "It was steady. Lord, it was steady. But in retrospect, no matter what deeds my life yielded ... no matter how many books I had written marched in a row on a library shelf,... I had done something rather extraordinary with my life as a mother."[5]

Then mid-life aroused new yearnings in Bombeck. She abandoned the role of dedicated mom and returned to journalism, although on a small scale. In *If Life Is a Bowl of Cherries—What Am I Doing in the Pits?*, she explained to other rebels the mild revolt that led to her resurrection: "...you can be like the woman I knew who sat at her kitchen window year after year and watched everyone else do it. Then one day she said, 'I do not feel fulfilled cleaning chrome faucets with a toothbrush. It's my turn.' I was thirty-seven years old at the time."[6]

At a portable typewriter perched atop a hunk of plywood on cinder block legs in her makeshift bedroom/office, the revitalized Bombeck typed a $3.00-per-week humor column for the *Kettering-Oakwood Times*. The work proved satisfrying, successful, and therapeutic. She returned full time to the *Journal-Herald* the next year and began producing two columns per week.

After the first six years of her resurgence, Erma Bombeck began establishing herself as something more than a writer of obituaries. Her column, *At Wit's End*, grew into a popular syndicated feature carried first by Newsday Syndicate (from 1964 to 1970), then by North American Syndicate (1970-1985), *Los Angeles Times* Syndicate for the next three years, and finally by Universal Press Syndicate. Obviously, Bombeck had arrived—and in grand style.

## Developing a Voice

The chronology of Erma Bombeck's arrival proved significant. Having acquired the basics of journalism during her first career, she became a competent writer. Next, the years of motherhood provided her with a steady flow of experiences as fodder for her rapid-fire wit. As she commented later, "I was overwhelmed [by parenthood]. We all were. That's the core of laughter. If you can't make it better, you can laugh at it."[7] From an amalgamation of the three—parenthood, journalism, and humor—came the unique style that is Bombeck.

The Bombeck canon reflects rare and insightful style from the title to the last hurrah. Even the chapter headings summon a chuckle. In wry, non-threatening satire, she covers the following topics in *Aunt Erma's Cope Book*: "A House Divided Against Itself Cannot Stand One Another," "How to Tell Your Best Friend She Has Bad Body English," "Go Suck an Egg," and "I Don't Care What I Say ... I Still Like Me."[8] The magic of Bombeck is her ability to tap into instant reader appreciation.

She quickly came into demand. Even seasoned pros like Art Buchwald confessed to being Bombeck fans. After hearing Arthur Godfrey read from her first book on the air, she soon became a regular on his radio program, then accepted an invitation to perform on "The Tonight Show." In a humorous reminiscence about that early appearance, Bombeck quipped about her mother's advice to be herself: "I was myself. And I bombed so bad it was ten years before I ever got on the show again."[9]

## Creeping Success

By the 1970s, Bombeck emerged as one of America's funniest women. In 1971 she created a private nest for herself in a converted garage adjacent to her new nine-room ranch house in Paradise Valley, outside Phoenix, Arizona. By 1978 she was earning $500,000 per year and employed both a secretary and a housekeeper. Her husband, who gave up journalism and worked as a high school principal, was her mainstay.

Today, the subject matter of her column and books ranges from where the lost socks go to how coat hangers breed in dark closets. Developing each segment from a single impression of the dull, mundane banality of housekeeping, she fires rapid one-liners, exaggerations, incongruencies, and self-accusatory satire. Her perusal of simple home quandaries, such as how to keep leftovers from sprouting green fuzz or quiet a whiny child, spark sympathetic snickers in her readers, most of whom are housewives. Whatever the subject—PTA, appointments with the orthodontist, dealing with visiting relatives, suburban politics, training a recalcitrant puppy, or cooking meals that please everybody—the theme remains uniquely American in tone and content. Summarizing her strengths, Bombeck observed: "I pride myself on being able to handle trauma, natural disasters, deep depression, misfortune, hardship, discomfort, and readily adjust when they run out of extra crispy chicken at the carry-out."[10]

## Erma As Social Critic

A large number of Erma Bombeck's columns deal with women's topics. Frequent among the objects of her lampoons are confronting fat around the thighs, counting calories, buying a bathing suit, and battling incipient middle age with no-holds-barred style. Although she counters some of society's most prevalent problems, Bombeck manages to control the field without wounding her audience.

Occasionally, Bombeck speaks in a straightforward voice, as in the conclusion of *I Lost Everything in the Post-natal Depression*, where the author castigates violence in American society. She questions how anyone can coddle children who grew up in the time of the Kent State massacre, President Kennedy's assassination, and the Attica prison riots. On kids who view movies like *Bonnie and Clyde, Willard,* and *Butch Cassidy and the Sundance Kid* as entertainment, she comments, "It's the reality that frightens them and gives them nightmares. God help us. It does me too."[11]

A second example of her ability to write serious commentary occurs in the introduction to *Motherhood: The Second Oldest Profession*. After describing the misery of one fan who read her books while serving time in solitary confinement in a southern prison, Bombeck gently reminded her audience: "It is not until you become a mother that your judgment slowly turns to compassion and understanding. Let none of you who read about the mothers in this book judge them until you have walked in their shoes of clay."[12]

## Keep On Keeping On

But Bombeck has not grown testy or thin-skinned as she changes with the times. In a recent column, she teased the talk show hosts—Oprah Winfrey, Sally Jessy Raphael, Geraldo, Joan Rivers, and Phil Donahue. Her premise was that these purveyors of human perversion had created a kind of "Aberrational Pursuit." As Bombeck saw it, "Nazi nuns with eating disorders is gone. So is terrorists as good fathers. Grandmothers who married their grandsons' ski instructors has been done to death. I find myself grabbing for the listings every day to see what will come up next."[13] As usual, her short perusal of the subject produces just enough humor for a brief but revealing essay.

Dedicated to light humor as opposed to sober analysis, Bombeck leaves social commentary to Dear Abby and Ann Landers. For her, the key to lively humor is a light pen undipped in the more acerbic wit of her fellow columnists. Her bailiwick remains the incongruencies and crazy-making scenes found in "everyfamily." As she explains, "I stick close to home—I'm still exploiting my children, husband, and family life. I know what my domain is."[14]

## Success at 40

By 1967, Bombeck was a household name and was published in more than 200 newspapers. Groups clambered to hire her for informal lectures. In 1971, a collection of her columns appeared in *Just Wait Till You Have Children of Your Own!*, the first of a series of books she wrote in collaboration with artist Bil Keane, a cartoonist who draws *Family Circus*. She followed in 1973 with *I Lost Everything in the Post-natal Depression* and three years later *The Grass Is Always Greener Over the Septic Tank*. By October 1978, CBS premiered a television series based on *The Grass Is Always Greener*, starring Carol Burnett and Charles Grodin, but jettisoned it as unwieldy and contrived. The fiasco was clear evidence that Bombeck's words belong on the printed page and not in a TV sitcom.

## What the Critics Say

On the whole, critics champion Bombeck's humor. Most realize that she is more than just naturally funny. Her drollery, carefully balanced and controlled, springs from real precision and awareness of human foibles. In her hymn to suburbia, she creates thorny, eccentric characters. Most memorable are Ralph the Little League coach and Wanda the school bus driver. A serious reader of America's symptoms, she understands that some everyday harassments, beyond their misery, are capable of producing a therapeutic laugh. And that very perception is Bombeck's strength—she delves beneath the pungent upper layers to the rich goodies at the bottom of the pot.

Her development as humorist and spokeswoman for middle America continues to evolve. By the late 1970s Bombeck's cheery little essays had achieved best-seller status. Her frequent television appearances substantiated a simple truth—that she belonged in her own rogue's gallery as a dyed-in-the-wool member of the suburban set.

Later Bombeckian triumphs include more zaniness: *If Life Is a Bowl of Cherries—What Am I Doing in the Pits?* (1978), *Aunt Erma's Cope Book: How to Get from Monday to Friday in Twelve Days* (1979), *Motherhood: The Second Oldest Profession* (1984), *Four of a Kind: A Treasury of Favorite Works by America's Best-Loved Humorist* (1985), and *Family: The Ties That Bind ... and Gag!* (1988). She outshines her colleague Art Buchwald with columns three times per week in 900 newspapers and even a record album, *The Family That Plays Together ... Gets on Each Other's Nerves.* She continues to hit best-seller charts, writes for *Good Housekeeping*, which she edited from 1969-1974, and appears as a twice-weekly columnist on "Good Morning, America." Her whimsical musings also appear in *McCall's, Reader's Digest, Redbook*, and *Family Circle.*

In 1989, Bombeck left her usual zany domain to produce a compassionate view of the effects of cancer on children with *I Want to Grow Hair, I Want to Grow Up, I Want to Go to Boise.* In the introduction, she explained her emotions, "As they talked and laughed about their lives, suddenly I felt like I was the innocent child and they were the adults, dispensing wisdom. And I knew then these kids deserved better than buckets of tears and public pity."[15]

## Reaping the Rewards

For her dedication to lifting America's spirits, Erma Bombeck has received a number of awards. She has won the National Headliner prize from Theta Sigma Phi and the Mark Twain humor award in addition to fourteen honorary doctorates and numerous honoraria from colleges and universities, notably Bowling Green University, Scholastica College, and Rosary College. Her name is a fixture on the annual list of the twenty-five most influential American women in *The World Almanac.*

Some of Bombeck's long-standing witticisms about herself remain true. She does take a daily nap and really does quail at the sight of her ample body in a bathing suit. Her gap-toothed smile warms a real family, although the children have long since outgrown adolescent messiness and mealtime chaos. Erma and husband Bill endure the empty-nest syndrome at their residence in Paradise Valley. In her mature years, she has outgrown PTA, car pools, and den mother status, but remains interested in community affairs. She serves on the board of the Kidney Foundation and other Arizona charities.

Bombeck keeps her distance from activism. She served on the President's National Advisory Committee for Women in 1978. In general, she supports women's rights, yet maintains that liberated women have shortchanged house-wives by making them feel less important to society. Yet, this stance on the issue of feminism has scarcely made a dent in her popularity with the 31 million readers who look to her for daily uplift.

## Notes

[1] John Skow. "Erma Bombeck: Syndicated Soul of Suburbia," *Reader's Digest*, February 1984, 40.

[2] Erma Bombeck. *Family: The Ties That Bind ... and Gag!* New York: McGraw-Hill, 1987, 2.

[3] Erma Bombeck. *Motherhood: The Second Oldest Profession.* New York: McGraw-Hill, 1983, 172.

[4] Skow, 44.

[5] *Family*, 198.

[6] Erma Bombeck. *If Life Is a Bowl of Cherries—What Am I Doing in the Pits?* New York: McGraw-Hill, 1978, 192-193.

[7] Skow, 44.

[8] Erma Bombeck. *Aunt Erma's Cope Book.* New York: McGraw-Hill, 1979.

[9] *Motherhood*, 4.

[10] *Cherries*, 201.

[11] Erma Bombeck. *I Lost Everything in the Post-natal Depression.* Garden City, New York: Doubleday, 1970, 161.

[12] *Motherhood*, 4.

[13] Erma Bombeck. "Let's Play 'How Did Talk Shows Get That'?," *Charlotte Observer*, January 22, 1991, 8D.

[14] *Current Biography*. Detroit: Gale Research, 1979, 41.

[15] Erma Bombeck. *I Want to Grow Hair, I Want to Grow Up, I Want to Go to Boise.* New York: Harper & Row, 1989, xviii.

# Sources

Battelle, Phyllis. "Erma Bombeck: Worries Behind Her Wit," *Woman's Day*, January 21, 1986, 75-80.

Bombeck, Erma. *Aunt Erma's Cope Book.* New York: McGraw-Hill, 1979.

_____. *Family: The Ties That Bind ... and Gag!* New York: McGraw-Hill, 1987.

_____. *I Lost Everything in the Post-natal Depression.* Garden City, New York: Doubleday, 1970.

_____. *I Want to Grow Hair, I Want to Grow Up, I Want to Go to Boise.* New York: Harper & Row, 1989.

_____. *If Life Is a Bowl of Cherries—What Am I Doing in the Pits?* New York: McGraw-Hill, 1978.

_____. *Just Wait till You Have Children of Your Own!* Garden City, New York: Doubleday, 1971.

_____. "Let's Play 'How Did Talk Shows Get That'?," *Charlotte Observer*, January 22, 1991, 8D.

_____. *Motherhood: The Second Oldest Profession.* New York: McGraw-Hill, 1983.

*Current Biography.* Detroit: Gale Research, 1979.

Skow, John. "Erma Bombeck: Dingbat Neighbor Supreme," *Reader's Digest* (Canadian Edition), February 1985, 65.

_____. "Erma in Bomburbia: For a Survivor of Housework and Motherhood, Laughter Is Still the Best Revenge," *Time*, July 2, 1981, 56-63.

_____. "Erma Bombeck: Syndicated Soul of Suburbia," *Reader's Digest*, February 1984, 39-46.

*Who's Who.* Detroit: Gale Research, 1991.

# Sir Francis Charles Chichester

Sometimes success comes to those late bloomers who seem least like achievers. The accomplishments of Sir Francis Chichester are prime examples. In fulfilling the role of daredevil, Chichester looked anything but rugged or daring. According to a special report in *Newsweek*, he was "an ordinary-looking bloke, a thin old man with big ears, broken teeth and spectacles."[1] He took up sailing at the age of 52 after a rather sedentary career as a London map publisher.

Aboard the *Gipsy Moth III*, the wiry, competitive Chichester sailed from Plymouth, Devon, to New York City in 40 days. On a second attempt, he shaved seven days off his record. At the age of 65, he went for broke and sailed around the world from Plymouth, arriving back in Greenwich for a knighting by Queen Elizabeth II, who touched his shoulder with the sword that Queen Elizabeth I used in knighting Sir Francis Drake.

Chichester graciously accepted acclaim from major newspapers and magazines around the world, who named the public clamor for him "Chichysteria."[2] One admiring interviewer voiced his appreciation that Chichester represents the driven individual who stands out from would-be adventurers who are "only able to coddle—rather than enact—their Walter Mitty fantasies."[3] In explanation of his extraordinary response to the challenge of the seas, Chichester claimed that fear brought out the macho in him: "If anything terrifies me, I must try to conquer it."[4]

## Early Promise

Francis Charles Chichester was born on September 17, 1901, in Barnstable, Devon, and received his education at Marlborough College, dropping out of public school in 1918. His father, a prim minister, was a spiritless man who tried to quash the boy's enthusiasm for adventure. In response to these family pressures to conform, Chichester became a loner and ultimately left home to make his way in the world.

An adventurer from a young age, he emigrated to New Zealand with only $50 to his name. He proved flexible, working as a coal miner, farmer, gold prospector, amateur boxer, salesman, lumberjack, and realtor. Within ten years, he returned to England with $100,000 in savings.

Obtaining his pilot's license in 1929, Chichester became the first man to fly solo to Australia, which he accomplished aboard a frail single-engine Gipsy Moth biplane in 180.5 hours. He then fitted his aircraft with flotation devices and continued 1,200 miles over the Tasman Sea and on to Japan, where a collision with a half-mile span of telephone wires ended his feat, catapulting him into a stone wall in Katsuura harbor and landing him in the hospital. Despite thirteen broken bones and the pronouncement that he had to give up flying, he co-piloted a plane back to England.

## A Change in Craft

During World War II, the war board rejected Chichester for active combat duty because of residual impairment from his crash. To compensate, he served as an air-navigation expert for the RAF from 1941 to 1945. His career as a map publisher filled the hiatus between youthful air and land adventures and his daring sea voyages. It was in 1953 that he decided to take up yacht racing. The next year, he bought and refinished his first sailing vessel, *Gipsy Moth II*.

Reciting from earlier times his favorite poem, John Masefield's "Sea Fever," Chichester kept alive the characteristically British adoration of a life at sea. As he phrased his urge, it lay in him like a seed lying fallow for fifty years until air and light brought it to life. To express his new love, he published *The Lonely Sea and the Sky* in 1964; two years later he followed with *Along the Clipper Way*.

When a bad cough presaged lung cancer, Chichester, with the backing of his loyal wife Sheila, rejected surgery. He opted instead for naturopathic treatment. Hovering near death for a time, he began a slow convalescence. The couple moved to the south of France, where Chichester regained his former vigor. In 1959, he purchased his second boat, *Gipsy Moth III*. He proved himself seaworthy once more by entering a solo race from England to New York and beat the competition soundly, covering the distance in 40 days. Intrigued with the experience, he repeated it three times.

## Plotting the Course

Undeterred by the close call with cancer, in 1960 he began plotting his ultimate course, which he financed with personal funds, a donation from a brewery, and twice-weekly radio reports to the *Sunday Times* and *The Manchester Guardian*. On his around-the-world trek in 1966, Chichester departed from the usual route, following the Trade Winds belts, and chose instead to round Cape Horn, an itinerary chosen by only nine predecessors. Bolstered by his wife Sheila's faith in prayer, he stuck to his plan.

Chichester, aboard *Gipsy Moth IV*, an $84,000 fifty-three-foot ketch with fore and aft rigging, sailed from Plymouth through the Bass Strait toward Sydney, Australia, his only port of call. A stroke of ill fortune befell him on the seventy-fifth day at sea when raging waves destroyed his automatic steering device, which linked up the wind vane to the rudder by means of pulleys. To complicate his woes, he broke a molar and had to smooth the jagged edge with a file from his toolbox. But the challenge failed to dissuade his determination.

To stick to the goal of completing the first leg of the trek in 100 days, Chichester had to forego regular sleep, nap when he could, and man the helm at all times. He grew so weak that he was nearly incapable of hoisting the mainsail.

He headed for Fremantle. Then, stodgily returning to his original plan, he pushed on toward Sydney by improvising a makeshift steering device. As he said, "The more I thought about it, the more it stuck in my gullet."[5] The success of his tinkering gave him new self-confidence: he felt elated that he was facing each challenge alone.

## In the Wake of the Great Sailors

Following the old square-rigger wool and tea routes, he completed the first leg of his odyssey—14,100 miles—in 107 days, remaining in radio contact with passing vessels, planes, and amateur radio operators. By December 12, 1966, he had accomplished something that no other sailor could boast. He had sailed twice as far as any single person had ever gone. Chichester was proud, but completely candid about his fears. At times he lay awake in his bunk awaiting the crash of each wave.

At the Royal Sidney Yacht Club, Chichester limped ashore, forty pounds shy of his normal weight. At an ebb of spiritual and physical strength, he also suffered from malnutrition. He was greeted by a corps of news reporters and began an immediate recovery from his hundred-day isolation from human contact. Even at the extent of his endurance, he was already a hero.

## Phase Two

Six weeks' rest and recuperation were necessary before the elderly sailor could tackle the next phase of his project, the treacherous second half around Cape Horn and some 14,000 miles back to Plymouth. To assure better nutrition on the remaining days at sea, he purchased foods that required less fuss and time. To correct some unmanageability in the steering mechanism, he made his yacht self-steering, then concluded his seven-week layover with a press conference.

Chichester set sail on January 29, 1967, weathered Cyclone Diana, and proceeded north of New Zealand and south of Cape Horn in four months. On the way, his ketch, at the buffeting of a freak wave, flipped over in gale-force winds and took on heavy seas. In the roll, a sharp knife imbedded itself in the woodwork overhead. Suffering only a minor cut on his lip, the doughty Chichester waited for the *Gipsy Moth* to right herself, then set her back on course, baled her dry, and tidied up the mess.

The real fascination of his route—the rounding of the Cape in a hellish zone known as the Roaring Forties—held a kind of forbidden lure, for Chichester knew in advance of the countless lone adventurers who had capsized or somersaulted in the terrifying storms characteristic of the region. In the days of the tall ships, it took a crew of twelve men to pilot a boat through these treacherous shoals. Chichester described the passage graphically: "You've got all the water being squeezed between South America and the Antarctic through this narrow, shallow gap. You get waves 50 feet high; you get the fury of hell loose at times there."[6] But against the advice of naysayers, he hung on.

## Around the Horn

On March 19, as he approached the crucial point of his journey, he was tingling with excitement. A plane passed over carrying representatives of the *Sunday Times* and the BBC, annoying Chichester by breaking in on his solitude. At 6:05 P.M., he wrote in his journal that he planned to celebrate with a bottle of champagne and sleep. At that point, Chichester had been without food or sustained rest for four days.

Somewhat awed by his own temerity, he decided against a celebration with all the trimmings. "It's always the same with any big effort," he concludes. "If you succeed, it seems slack at the time. You've made so much effort that success at the end means nothing. It's the effort that counts, not the success."[7]

Thirty reporters scrambled to record his impressions. Two from the BBC risked crashing in gale winds under a 600-foot ceiling to get a closer view of Chichester's ketch battling the cape. After a harrowing return to the ground, they published their scoop in the *Times*, noting, "The sight of *Gipsy Moth* plowing bravely through the wilderness of rain and sea was well worth it."[8]

## Alone with Himself

Most days, he kept busy with navigation, maintenance, sail repair, cooking, photography, observation of sea birds and fish, and treatment of bursitis and a chipped elbow. His quarters, laid out to Sheila's tastes, featured a galley, a red chair complete with safety belt, and a radio transmitter to connect him with the outside world. In addition, he packed a barrel of beer and a selection of liquors. To the assembled press, he noted sheepishly that running out of drink was a major hindrance near the end of the voyage.

Chichester, a vegetarian, baked bread in his galley and grew salad greens, which he spiked with garlic and Dutch cheese. On his sixty-fifth birthday, he celebrated in a green velvet smoking jacket by popping the cork on a bottle of champagne and opening gifts from Sheila and friends. He declared that, alone in the cockpit, he drank toasts to absent family members and friends. As an appropriate capper for an old seadog, the day ended with a spectacular sunset. Chichester carried with him tapes of Tchaikovsky, Beethoven, and Gershwin, but held back from enjoying them. He explained that the demands of the voyage turned him into a machine.

As he neared his landing point, the same spot where Sir Francis Drake returned the *Golden Hind* in the days of Elizabeth I, Chichester pondered the changes that had taken place in him during his months alone on the little craft and rejoiced that he still had two gallons of fuel in reserve. He chuckled at his habit of conversing with himself and his sporadic need for catnaps, even during meals. With typical British courtesy, he saluted cheers emanating from HMS *Eagle* and followed with a second greeting to a passing minesweeper.

## Ready for Kudos

Sir Francis arrived home bearing two token bales of wool from Australia and eight logbooks filled with 200,000 words describing his experiences, including the extensive periods when he traveled at a speed of over 130 miles per day. In all, he saw land only four times during the voyage. The span of 15,517 miles was the longest ever completed at a stretch by a small vessel. He ended his 226-day voyage with 250,000 well-wishers waving flags and escorting him to the Plymouth Guildhall and millions more watching on television.

Souvenir stands sold plastic models of the *Gipsy Moth IV* alongside humbler trinkets bearing his likeness, such as picture puzzles, health food, tea towels, postcards, mugs, and even pink panties decorated with a black anchor. The *Cutty Sark*, the famous clipper ship, was decorated in his honor. A songwriter immortalized Chichester with "A Man Alone."[9] Church bells rang an insistent hurrah; guns fired a salute. The Queen dashed out a telegraphed welcome. Along with hordes of curious fans, she inspected the *Gipsy Moth IV* at quayside.

At his press conference, the crowd gave Chichester a standing ovation, although he demurred, "I honestly can't say that I enjoy mass fame."[10] Though Lindbergh, Hillary, and Tensing were more famous, few men touched the human imagination as Chichester had. As *Newsweek* explained, "Sorely diminished in power and unsure of its future role, the British nation likes to be reminded that it can still produce men of daring and resource. Sir Francis has grandly filled that need."[11]

In London awaited Chichester's advancement to knight commander of the Order of the British Empire at the Royal Naval College at Greenwich and lunch with the Lord Mayor of London. Accolades lauded his self-discipline, perseverance, courage, and endurance. In true form the muscular, bespectacled, weather-beaten old man gave most of the credit to his wife Sheila and junior partner, son Giles.

# A View of the Hero

Chichester shrugged off the concept of heroism with the quaint notion that "it's nothing to do with one personally. It's some sort of an idea they are applauding. It's a wonderful thing."[12] In a later interview with *Time* magazine, he appended: "I have no interest in meeting a better class of person than the friends I already have. I still much prefer to be appreciated by the connoisseurs."[13]

The voyage took its toll; a week after Chichester's triumph, he was hospitalized with a duodenal ulcer and remained in bed for a month. The following year, he narrated his adventures in *The Gipsy Moth Circles the World*. At the age of seventy, he put *Gipsy Moth IV* to further use by sailing alone in twenty-two days from Bissau in Portuguese Guinea to San Juan, Nicaragua, a total of 4,000 miles. At the time of his final illness, Sir Francis was contemplating a solo transatlantic race. Mountain climber Sir Toni Hiebeler made a fitting tribute to his spunk: "When I was reading about the old man, Chichester, I told my wife—see, people who are a little crazy stay young."[14]

## Notes

[1] "The Old Man and the Sea," *Newsweek*, June 12, 1967, 61.

[2] "Treasure from the Sea," *Time*, June 9, 1967, 48.

[3] *Newsweek*, 62.

[4] Sir Francis Chichester. "Around the World with Gipsy Moth IV," *Reader's Digest*, June 1967, 46.

[5] *Time*, 48.

[6] Chichester, 46.

[7] Chichester, 51.

[8] *Time*, 48.

[9] *Newsweek*, 61.

[10] *Time*, 48.

[11] *Time*, 48.

[12] *Newsweek*, 61.

[13] *Time*, 48.

[14] *Time*, 64-65.

## Sources

Chichester, Sir Francis. "Around the World with Gipsy Moth IV," *Reader's Digest*, June 1967, 46-52.

_____. *Gipsy Moth Circles the World.* London: Hodder Stoughton, 1988.

"Derring-do off Cape Horn," *Time*, March 31, 1967, 27.

"The Old Man and the Sea," *Newsweek*, June 12, 1967, 61-65.

"Treasure from the Sea," *Time*, June 9, 1967, 48.

# Julia Child

Achievers in the kitchen are common enough, but only a select few reach their pinnacle in French cookery, considered by some the height of European cuisine. A notable example is Julia Child, doyenne of food preparation from A to Z. Noted for hard work and determination, she taught herself to cook, then set about proving to American audiences that they, too, could complete difficult Continental dinners while having a good time and enjoying nutritious, attractive food. Her first book, which she wrote in collaboration with two French women, has been labeled the "premiere guide to classic French cooking."[1]

A staple on American educational television, Julia Child became a symbol of no-nonsense cookery and trounced the myth that only Continental chefs could succeed with French recipes. Appearing in her studio kitchen in an impeccable denim apron with a sporty cooking school insignia, she tackled everything from giant lobsters to delicate *fines herbes*. In good spirits, whatever the challenge, she ended each installment with her familiar rallying cry, "This is Julia Child. Bon appétit!"

## Dry Beginnings

A native of Pasadena, California, blue-eyed, brown-haired Julia McWilliams was born to John McWilliams and Julia Carolyn Weston on August 15, 1912. Her father was a farm consultant. The Weston side of the family has been in the United States since Pilgrim days and provided Julia with her stalwart pioneering spirit. She and her brother John and sister Dorothy, all spirited six-footers, took a hearty interest in good eating, but had little need to learn cooking because the family had a hired cook. Instead, the McWilliams children, who maintained a close relationship, preferred outdoor games. Of her lanky, athletic brood, Julia's mother crowed, "I have produced eighteen feet of children."[2]

Julia received traditional upbringing, yet attended a Montessori kindergarten and the Katherine Brandon School in Ross, north of San Francisco and five miles from the Pacific Ocean. An average student, she graduated in 1930 and moved on to Smith College, majoring in history and considering both fiction writing and basketball as possible vocations. She roomed in a tiny efficiency apartment in New York City and served as a copywriter in the advertising department of W. & J. Sloane, a noted furniture dealer.

## A Dash of Adventure

Hoping for more challenge during the war years, Julia signed up for the Office of Strategic Services (OSS), a short-lived wartime spying operation which eventually developed into the CIA. Her assignment as a file clerk in Washington, D.C., and Sri Lanka proved less than rapturous. Julia and the other female OSS members traveled by troop carrier, slept on cots, and wore baggy fatigues. She recalled her girlish philosophy during those days with characteristic humor: "I was a playgirl, looking for the light. I remember pulling into Bombay. It was very early dawn... 'Oh, my God,' I thought, 'what have I gotten myself into?' "[3]

Then in 1943, Julia met cartographer and fellow OSS member Paul Cushing Child, ten years her senior and several inches shorter. Because of his artistic flair, he had been hired to decorate the headquarters of Lord Mountbatten. A sophisticated member of a prestigious Boston family and an epicure at heart, Paul became her life-long beau. Romance blossomed between Paul and Julia during a mutual assignment to China, where Paul, adept at food preparation, introduced his girl to the subtleties of oriental cuisine.

After the war, Julia, while smitten and eager to settle down, was cautious in committing to a life with Paul. She returned to California and began studying in earnest in Beverly Hills at the Hillcliffe School of Cookery. Gradually, she introduced her staunch Republican father to the notion of having an artist for a son-in-law. When her father bridled at the suggestion, she did what she is famous for—made up her own mind and defied authority.

Julia married Paul in New Hope, Pennsylvania, in September 1946. Still a neophyte cook, she maintained a Washington apartment and cooked for her husband, who worked for the Foreign Service. Perhaps the most important move in her life occurred in 1948, when Paul was transferred to France to serve as exhibits officer for the United States Information Agency in the American Embassy in Paris.

The couple settled in an apartment in a choice neighborhood on the Left Bank, cultural center for artists, writers, philosophers, and cooks. There Julia thrilled to a ready supply of taste treats. With scholarly attention to research, she tried to learn every aspect of French cooking methods so that she could duplicate the recipes.

# The French Chef

Child was by no means ready to conquer the frontiers of cuisine until she had mastered the French language. After intensive daily study at the Berlitz School, she entered the Cordon Bleu, an exclusive school founded in 1895 and originally intended to teach the rudiments of fine cooking to young ladies from elite families. In addition to the small classes of six to eight students, Julia sought private tutoring under master chefs, particularly Max Bugnard, noted Belgian restaurateur. With this preparation, she was ready for greater challenges. Under the guidance of her friend and mentor, Simone "Simca" Beck, Child gained entrance to French society and a group of food appreciators known as Le Cercle des Gourmettes.

Julia joined Louisette Bertholle and Simone Beck to form L'Ecole des Trois Gourmandes, a cooking school held in the Childs' apartment. For a modest $5 per lesson, students attempted the challenging recipes that made Paris famous to world-class gastronomes. Child's advice to those few beginners reflected her understanding of the learning process as well as her appreciation of the beginner's quandary: "First learn the basics—learn to make chicken stew. From there you can make coq au vin."[4]

A second product of the trio's school was Child's definitive book, *Mastering the Art of French Cooking*, which she compiled during Paul's various assignments in Oslo, Marseilles, and Bonn and completed in 1961 at the age of forty-nine. The book was a critical masterpiece, lauded by the great names in cooking as a primer for chefs. Child explained its phenomenal sales in her usual modest style, "It came out at just the right time. People were getting interested in traveling to France and eating good food."[5]

# Success and Then Some

Child did not move into the media until after Paul retired from the diplomatic corps in 1961. The couple established a permanent residence in a three-story gray clapboard country house in Cambridge, Massachusetts, known to insiders for its six-eye gas stove, raised chopping block, array of cookware and cutlery, and state-of-the-art appliances. She began writing magazine articles for *House and Garden* and *House Beautiful* in the early 1960s, followed by a regular column in the *Boston Globe*.

She made a brief appearance on a panel show on station WGBH in Boston to demonstrate a lesson from her book. On February 11, 1963, the success of an on-air omelette led to Child's legendary thirty-minute hands-on cooking program, "The French Chef," an instant smash with viewers which was soon carried by 100 stations. With arms pumping and hands gesturing the exact way to whip up recipes with a Continental flair, she treated her audience to entertaining lessons laced with wit, occasional gaffes, and sound advice. Producer Russ Morash commented, "It's difficult to think and react on TV at the same time. But Julia knew her stuff and didn't have to fake it. We just had to point her in the direction of the camera."[6]

As a chef, Child exuded confidence, which she communicated to her fans. Believing that anybody could succeed at French cooking, she moved unhesitatingly from simple kitchen maneuvers to the subtler touches, particularly the preparation of sauces, soufflés, sculpted chocolates, soup stock, and puff pastry. Her unwavering philosophy called for the best ingredients and appropriate utensils, meticulous adherence to instructions, careful timing, and a sense of daring.

To assure authenticity for each segment, Child purchased the ingredients herself, often commenting on the availability and quality of American produce, meat, seafood, and fowl as compared with their European counterparts. Likewise, she suggested American equivalents for French saucepans and casseroles as well as replacements for species of wheat, artichokes, mushrooms, and other specialty items not found in American markets. She taped demonstrations before live audiences, who paid $5 each for front-row seats.

Each segment of "The French Chef" and its sequel, "Dinner at Julia's," required ten hours of rehearsal and was underwritten by Hills Brothers and Polaroid. Child received a pittance of $50 for each step-by-step lesson, then either fed the results to the taping crew or else auctioned off the meal and donated the proceeds to the station, which paid for the groceries. She allowed no commercialization or free advertising and derived profit only from promotion of her book. For her professional approach to educational television, she earned the George Foster Peabody award in 1965 and, the next year, an Emmy, followed by honorary doctorates and other accolades.

## Follow-up to Success

The Childs enjoyed the financial rewards of Julia's television success. They built a home at Grasse a few miles west of Nice in southern France and maintained a winter condominium on the American West Coast near Santa Barbara with a view of both mountains and the Pacific. Child continued making public appearances and writing books on food. Her later titles include an illustrated volume, *The French Chef Cookbook* (1968), *From Julia Child's Kitchen* (1975), *Julia Child & Company* (1978), *Julia Child & More Company* (1979), and, at the age of seventy-seven, *The Way to Cook* (1989), complete with color photographs and columns lifted from *Parade* magazine, to which she contributed from 1982 to 1986.

To promote her last book, Child toured the country from San Francisco to New York, stopping for interviews along the way. She discussed the book business with the aplomb of a pro: "You've got to go out and sell it. No sense spending all that time—five years on this one—and then hiding your light under a bushel.... Besides, I'm a ham."[7]

Child was never chary with advice about food. She appeared regularly on "Good Morning, America" on ABC-TV and wrote columns for *McCall's* magazine. During the Carter administration, she urged the First Lady to upgrade White House menus. When Michael Dukakis assumed the governorship of Massachusetts, aides sought Child's word on what to serve inauguration officials. Even at the age of seventy-seven, following hip replacement and new kneecaps, she appeared as a chipper, optimistic speaker at the Eighth Annual Food and Wine Classic in Aspen, Colorado.

## Challenges in the 1990s

After the advent of French cooking, Americans continued sampling and changing their diets through *nouvelle cuisine*, organic food, and health diets. As consumers began turning from salt, eggs, butter, cream, and the other taboo ingredients of traditional recipes, Child supported sensible eating, variety, and moderation. However, upon encountering unsauced, undressed, unsalted foods in five-star establishments, Julia feared that paranoia would lead to the demise of gastronomy in American restaurants. In assessment of the abrupt shift toward bland health-conscious diets, she noted with distaste: "It's unrealistic, unscientific. I think people will die sooner just because life will be so boring."[8] To Amy Rennert she added a personal opinion: "What I'd like to find is a healthy normal nutritionist who loves to eat and I haven't run into one yet. Just as people who go into psychology are a little nutty, the people who go into nutrition just aren't healthy."[9]

Even though Child continued to tout red meat, gin, butter, and McDonald's french fries, she began modifying her style in the 1980s to accommodate nutrition consciousness as well as two-income families who had little time for tricky preparations. Even though she simplified earlier creations, she rejected any notion that her cooking had become trendy. As a compromise, she suggested that Americans continue sampling artistic, creative foods and protect their health the French way, by cutting down on portions.

Child's dream was to establish an American-style institution to train students the European way, through apprenticeship under master chefs. "If you can get a degree in the fine arts for drama, architecture, or dance, then you certainly should be able to get a degree in gastronomy," she declared. "Food is very much more important than any of them."[10] She wanted a blue ribbon training facility complete with library, video lab, and test kitchens and recommended a thorough academic background including four years of French, literature, history, physics, chemistry, art, and nutrition.

Another of Child's outreach efforts was the establishment of the American Institute of Wine and Food (AIWF), a 5,000-member restaurant league dedicated to the advancement of food and wine. The group, first envisioned in the 1970s, gelled in the 1980s under the leadership of major cooking stars James Beard, Alice Waters, Jeremiah Tower, and Richard Graff. Child co-chaired the group with wine expert Robert Mondavi, then toured the country to scout for prospective members. With typical enthusiasm, she explained, "We wanted some kind of organization for growers, distributors, chefs, and passionate amateurs. Anyone who is passionate about food is welcome to join."[11]

The group was successful. Bolstered by the prize book collection of Eleanor Lowenstein, the non-profit AIWF created a substantial library at the University of California at Santa Barbara. To lure members, it offered two publications, *American Wine and Food* and *The Journal of Gastronomy*, and a sliding scale of annual fees from $35 for students to $1,000 for corporations.

## Changes and Reflections

Child's busy life altered significantly in 1989 after Paul suffered a stroke at eighty-seven. A dependable prop and indefatigable dishwasher throughout their marriage, he began failing in health and had to move to a nursing home a half hour's drive from their home. She continued traveling and conducting her career interests, but visited regularly and called morning and evening.

As she looked over her meteoric rise to food stardom, Julia credited serendipity for much of her success. She noted that the publication of her first book coincided with a new awareness of French culture, mainly because Jack and Jackie Kennedy occupied the White House and maintained a steady flow of cultivated visitors to America. She added that she never acted too refined or expert on television so she could put viewers at ease and encourage them to try a hand at cooking. She concluded, "I had learned to cook at a mature age myself, so I understood that beginners need lots of details."[12]

To explain her lengthy cooking instructions, Child noted that each entry in her book was meant as a lesson, an educative experience. To talk a timid beginner through the steps required explicit details, such as how far from the flame to place a dish or how high to turn the temperature. But overall she wanted to relax cooks so that they could enjoy the pleasure of preparing and eating good food. Her summation to *Cosmopolitan* magazine gives a clear picture of the Julia Child philosophy: "...most people don't know the difference between feeding and dining.... That's why I want to give people a sense of the joy of preparing something delicious to eat. We all have to eat, so why not do it in the most attractive way possible?"[13]

## Notes

[1] Robin Mather. "Child's Play," *Detroit News*, October 4, 1989, n.p.

[2] "A Holiday Bird and a Free-Range Chat with Julia," *Life*, December 1989, 96.

[3] Roberta Wallace Coffey. "Julia and Paul Child: Their Recipe for Love," *McCall's*, October 1988, 98.

[4] Leslie Weddell. "Renowned Cook Rises to Defense of Food As Gastronomic Bliss," *Colorado Springs Gazette Telegraph*, June 29, 1990, n.p.

[5] Coffey, 97.

[6] "Julia's Crusade," *Boston Herald*, March 5, 1989, n.p.

[7] Charles Grandee. "Grandee at Large," *House and Garden*, June 1989, 174.

[8] Mather, n.p.

[9] Rennert, n.p.

[10] Crusade, n.p.

[11] Weddell, n.p.

[12] Beverly Stephen. "Cosmo Talks to Julia Child," *Cosmopolitan*, May 1990, 246.

[13] Stephen, 247.

## Sources

Coffey, Roberta Wallace. "Julia and Paul Child: Their Recipe for Love," *McCall's*, October 1988, 96-99.

Grandee, Charles. "Grandee at Large," *House and Garden*, June 1989, 174.

"A Holiday Bird and a Free-Range Chat with Julia," *Life*, December 1989, 95-100.

"Julia's Crusade," *Boston Herald*, March 5, 1989, n.p.

Mather, Robin. "Child's Play," *Detroit News*, October 4, 1989, n.p.

Rennert, Amy. "The West Interview: Julia Child," *San Jose Mercury News*, March 30, 1986, n.p.

Stephen, Beverly. "Cosmo Talks to Julia Child," *Cosmopolitan*, May 1990, 246-248.

Weddell, Leslie. "Renowned Cook Rises to Defense of Food As Gastronomic Bliss," *Colorado Springs Gazette Telegraph*, June 29, 1990, n.p.

# Norman Cousins

Like other achievers, Norman Cousins left the starting gate on a sweep to victory. He won accolades with ease in writing and editing and for being a step ahead of other pundits criticizing modern society. He undertook presidential missions and interviewed some of the great names of his day, including Winston Churchill, Albert Einstein, Nikita Khrushchev, Pablo Casals, Buckminster Fuller, Bertrand Russell, and Mohandas Gandhi. When life brought hard times, however, Cousins found himself plying unfamiliar waters. True to the nature of an achiever, he adapted his talents to new challenges and again came up a winner.

From thirty years of overseeing the editorial policies and outreach of *Saturday Review*, Cousins attained a worldwide reputation for innovation and courage, particularly in matters that affected humanity and threatened its survival. Not one to shirk difficult undertakings, he was an active citizen of the world while maintaining the quiet role of husband to Eleanor Kopf and father of four girls. Then, when debilitating illness threatened his many interests, Cousins made a bold move in a new direction—he brought hope to his readers through a series of books on the mind's control of illness.

## Strong Beginnings

Cousins was born on June 24, 1912, in Union City, New Jersey, on the west bank of the Hudson River directly across from Manhattan. The son of Samuel and Sara Barry Miller Cousins, he displayed keen intelligence before the age of five and earned the nickname "The Professor." In New York public schools, he played baseball and achieved his best marks in English composition. At the age of eleven, he underwent a harrowing year in a sanitarium because of a misdiagnosis of tuberculosis. This experience foreshadowed his late-in-life role as a healer and confidence-builder for patients facing terminal illness.

In 1934, after obtaining a degree from Teachers College, Columbia University, Norman Cousins moved directly into the job of education editor for the *New York Post*. A slim, self-assured man, he combined intense concentration with jovial humor. His cheerful nature and devotion to music, photography, and good company led him to early success with colleagues and the world at large. By the age of twenty-three, he was editor and book reviewer for *Current History*. Five years later he moved to his most famous editorial post at the *Saturday Review of Literature*.

As editor-in-chief, Cousins took on the onus of revitalizing the magazine by extending its cultural range. In 1942, he renamed the magazine *Saturday Review* to indicate that literature was no longer its sole purpose. By reaching out to art, science, education, travel, world events, and contemporary culture, he gave the publication new life. To further strengthen it, he hired such talents as Bennett Cerf and Cleveland Amory as well as regular music, education, communications, and science editors. In the magazine's heyday, Cousins boosted its readership from 20,000 to 650,000 and established it as an influential voice in current affairs.

## Man of Many Talents

Cousins, a benign workaholic, did not allow his devotion to *Saturday Review* to dominate his many talents and interests. During World War II, he displayed his patriotism by editing *U.S.A.*, co-chairing the Victory Book Campaign, and serving on the Overseas Bureau of the Office of War Information. He published *The Good Inheritance: The Democratic Chance* (1942) and edited two anthologies, *A Treasury of Democracy* (1941) and *The Poetry of Freedom* (1945).

At this point in his career, Cousins was an early voice against pollution and against violence in the media. He championed the consumer by publishing incisive articles questioning fluoridation, tobacco use, miracle drugs, and atomic energy. His prophetic 1945 essay, "Modern Man Is Obsolete," which was written immediately after the U.S. bombing of Hiroshima (often appearing in anthologies), urged humanity to develop effective controls of atomic power. The essay, which calls for a global government, also figured in two later works, *Who Speaks for Man?* (1953) and *In Place of Folly* (1961).

In addition, Cousins backed worthwhile efforts. He advocated American sponsorship of children orphaned by the atomic bombings of Japan in addition to treatment for people severely disfigured by the experience and for those who survived Nazi medical experimentation at the Ravensbruck death camp. He bolstered hospital care for veterans, encouraged the creation of public television, and rounded up supplies to combat famine in Biafra. With little fanfare, Cousins managed to be on the front lines when there was a need.

## Becoming an Activist

By the early 1950s, Norman Cousins had become a strong force for a lawful world alliance. A follower of one-world advocate Wendell Willkie, he presided over the United World Federalists from 1952 to 1954 as well as the National Committee for a Sane Nuclear Policy. This early advocacy led to his push for American-Soviet cultural exchange, which took shape as the Dartmouth Conferences in the early 1960s.

As a lay ambassador, Cousins was instrumental in arranging release for two Catholic priests imprisoned in Russia and pushed for a nuclear test ban treaty. His 1972 book, *The Improbable Triumvirate: John F. Kennedy, Pope John, Nikita Khrushchev*, described his years of public activism. For his determination to save humanity from nuclear holocaust, Cousins received a Vatican medallion, the Eleanor Roosevelt Peace Award, the Family of Man Award, the United Nations Peace Medal, and public thanks from President Kennedy.

In the late 1940s Cousins often left his desk job in favor of covering newsworthy events on the spot. He reported on the Berlin airlift in 1948, the India-Pakistan border clash in 1954, the Israeli occupation of the Gaza Strip in 1956, and the revelation of war-torn Laos to western readers in 1961. Other headline scenes found him in close attendance, particularly Ceylon, India, Pakistan, Africa, Japan, and Indonesia. From these junkets came his insightful works *Talks with Nehru* (1951) and *Dr. Schweitzer of Lambaréné* (1960). During this motivated era of his life, Cousins earned honorary degrees from fourteen institutions of higher learning, along with the Thomas Jefferson Award for the Advancement of Democracy in Journalism, recognition for outstanding service to American education, a New York State Citizens Education Commission Award, and the John Dewey Award for Education.

## Changing Times

Under Cousin's editorship, the *Saturday Review* rose in prestige and readership. He lightened its weighty pages with occasional literary pranks and continued its traditional double-crostics, cartoons, columns, and editorials. By 1958, Cousins inherited full ownership of the magazine from Everett de Golyer.

The magazine experienced vicissitudes common in the publishing world when it was sold to *McCall's*. Cousins attempted to guide *McCall's* magazine for a fourteen-month period, but relinquished the job after admitting his failings on women's issues. After the *Saturday Review* was sold to Nicolas H. Charney and John J. Veronis in 1971, Cousins found himself at odds with the new management. He continued to edit the magazine for a while after it was divided into four smaller magazines, then decided to seek new avenues of expression. He took some of his former staff with him and in 1972 initiated *World*, which later became an anti-pollution magazine. The experiment proved short-lived. The following year the new owners of *Saturday Review* admitted defeat and Cousins resumed his position as editor.

## From Familiar to New Territory

The last years of Cousin's life were perhaps his most demanding. He was content with the return to "his" magazine, but he did not allow complacency to spawn slipshod editing. He continued to strive for better coverage of topics of cultural and literary significance. Because he persevered in bringing insightful writing to his audience, the Magazine Publishers Association named him publisher of the year.

A rare collagen disease, ankylosing spondylitis, struck Cousins in his late forties. He suffered a flu-like malaise, fever, and general achiness which developed into nearly total paralysis. His search for ways of harnessing his body's regenerative powers resulted in a new direction for his talents. In 1974, ten years after the onset of his malady, he produced *The Celebration of Life: A Dialogue on Immortality and Infinity*, followed by *Anatomy of an Illness As Perceived by the Patient* (1979), *Healing and Belief* (1982), and *The Healing Heart* (1983). The thrust of his new endeavor was a promotion of positivism in combatting catastrophic illness.

At the age of 65, Cousins sold the *Saturday Review* to a consortium that he handpicked as his successors. He continued studying and writing about mental control of the healing process, about which he became a self-made expert. Even a heart attack in 1980 failed to daunt his courage or enthusiasm. He probed the efficacy of a hopeful attitude in healing until his death from a subsequent heart attack in Los Angeles on November 30, 1990.

## A Voice in the Wilderness

From the beginning of Norman Cousins's interest in self-motivated healing, he found an audience. Some of his listeners were fellow sufferers, some were doctors or critics of health care service, and some were notable voices of the publishing world. In 1982 in *Prevention* magazine, Robert Rodale remarked, "Norman Cousins ... stands almost as a monument to the little-known power within oneself to generate an enormous curative force. By taking large doses of vitamin C and watching comic movies that forced him to laugh while resting on what doctors said was his deathbed, [he] literally saved his own life."[1]

In an article for *The Saturday Evening Post*, Cousins's wife Eleanor reported that her husband had defied doctors' predictions that he would die without a heart bypass operation. To heal himself, she said, Cousins chose to exercise, improve his diet, read humor by authors such as Ogden Nash and James Thurber, and avoid undue stress. He studied the 15 billion neurons in the brain that convert positive emotions to chemical medicines. And most important of all his regimen, he cultivated self-esteem and believed that he would prevail over his impairment.

In his writings about healing and regeneration, Cousins stated his hypotheses in simple terms. He envisioned the will to live as a "window on the future. It opens the individual to such help as the outside world has to offer, and it connects that help to the body's own capability for fighting disease. It enables the human body to make the most of itself."[2]

As a result of Cousins's successful fight against disease, he accepted a post as adjunct professor in the Program of Medicine, Law and Human Values of the Medical School at the University of California at Los Angeles and served as consulting editor to *Man & Medicine*, a medical journal published by Columbia University. He proved to many doubters that self-confidence and a belief in the human spirit are enough to alter the body's response to disease. In his words, "We are not being called upon to rearrange the planets in the sky or to alter the composition of the sun. We are called upon to make decisions affecting our own welfare. The only price we have to pay for survival is decision."[3]

In his early seventies, Cousins spent time learning the biochemistry of the emotions. He became convinced that the brain can mobilize forces in the body to combat illness and protect it from further erosion. He referred to this internal system as the "built-in apothecary."[4] To actuate this innate power, Cousins realized that the human sufferer had to do two things: face the problem and believe that the body can heal.

## Applying the Force

One of Cousins's greatest discoveries about self-healing was that a helpless, hopeless vulnerability can actually trigger life-threatening disease. Because he realized that the immune system is stymied by negative emotions, particularly depression and grief, he touted the salutary effect of cheerfulness, anticipation, and other positive feelings. One discovery that supported his philosophy of self-healing was the fact that in the 370 cancer patients he studied, the intensity of the disease increased at the time of diagnosis. He concluded that the patient, upon hearing a death knell in the doctor's words, prepared for death by giving in to the disease.

In place of acquiescence to a death sentence, Cousins advocated immediate action. He called for a protest against "the arrogance of any human being who would make a pronouncement of doom upon another human being."[5] He noted a significant lapse in health care in that doctors are more likely to test and treat than to talk with patients. Because the nation has come to depend on abstract technology, its citizens have lost important personal values. As he concluded, "We stop thinking ... we stop talking ... and we live by numbers."[6]

In spite of his disillusionment with modern medical practice, Cousins maintained respect for and sympathy with physicians, whom he thought overworked. His sanguine outlook on pioneering developments in the medical world led to an influential role in the training of doctors. At an address to graduates of Tulane School of Medicine in New Orleans, he verbalized his belief that the human touch is the real answer to life-threatening illness: "The conclusion is clear: doctors who spend more time with their patients may have to spend less money on malpractice insurance policies."[7]

Cousins's remedy for lapses in the practice of medicine was a clearly defined program of improvement. He recommended that interns spend more time learning about patient relations. He also prophesied a time when medicines would serve as triggers for the body's internal powers rather than as an external force usurping control. And perhaps most important to his philosophy was a restatement of Albert Schweitzer's emphasis on "reverence for life."[8] Overall, Cousins advocated that doctors return to ancient Hippocratic values, especially a belief in the uniqueness of each human life.

## A Message to the Patient

In his role as healer, Cousins made regular visits to cancer patients. He tried to overcome their panic, to stop what he termed a "mad toboggan ride" in which the progression of fear and desolation led to a despair that worsened the body's state of health.[9] One of his demonstrations of self-healing involved the use of a skin thermometer to illustrate to patients that they could raise skin temperature by an effort of the will. In convincing sufferers that they had some degree of control over autonomic responses, he paved the way for greater revelations about how they could will themselves back to health.

Cousins indicated in his writings that doctors must play an important part in the healing of disease. In *Healing and Belief*, he characterized physical recovery in two parts: "The belief system converts hope, robust expectations and the will to live into plus factors in any contest of forces involving disease. The belief system is no substitute for competent medical attention in serious illness or vice versa. Both are essential."[10]

Cousins also believed that a study of disease required a recognition of the place of death. He acknowledged that, at some point, a patient has the right to let go and embrace death, which is a natural part of human existence. Yet, implicit in his philosophy was a determination to stave off death by homing in on life processes and the accomplishments which the human body could achieve.

At his death, Norman Cousins's family received outpourings of love and thanks from the people whose lives he had improved. Among the messages that appeared in news stories and reflective articles were recaps of his many political achievements. But even greater numbers of accolades noted his flare for life and his dedication to helping others share it with him.

## Notes

[1] Robert Rodale. "The Experimental Force within You," *Prevention*, March 1982, 8.

[2] Norman Cousins. "Healing and Belief," *The Saturday Evening Post*, April 1982, 32.

[3] "Norman Cousins: A Spokesman for the Human Race," *The Mother Earth News*, November-December 1984, 15.

[4] *Mother Earth*, 20.

[5] *Mother Earth*, 20.

[6] *Mother Earth*, 20.

[7] "Parting Words, Mostly Somber," *Time*, June 21, 1982, 83.

[8] Cousins, 48.

[9] *Mother Earth*, 22.

[10] Cousins, 31.

## Sources

*Contemporary Authors*. Volumes 17-18. Detroit: Gale Research, 1967.

Cousins, Eleanor. "The Irrepressible Spoofer Strikes Again," *The Saturday Evening Post*, April 1982, 26-30.

_____. "The Strange Appearance of Norman Cousins," *The Saturday Evening Post*, July/August 1984, 26-28.

Cousins, Norman. *Anatomy of an Illness As Perceived by the Patient*. New York: W. W. Norton, 1979.

_____. "Healing and Belief," *The Saturday Evening Post*, April 1982, 31-111.

_____. *The Healing Heart*. New York: W. W. Norton, 1983.

*Current Biography*. Detroit: Gale Research, 1977.

"Norman Cousins: A Spokesman for the Human Race," *The Mother Earth News*, November-December 1984, 15-22.

"Parting Words, Mostly Somber," *Time*, June 21, 1982, 82-84.

Rodale, Robert. "The Experimental Force within You," *Prevention*, March 1982, 6-10.

# Dorothy Day

The accomplishments of middle and old age often reflect the directions of youth. For Dorothy Day, co-founder of the Catholic Worker Movement, the addition of faith to a passionate, radical spirit produced a no less passionate, radical achiever. Indeed, belief in Christian tenets led her to channel concern for poor, dispossessed people into mainstream religious outreach.

The upshot of so dedicated a life was nothing short of miraculous. With deft guidance, Dorothy Day, whom biographer William Miller characterized as "quietly heroic," helped change the thinking of metropolitan New York about the marginal people who never enjoyed America's bounty.[1] Equally influential in the growth and development of Catholicism, Day held a key role in the fostering of social thought during the twentieth century.

## Early Life

Born November 8, 1897, in sight of the Brooklyn Bridge at 71 Pineapple Street, Bath Beach, Brooklyn, New York, Dorothy Day was the child of horse-racing fan John Isaac Day, who produced the column "On and Off the Turf" for the *New York Morning Telegraph*. Dorothy's mother, Grace Satterlee Day, was a native of Marlboro, New York, and a staunch, but joyful woman.

Dorothy's ancestry was mainstream American. On the Satterlee side of the family were a whaler and Union hero of the Civil War. On the Day side, the family's Tennessee connections bragged of heroes at the Battle of King's Mountain and kinship with Daniel Boone.

In the lineup of five children, Dorothy came between older brothers Donald and Sam Houston and younger siblings Della and John. Dorothy learned early how to ward off tussles with her older brothers by biting, scratching, and screeching foul language, for which she was punished. Her family lived well and tenuously associated with the Episcopal and Congregational churches. They practiced no religion at home, but their live-in Irish maid introduced Dorothy to Catholic mass.

In 1904, the Days moved to Berkeley, and then Oakland, California. John edited a newspaper and reported racetrack news. After the San Francisco earthquake, he moved his family to a dismal row tenement over a saloon on Cottage Avenue and Thirty-seventh Street in Chicago, where they lived in poverty while he drank heavily and tried to write a novel. The bad years ended in 1907 when he found work on *The Inter Ocean*. The family moved four more times.

The Days made little show of affection and took their communal Sunday meals in silence. From early childhood, Dorothy, a lonely, introspective child, was affable, but cultivated no social life. To vent her feelings, she kept a journal, which she hid under the stairs to safeguard her private thoughts from prying brothers. She was an ardent reader and moved from girlish romance to naturalism and philosophy by her mid-teens. In adolescence, moved to seek answers to her restless spirit, she became a fervent Episcopalian and read John Wesley, *The Imitation of Christ*, Jonathan Edwards, and saints' lives.

## New Interests

Dorothy studied Latin and Greek and graduated from Robert Waller High School in 1914. On scholarship earned from an essay contest sponsored by the *Chicago Examiner*, she spent two years at the University of Illinois at Urbana, where she worked in the dining hall, served as a governess, and did light housework for faculty members. During this period, she was bold and bohemian and began to smoke, drink, and swear to accentuate her growing independence.

Day took little interest in her classes and professed no major. Instead, she immersed herself in labor history and heroes of the workers' movement as well as voting rights and sexual freedom for women. Under the influence of more sophisticated personalities, she joined the Socialist party. As an outlet for her opinions, she wrote for a campus group called the Scribblers. At age eighteen she was working as a book critic and reviewer for the *Examiner*.

In 1915, the Day family moved to New York because John was once again out of work. Dorothy left school and joined her parents, but her father's objections to her career choice alienated her. A believer in women's rights to work, she moved out and got a job on the socialist *Call*, found a flat on the East Side, and fell under the sway of romantic radicals, including Emma Goldman, Jack Reed, Max Eastman, and other idealistic left-wing agitators who were vicariously living out the Russian Revolution. At a demonstration for women's suffrage in Washington, D.C., she took part in a scuffle and was jailed.

As an active socialist and communist, Day wrote for the *Masses* and the *Liberator* and involved herself in politics. She was a striking woman, tall and slant-eyed with braided hair wrapped around the crown of her head. Attracted to hard-drinking, forceful male personalities, including playwright Eugene O'Neill, she developed a reputation for aggressive behavior.

During World War I, Day and sister Della, who became her best friend, studied nursing at Kings County Hospital in Brooklyn and volunteered during the great influenza epidemic. The experience focused Day's attitudes toward benevolence. While working with patients, she discovered that the reality of charity differs from the ideal. Once, an old reclusive woman, disfigured by disease, dumped a bedpan on her. The experience led to Day's reassignment to the men's ward.

## Marriage and Beyond

In her early twenties, Day changed direction, choosing life with her moody lover, Lionel Moise. The relationship seemed doomed from the start because of his inflexibility and stifling possessiveness. When the affair ended abruptly, Day gave up nursing and married Barkeley Tobey on the rebound in the spring of 1920. The newlyweds traveled in Europe and were, for a time, content, but broke up on their return home when they realized their incompatibility.

This era brought both loneliness and hardship to Day, who did not enjoy living alone. At one point, her landlady summoned her mother to care for her during a short bout of illness. Arrested a second time for consorting with unsavory characters from the IWW, she spent two days behind bars. She returned to an unhappy daily grind, made more wretched by her longing for Moise.

## Moving Toward Peace

Her luck took an upward turn in 1923 when she moved to New Orleans with Della, wrote for the *New Orleans Item*, and worked on her novel *The Eleventh Virgin*. The book, a minor success, was published in April 1924. She then made a more significant transition by returning to New York, abandoning the pseudo-sophisticated literati of Greenwich Village, and settling in a cottage on Raritan Bay at Huguenot, Staten Island. In relative contentment, she lived with Forster Batterham and wrote columns and books.

Day's unforeseen conversion to Catholicism came in 1927. Filled with joy over the impending birth of her daughter, Tamar Teresa, she found peace in rural existence and impending motherhood even though Forster ridiculed her newfound religiosity and left her. Day turned to a nearby Catholic community, where nuns encouraged her daughter's baptism. Allying with Catholicism on December 28, 1927, she recanted earlier radicalism and devoted herself to spirituality, saying, "All my life I have been haunted by God ... I do believe every soul has a tendency toward God.[2]

During her early Christian fervor, Day suffered alienation from her agnostic friends. Though she shared nothing in common with local Catholics, her conversion brought her peace and satisfaction that she had lacked during her wilder years. To stave off loneliness, she turned to her daughter for companionship. To feed them both she wrote scripts for Pathé Films in Hollywood and was appalled that the red scare connected her beliefs inextricably with communism.

## The Catholic Worker

In December 1932, Day's life as a practicing Christian took on new meaning after she met writer Peter Maurin (1877-1949), a Catholic layman from Languedoc, France. Day later described Maurin as "a genius, a saint, an agitator, a writer, a lecturer, a poor man, and a shabby tramp, all in one."[3] Short and rather bedraggled, he had been radicalized by poverty in the Paris slum. He emigrated to Canada and followed New Testament doctrines, which denigrate materialism and encourage care for the needy. Seeking to align believers in an effort to help others, he delivered stirring public addresses and organized seminars composed of Catholic anti-capitalists.

With his assistance, Day began the *Catholic Worker* on May 1, 1933. This monthly newspaper, based on New Testament fundamentals, reached 2,500 readers and publicized Catholic home missions. Within three years, the readership grew to 150,000. It covered a wide range of topics, including race relations, hiring policies, and women's rights.

In response to readers, Day opened a store, some apartments, and a ramshackle building on Jackson Square to feed the hungry and shelter the sick, homeless, and unemployed who petitioned the staff for aid. Such personalized outreach was the embodiment of her philosophy. She declared, "Every house should have a Christ's room.... It is no use turning people away to an agency, to the city or the state or the Catholic charities. It is you yourself who must perform the works of mercy."[4]

In her writings, Day characterized the era: "Canned beef was being doled out and more people were going on home relief and work relief and were submitted to questionnaires and bureaucracy and the bitter worm of despair was gnawing at the human heart."[5] Day's charity, fueled by energy and Christian brotherhood, consisted of hot meals, clothing, beds, and comfort. It resulted in St. Joseph's House of Hospitality, a settlement way station near the Bowery in New York City. Shortly, thirty more centers appeared nationwide to alleviate the sufferings of the Great Depression.

As William D. Miller described Day during this significant phase in her life, she was the touchstone of strength that inspired others to help. With a controlled assertiveness, she expressed the needs of the poor in feasible terms. Her readers not only read her words, they took them to heart. In a few months, she transformed the *Catholic Worker* from a newspaper to a social impetus for change.

The appeal of the *Catholic Worker* waned as World War II approached in Europe. However, as mainstream American philosophy moved toward intervention with the coming of the Spanish Civil War, Day's pacifism remained firm. She encouraged readers to reject war by joining the Association of Catholic Conscientious Objectors.

# A Dedicated Life

Always concerned for social justice, Day supported labor unions, civil rights, anti-war efforts, and the suppression of firearms. Following World War II, she protested threats of nuclear annihilation. In 1955 she joined in a protest of civil defense drills. She was regularly arrested, booked, and jailed, yet bore her tribulations as a necessary part of actualizing her beliefs. In the sixties, she continued to support peace with an American version of the British PAX, an English Catholic anti-war effort. For ten years, PAX cranked out a quarterly newsletter and held conferences in the Gandhian tradition of social change through nonviolence.

In 1965, Day journeyed to Rome to carry the PAX message to a Vatican peace council. To demonstrate commitment, Dorothy fasted and prayed for ten days at the catacombs of Saint Priscilla while reading the works of Martin Luther King. On her physical deprivation she commented: "I had offered my fast in part for the victims of famine all over the world, and it seemed to me that I had very special pains. They ... seemed to pierce to the very marrow of my bones when I lay down at night."[6]

# Acting on Beliefs

Later, Day established a hospitality house on Chrystie Street in New York City to serve meals and contain the staff of the *Catholic Worker*. The house was large enough to sponsor a large closet for donated clothes and a round table for discussion, but did not offer temporary housing, as had her earlier establishment. In addition to the city house, she operated the 23-acre Peter Maurin Farm and two cottages at Pleasant Plains, Staten Island.

Dorothy Day's activism evidenced her beliefs, which she refused to leave on the pages of the Bible but incorporated in voluntary poverty and daily battle against oppression. Some branches of Catholicism rejected her witness and castigated her for what they interpreted as radical pro-communism. But Day proved indefatigably strong in her speaking, witnessing, and writing. In addition to journals she wrote *From Union Square to Rome* (1938), *House of Hospitality* (1939), *On Pilgrimage* (1948), *Thérèse* (1960), *Loaves and Fishes* (1963)—a history of the *Catholic Worker*—and *The Long Loneliness* (1981—an autobiography published posthumously).

In old age, Day suffered myriad ills, particularly arthritis, high blood pressure, and an enlarged heart. In 1968, under doctor's orders to take daily medication, she realized a dream in a trip around the world with stops for speeches and meetings in Australia, India, and Africa. By 1971, although thin and easily fatigued, she was eager to visit Russia to support Alexander Solzhenitsyn, dissident author and human rights activist. Even in 1973, at the age of 76, Day joined Cesar Chavez at a farm workers' demonstration against the Teamsters Union and was again jailed.

Near the end of her days, Day turned inward for strength to face some of the trends of the late 1970s, particularly the youth cult, departure of priests and nuns from religious orders, and rise in sexual freedom and gay rights. At the Staten Island Catholic house, she quieted her mental turmoil by contemplating God's love. She said, "We do have a gem of a chapel and permission for the Blessed Sacrament. What an immense consolation. And also I have to learn daily over and over not to judge."[7]

By 1976, Dorothy Day's active association with radical Catholicism was virtually ended. Weakened by frequent respiratory congestion, she spent time reflecting and enjoying her nine grandchildren. She died without pain or struggle on November 29, 1980. Her funeral, thronged with Indians, Hispanics, blacks, workers, friends, disciples, and other recipients of her charity and influence, was a testimonial to her good works. She was buried in a cemetery in Richmond, New York, near the spot where she was converted.

Whether visiting a Japanese internment camp, addressing Catholic students at a university campus, supporting striking steel workers, participating in the burning of draft cards, or helping evicted tenants gather their effects into a barrow, Dorothy Day made a difference with her life. The more time she spent with followers and the underprivileged, the stronger grew her commitment to the Catholic ideal. Father Dennis Geaney summed up her contributions: "Here is a woman who has placed her stamp on American Catholicism."[8]

## Notes

[1] William D. Miller. *Dorothy Day: A Biography.* New York: Harper & Row, 1984, flap copy.

[2] Miller, 199.

[3] Miller, 228.

[4] Miller, 259.

[5] Miller, 259.

[6] Miller, 481.

[7] Miller, 502.

[8] *Current Biography.* Detroit: Gale Research, 1962, 94.

## Sources

Coles, Robert. *Dorothy Day: A Radical Devotion.* New York: Addison-Wesley, 1987.

*Current Biography.* Detroit: Gale Research, 1962.

Day, Dorothy. *The Long Loneliness: An Autobiography.* New York: Harper & Row, 1981.

Klejment, Anne, and Alice Klejment. *Dorothy Day and the Catholic Worker.* New York: Garland Publications, 1985.

Miller, William D. *All Is Grace: The Spirituality of Dorothy Day.* New York: Doubleday, 1987.

_____. *Dorothy Day: A Biography.* New York: Harper & Row, 1984.

Roberts, Nancy L. *Dorothy Day and the Catholic Worker.* Albany, New York: State University of New York Press, 1985.

# George Dempster

In nearly every industrial parking lot and alongside almost every apartment and condominium complex stands a humble device attesting to the late achievement of one inventor, George Roby Dempster. With more than twenty-five patents for dumping, moving, and lifting equipment, George Dempster made himself a very rich man by lightening the work load for millions of heavy construction workers and trash haulers. His simple but effective mechanism, enabling a truck to maneuver a covered container of trash over a receptacle, dump it, and replace the emptied container at the ready for more loads, revolutionized refuse collection. In an age when waste management is a crucial environmental issue, the Dempster Dumpster is as familiar a brand name as Kleenex, Frigidaire, Xerox, Rolodex, Polaroid, or Jell-O.

Apart from his role as inventor, Dempster's biography reads like a who's who of civic sainthood. On the positive side of his workaholic ways were marathon stints as city manager, mayor, and town councilman of Knoxville, Tennessee, as well as support of a blue-ribbon list of charities, church activities, and community programs. Dempster was also a leader in healing racial tensions, hiring the handicapped, establishing recreational sites, and cleaning up pollution. Some projects bear his name, as is the case with the Dempster Memorial Sheltered Workshop; others he supported without publicity. Generous and supportive, he set the example for philanthropists of his era.

## Tennessee Born and Bred

Before earning fame as an inventor, George Dempster began his career as a construction worker at sites across the South. Born September 12, 1887, in humble circumstances in Knoxville, Tennessee, to John and Ann Doherty Dempster, he was the third of eleven children, five sons and six daughters. His mother was Irish, his father a Scottish immigrant who arrived in the New World in 1877 and took up the miller's trade. George graduated from high school in 1906 and studied at Knoxville's John R. Neal Law School for a year. By a small margin he failed the bar exam, giving up on law in favor of travel and other enterprises. Even though his ambitions took him to distant places, throughout his adult years he remained close to his large family, two of whom survived him.

During his schooling, Dempster tackled a variety of jobs, including orchard maintenance on a fruit farm, stable upkeep, and construction. At fourteen, he bummed around and worked for a short period as common laborer on the C & O Railroad. Two years later, he began traveling with crews of the W. J. Oliver Construction Company. He worked on railroads as a track laborer in Elkwood, Virginia, and locomotive fireman in Guilford, Indiana. Overall, he tackled most railroad jobs, from oiler to brakeman to water tender.

He tried his hand at flying, then gave it up during the Depression years as too expensive a hobby. He maintained a healthy curiosity in a vast number of fields, especially anything connected with engineering. In his later years, he gave speeches that drew on minute facts from his youth, astounding associates with his accurate memory of details.

One of Dempster's early adventures occurred on a voyage aboard a liner from Georgia to New York. While serving as an oiler and water tender, he was questioned by the chief engineer. When the truth came out that Dempster was only sixteen, his status changed from employee to unpaid guest. He enjoyed a free berth from Cape Hatteras to New York. But the story does not end at the docks. From New York he traveled on to New Jersey, then journeyed by train to Council Bluffs, Iowa, where his trek halted abruptly because of a strike on the Union Pacific Railroad. For ten days, Dempster was stranded in a vast hobo jungle of 5,000 residents.

## From Railroad to Canal

Upon his return home, Dempster set his sights on a construction job that evolved into a significant piece of American history—the Panama Canal. He and his brother Tom both sought jobs there. George was employed as a heavy equipment operator and engineer in Panama from 1907 to 1912. His chief responsibility was the manning of a steam shovel on the Pacific side of the operation. A severe bout of typhoid complicated by malaria brought him under the care of Colonel William G. Gorgas, the physician who followed Walter Reed's example and mobilized the American army against mosquitoes to whip yellow fever.

For George, the cure was slow in coming. His weight dropped to 86 pounds. He subsisted on cracked ice and two glasses of milk per day, yet refused the doctor's orders to drink eggnog laced with alcohol. After Gorgas warned the boy that he would soon die of disease and malnutrition, for the next four weeks Dempster made a conscious effort to eat from the tray of Jack Oberly, fellow steam shoveler who occupied the adjacent bed in the ward. Once Dempster recovered from his Panama experience, he remained in robust health until his death.

A later episode proved that Dempster was not a man to be trifled with. Under the steady verbal abuse of a Jamaican worker, he took all he could stand. Then he leaped aboard a train and fought the man with his fists. The upshot of the fray was a tumble into a watery ditch for the final blows. The engineer was so amazed at the two men's behavior that he stopped the train. Dempster's well placed punches landed his adversary in the hospital, but Dempster was unhurt and immediately returned to his steam shovel.

## Settling Down in Knoxville

In the midst of these post-adolescent Panama escapades, Dempster swept into Knoxville to marry his girl, Frances Mildred Seymour, the daughter of civil engineer Digby Gordon Seymour of Madisonville, Kentucky, on March 21, 1911. Immediately after the nuptials at the First Presbyterian Church, the Dempsters departed in their Buick and sped toward Panama, where the groom completed another year of work.

The Dempsters returned to a less harrowing lifestyle in 1912. Knoxville was the appropriate location for George, who proved to be the right man at the right moment in history. The city, in the eastern portion of the state, later developed into headquarters for the Tennessee Valley Authority and a center for experiments on the atomic power industry. Also, the area overlooked the Smoky Mountains, which in time became a vacation bonanza for American tourists. All these opportunities challenged the talents of an energetic go-getter like Dempster.

The Dempsters were model citizens and staunch members of the St. James Episcopal Church and the Democratic party. They had three children, George, Jr., Ann Gordon, and Josephine Frances. Both girls produced two children; George, Jr., remained a bachelor. Dempster built a succession of six homes in and around Knoxville. He maintained a 500-acre cattle ranch spread over two counties near the Maryville Pike. The Dempster family enjoyed his polled Hereford cattle, which grazed on prime grassland. However, after Mrs. Dempster's health failed in the 1950s, she was unable to drive, so the family moved back to town and settled on Cherokee Boulevard.

## From Worker to Inventor

At the age of 26, Dempster joined two of his brothers, Tom and John, in a contracting partnership called Dempster Construction Company. Later, brothers Bob and W. J. came in with them. Their aim was to construct railroads, highways, dams, and bridges during a flurry of transportation construction in the southern states. The sites were scattered throughout Kentucky, Tennessee, Virginia, North Carolina, and Georgia.

Within three years, the company began marketing earth-moving machinery and equipment. In three more, the Dempster company located on a large tract of prime land fronting on the Southern Railway. Then, at the age of thirty-nine, Dempster made his contribution to American technology and changed his life. The firm created the Dempster-Dumpster, a multi-purpose device capable of storing liquids or solids and of being emptied by movable lifts into a truck manned by a single operator. The machine was so versatile that it could be applied to over

3,000 types of containers, although Dempster evolved the device primarily to load stone as it was removed from quarries. At first, the machine served only the company's needs. Then demand from other firms resulted in a patent and a steady flow of Dempster collectors for sale.

This single innovation proved so lucrative to Dempster and his brothers that they gave up construction jobs in favor of their equipment line, marketed under the name Dempster Brothers, Inc. George Dempster served as president and company manager of the closed corporation, which remained in the tight grasp of the Dempster family. Until his death from a heart attack at the age of 77 on September 18, 1964, he was chairman of the board of the company, which became Tennessee's major steel-fabricator.

Not one to rest on past successes, Dempster perfected more labor-saving devices. First came the Dempster-Balester in 1939, a hydraulic press capable of baling scrap metal and popular with factories and junkyards handling loose items. From this second success Dempster moved on to the Dempster-Digster, a hydraulic scoop and front-end loader suitable for messy jobs like road construction and coal mining operations. With this innovation mounted on a truck or tractor, a construction crew could dump heavy loads directly into waiting vehicles.

These Dempster products were widely used through the war years. Reports indicate that 125 dumpsters were on the docks in Hawaii when the Japanese bombed Pearl Harbor on December 2, 1941. Because of huge orders from the Navy, Army, and Air Force, the Dempster brothers made millions of dollars worth of equipment. The company expanded to cover a 30-acre tract of land on Springdale Avenue. Although a move to open land might have made better business sense, Dempster took pride in the location, which produced a hefty amount of city tax for Knoxville.

The list of Dempster work savers grew in the 1940s and established the company's reputation worldwide for quality and innovation. First came the Dempster-Dumpmaster, then the Dempster-Dinosaur and the Dempster Compaction Trailer. To alleviate problems with the handling of car chassis, he designed scrap-metal baling presses and shears. At the prompting of the U.S. Navy, Dempster also manufactured 15,000 pontoons, which were used in massive engineering projects.

## Spin-Offs

George Dempster's success in his sphere of interest brought him more entrepreneurial opportunities and considerable notoriety. He expanded his business by adding the Dempster Coal Company, a strip-mining operation in western Kentucky, and a west coast warehouse. The firm forged agreements with outlets to market their products in Canada and England; it also upheld contracts with the federal government and sold to almost every country outside the communist bloc. In keeping with the lighter end of the industry, Dempster developed the 500-employee Dempster Motor Company in Knoxville, which produced Maxwell and Chalmers cars and trucks.

As an outlet for journalistic talent, Dempster began writing a daily column for the *Knoxville Journal* entitled "Like It or Not." To actualize political ambitions, he pursued local politics, then entered the race for governor. His oft-cited campaign speech revealed much about the courage and honesty of the man: "Pendergast is in the penitentiary, Huey Long is in his grave and his successor in jail. And now the day has come to round up and destroy the last bunch of political gangsters in the South—the Crump statewide machine."[1] However, daring words did not save the day for Dempster, who lost to his opponent 217,786 to 40,497.

Undeterred by overwhelming defeat, Dempster remained politically active. During the 1950s he aired his opinions on industry and development in speeches for the American Public Power Association, Naval Mobile Equipment Symposium, and District Transportation Conference. He took a keen interest in postwar growth during the Eisenhower years and debated ownership of power installations on "America's Town Meeting of the Air." Despite Mrs. Dempster's attempts to slow him down, he rose early and worked late, throwing himself into projects that kept his mind and body occupied. Often he would fortify himself with a candy bar and a quick nap so that he could attend meetings that lasted into the wee hours.

## A Contributing Citizen

Dempster was a multi-faceted man. Not only did he excel in manufacturing, he also understood the need for benevolence and philanthropy. He served on the President's Committee to improve hiring of the handicapped as well as boards supporting youth, mental health, civil rights, science education, and victims of arthritis, rheumatism, blindness, retardation, tuberculosis, and cerebral palsy. He served as state commissioner of finance and taxation and was an interested party in the creation of building codes. He was one of the early voices for strong anti-pollution measures and a supporter of the Great Smoky Mountains National Park and the Tennessee Valley Authority, a government program bringing cheap electric power to mountain residents.

Dempster supported desegregation efforts. Following the bombings of black churches in the mid-1960s, he raised funds to help worshippers rebuild. He continued bettering the area around Knoxville with public works projects, including a municipal garage, playgrounds, stadiums, bridges, sewage systems, schools, parks, libraries, and swimming pools. The rewards and honors poured in from all fronts, including the Jaycees, National Conference of Christians and Jews, Knights of Columbus, and Department of the Navy.

In his obituaries, local and state people remembered George Dempster as a hard scrapper, but a fair man. They emphasized his political acumen and his ability to accept whatever role he could fill to accomplish worthwhile projects. He had a reputation for sticking to a task, even when it proved controversial or difficult to manage. By delegating, questioning, and pushing it through, Dempster, to the dismay of his detractors, usually finished whatever he set out to do.

Lauded for his even handedness, Dempster evolved a massive following among all classes. Because of his democratic dealings with petitioners, people felt encouraged to seek his help during his days in office and in the many years he functioned as private citizen and businessman. Even strangers down on their luck could count on a free meal at the company cafeteria if Mr. George learned of their plight. He was a champion of blacks, whom he established in the local fire department with their own company. They returned his good will by giving him their votes.

Myriad stories circulated in the Knoxville area of George Dempster's good deeds. As a friend of the handicapped, he took pride that they comprised ten percent of his work force. He arranged a radio program for a blind pianist, bought a house for a widow whose husband was killed while serving the city as a police officer, paid for a heart operation for a university student, donated his corneas for transplant after his death, and appeared on a television quiz program, "The $64,000 Question," in order to raise money to pass on to a Maryland woman in the audience whose name was drawn at random.

A jolly, round-faced man with little hair and a Santa Claus smile, George Dempster was a spiffy dresser. He rejected both tobacco and alcohol and enjoyed a reputation for caring. From his extended era of political service, he made enemies, whom he battled without rancor. He took pride in the number of lives he influenced, rose in the ranks of Masons and Shriners, and was a member of the Executives Club. Despite a hot temper that sometimes erupted in aggressive gestures and crude language, his example of hard work, family values, religious faith, and response to civic needs brought him accolades from an entire city and beyond.

## Notes

[1] Carson Brewer. "Dempster, Ex-Mayor, Is Dead," *Knoxville News-Sentinel*, September 19, 1964, 4.

## Sources

Brewer, Carson. "Dempster, Ex-Mayor, Is Dead," *Knoxville News-Sentinel*, September 19, 1964, 1-4.

*National Cyclopedia of American Biography*, Volume 53. New York: James T. White, 1971.

# Ellen Gilchrist

The sweet reward for preparation often does not come in the youthful twenties or staid thirties. It arrives—with accrued interest—in the mature years. Such is the case with Ellen Gilchrist, noteworthy southern essayist, novelist, poet, short story writer, and scriptwriter. She got a late start in professional writing after half a lifetime of doing it for fun. Her canon includes volumes of poems, short stories, novels, and essays as well as numerous contributions to a variety of literary journals.

At the New York Public Library in 1985, Gilchrist, dressed confidently in a red velvet suit, accepted her first major honor, the American Book Award and the accompanying $10,000 purse. Shortly afterward, she celebrated her fiftieth birthday at a party given by Mississippi Governor Bill Clinton and his wife. During this period of attention from the media and public, she was offered a post as a radio commentator and began tickling the funny bones of millions of listeners.

## Early Life

The daughter of William Garth and Aurora Alford Gilchrist, Ellen Louise Gilchrist was born February 20, 1935, in Vicksburg, Mississippi. She was named for her great-great-grandmother, Ellen Connell Biggs Martin, a Philadelphia milliner. Of her love for her rural home on Hopedale Plantation in Issaquena County near Greenville, Mississippi, Gilchrist comments, "I could never live in a city. I need to smell the earth. I need to be here when it storms."[1] She recalls the births of lambs, colts, piglets, and biddies alongside the arrival of well-loved children, both black and white.

Gilchrist's extended family is important to her career. Her journal records the polite veneer that coats her family's interactions and the "exciting undercurrents, alliances, power and usurpations of power, statements and allegations and rumors"[2] that lie underneath. She notes with joy that her generation of southern children was reared by blacks, a memory she describes as wonderful.

Her childhood activities stemmed from a fathomless curiosity that led her to examine a broad spectrum of life, from the making of mayonnaise, pinch cakes, and wars, to the causes of marital unrest, undying friendships, and suicide. Of this era of growth and personal development she remarks: "We live at the level of our language. Whatever we can articulate we can imagine or understand or explore. All you have to do to educate a child is leave him alone and teach him to read. The rest is brainwashing."[3]

Gilchrist's autobiographical *Falling Through Space* is a generous family album, offering glimpses of her Aunt Roberta, who raised angora rabbits; Great Uncle Robert, the country doctor; her cousin Nell, who practiced cheerleading, and her tall, proud, brave, civilized grandfather, who considered himself an Englishman. Many of her recollections of childhood are gentle and sweet—a sandpile under a tree where she spent time sculpting forts as a place for the fairies to dance under the moon. Recalling her mother's support of these fantasies, she adds, "At night, after I was asleep, my mother would come out here and dance her fingers all over my sand forts so that in the morning I would see the prints and believe that fairies dance at night in the sand."[4]

Gilchrist's mother, a one-time beauty queen, made half-hearted attempts to discipline her daughter's wildness and craziness, but was never truly dedicated to bridling the little girl's bumptious, free-spirited ways. She humored Ellen's make-believe companion, Jimmy, by setting a place for him at the table and often allowed Ellen to remain home from school on some frail excuse so that she could read. She even prepared special sick-bed trays. Like her daughter, Aurora Gilchrist loved literature, particularly the classics, which she shared with Ellen. From an adult perspective, Gilchrist looks back on her mother as a major influence on her development of imagination.

Of her father, nicknamed Dooley, a pro-baseball infielder for the Nashville Volunteers and an engineer, Gilchrist tells that he helped build the levee that holds back the waters of the Mississippi. During World War II, he labored on airports for the Army. She remembers his interest in finance and his wish that she take a course in the stock market. But she recalls that the interference of a campus hunk lured her from serious study, thus ending all hope of her challenging Wall Street.

## A Southern Girlhood

Much of Gilchrist's girlhood reflects the mores of the 1950s. In 1949, she got her first writing job as a columnist for a Franklin, Kentucky, newspaper. She called her column "Chit and Chat About This and That." The next year, she served as feature editor of the Harrisburg High School paper. This creative era ended after she eloped to Georgia at the age of nineteen with Marshall Walker, an engineering student. In rollicking fashion, she typifies her early marriage: "I did what every healthy human being does—I married the first good-looking man who wanted to marry me back and had three beautiful children. I thought I didn't want to be pregnant, but I did."[5]

Her first marriage existed in a perpetual state of separation. With the birth of each of her three red-haired children—Marshall Peteet, Jr., Garth Gilchrist, and Pierre Gautier—she returned to her parents' Mississippi home for solace. While the children raised themselves under her lenient hand, she turned to a life of reading and tennis to keep the status of her household out of mind.

An eclectic reader, Gilchrist delved into the arcane corners of philosophy as well as the biology of Charles Darwin, the poems of Dylan Thomas, and the science and philosophy of Albert Einstein. In those days, when she immersed herself in T.S. Eliot's poetry, she considered herself "too easily influenced to know there are other ways to grow old, that it can mean having the world grow simpler, clearer, more beautiful, less complicated."[6]

While her parents tended the children, Gilchrist obtained her bachelor's degree in philosophy from Millsaps College in 1967. During these late-in-life school years she studied under her idol and chief mentor, southern short story writer Eudora Welty. Her personal life faltered as her literary skills took shape. Divorced from Walker, Gilchrist married an Alabama judge, divorced, remarried Walker, divorced, married a New Orleans lawyer, and divorced a fourth time in 1980.

At forty, she was working full-time as an editor for the *New Orleans Vieux Carré Courier*. During this period, her sporadic creative writing centered on short stories and poems. Her work remained closeted until she submitted poetry to Jim Whitehead, who encouraged her to enter the University of Arkansas.

## Kindred Hearts in Fayetteville

Of her arrival on campus in 1976, Gilchrist rhapsodizes that, wearied of the snooty New Orleans elite, she fell in love at first sight with Fayetteville, where scholars hobnobbed with hardhats. In contrast to New Orleans, she found no cloying social restrictions and no class-conscious phoniness. During what she calls her hippie period, she settled in a frame house in the mountains, exulting in an environment that encouraged her growth.

The resulting fiction was a tapestry of experiences, including her four marriages and divorces alongside the maneuverings of the southern aristocrats to maintain a hold on the top rung of social prominence. Exuberantly, she explains her creative method: "I just have a vision of a story. I'll be sitting in the bath and I'll hear Traceleen's voice: 'Another time Miss Crystal did a real bad thing at a wedding,' she'll say, and I just jump right out and start writing."[7] Her works achieved a success atypical of fiction published by a small university press.

In 1980, Gilchrist received an offer of $65,000 to adapt plots into scripts for a Hollywood producer. Her better inclinations advised her to turn down easy money and continue toward her own destinations. Temptation behind her, nine years after leaving college, she completed postgraduate work at the University of Arkansas. Then, at the age of 49, she began a successful career as a commentator on National Public Radio's "Morning Edition."

# A Published Author

In addition to her journalism work and authorship of a play for the National Educational Television network, Gilchrist has published poems (*The Land Surveyor's Daughter*, 1979), novels (*The Annunciation*, 1983; and *The Anna Papers*, 1988), an autobiographical journal (*Falling Through Space*, 1987), and story collections (*In the Land of Dreamy Dreams*, 1981; *Victory Over Japan*, 1984; *Drunk With Love*, 1986; and *Light Can Be Both Wave and Particle*, 1989). In 1979 she won a grant from the NEA and earned a Book of the Month Club selection for *The Annunciation*, as well as an American Book Award. She has contributed poetry and short stories to *Atlantic Monthly*, *Mademoiselle*, *Cosmopolitan*, *New York Quarterly*, and *Southern Living*. In the field of poetry and fiction she has received awards from the University of Arkansas, *New York Quarterly*, Mississippi Arts Festival, Saxifrage, *The Prairie Schooner*, J. William Fulbright fund, Mississippi Institute of Arts and Letters, and twice from Pushcart Press. To top it off, she bears the title of Mississippi's poet laureate.

Much of Gilchrist's short fiction, which ranks above her novels, details the downward spiral of the southern blueblood. Frequently set in the lush, languid background of New Orleans or the Mississippi Delta, her stories contrast the idealism of aristocratic heroines with the reality of less-than-sparkling lives. At times she reintroduces a character, examining a different stage in his or her life in order to demonstrate growth. Of these characters she murmurs affectionately, "I give them things that belong to me. I give them my old black lace dress or my best friend's eyes or a poem I wrote a year ago or one of my old boyfriends or whatever I think they need."[8]

Among her memorable creations is Nora Jane Whittington, who, with characteristic aplomb, purchases a stage pistol, dresses up like a nun, and robs a bar so that she can flee New Orleans and join her lover, Sandy Halter, in California. Along the way, wires get crossed and Nora Jane arrives at an empty house, running across evidence that Sandy has taken a new love. Undismayed, Nora Jane forms a second liaison with Freddie Harwood, a book store owner, and takes a job at an art gallery before reconnecting with Sandy. Later adventures detail her decision to have a test to determine which of the two men sired her twins.

A second vibrant individual in her stories is Traceleen, personal servant of Miss Crystal, who married into a wealthy Jewish clan, admittedly for the money. Through Traceleen's eyes—often bulging in amazement at her mistress's adventures—the stories of Miss Crystal's escapades spread like succulent honey spilled from the jar. Gilchrist loses no opportunity to lampoon the amorality of the upper crust, whose uproarious clashes over family, greed, lust, and power keep Traceleen enthralled.

Then there's Rhoda Manning, a smart-mouthed adolescent who manipulates her father's guilt by downgrading his working class friends. To complete her victory over Dad, she renews her acquaintance with the joys of smoking Lucky Strikes, steals a jeep, drives without a license, then beds down with a poolroom drifter.

## Critical Response

Critics praise Gilchrist's tawdry cast, realistic dialogue, vibrant language, and powerful re-creation of human emotion, notably adolescent frustration. As Bruce Allen describes her characterizations, "These are vividly nasty portraits of adolescents pleasuring themselves with monstrous lies, spoiled Southern belles who get their doting rich daddies to pay for their abortions, lamebrained nouveaux riches who can't handle the consequences of their prosperity."[9] Like Flannery O'Connor and Eudora Welty, Ellen Gilchrist does a notable job of delineating southern womanhood. Jeannie Thompson and Anita Miller Garner state in their critique of her work, "She seems convinced that a woman's life is often like an extended downhill sled ride, starting out with much promise for excitement and speed, but troubled by ill-placed obstacles, icy spots, and a fizzle at the end."[10]

## Speaking Her Mind

Perhaps more than her short stories and books, Ellen Gilchrist is known for speaking her thoughts. In her job as a radio commentator, she sat in a soundproof room with earphones clamped to her head, read the short philosophical essays that are her trademark, and amassed a loyal following. Many of her short radio pieces began in her journals. Others originated in public speeches, some of which sting her audiences with caustic wit and undiluted opinions.

In 1985, Gilchrist addressed the students at the Arkansas Governor's School for the gifted, located at the Hendrix College campus. She stirred listeners from their complacency with a single remark: "My father ... meant to pay me a compliment by sending me an American flag once given to him by President Nixon during the Vietnam war. One of my children made a pair of pants out of it."[11]

A second example of her wordcraft comes from a baccalaureate address at the J. William Fulbright College of Arts and Sciences at the University of Arkansas. In it she denigrated the effect of money on her life and raised above it her love of reading. To the graduates, she spoke directly and earnestly, urging them not to immerse themselves entirely in temporal forms of literature, such as newspapers and magazines, or in vapid, unfulfilling televised pap.

Gilchrist noted that, having worked for these media, she was aware of their shortcomings and contrasted them with more stimulating, honest literature. She concluded with a telling picture of popular writers, whom she characterized as clever, but not necessarily wise. As a warning to students about the power of persuasive voices, she contended that most writers are just as befuddled and frightened as other human beings.

## Self-Analysis

Ellen Gilchrist is not always so intense or analytical. In her spare time she relaxes with sports, music, enjoyment of the outdoors, and marathon running. She seems content with her persona as a writer and observer of life—but not too content. As she has pointed out, artists lose their zip when life loses its mystery. For Founder's Day at Scripps College in Claremont, California, she stated her humanistic concerns with style: "Who am I? Where did I come from? What am I doing here? Is this right?... Clearly, we have been human for a long time. Clearly the first thing we did was probe the mystery and the last thing we will ever do is probe that same mystery."[12]

In her statement of purpose to *Contemporary Authors*, Gilchrist declared that she writes to entertain herself as well as to understand. And her method of understanding is to express dilemmas and doubts in as many ways as she can find words for. She relies heavily on intuition and chooses for each collection the stories that she herself likes to read. She writes as though she were talking to friends, then gives her stories like gifts. An unpretentious thinker and talker, she loves the sound and feel of language, which she eventually reworks and shapes into sublime, but tangible expression. In her autographs, she includes the injunction, "Dance in the fullness of time," a summation of her own exuberance.[13]

When the possibility of a teaching job comes up, Gilchrist pushes it aside. She disdains the task of the writing teacher by conjuring up a hypothetical situation in which she would have to crush someone's dream of one day succeeding as a writer.

Gilchrist holds fast to her roots by remaining firm in the bosom of her family, even though she differs with her conservative father. She expresses gratitude that her parents are alive and well, that she lives across the street from brother Dooley, Jr., and that her two grandchildren live close enough for her to enjoy them. She remains down-to-earth by rejecting the trappings of fame, commenting: "Celebrity is a real terrible cardboard thing to happen to you. You can refuse that gamut. If you don't want anybody to treat you like a celebrity, they won't."[14]

## Notes

[1] Ellen Gilchrist. *Falling Through Space*. Boston: Little, Brown, 1987, 13.

[2] Gilchrist, 27.

[3] Gilchrist, 30.

[4] Gilchrist, 12.

[5] Gene Lyons. "First Person Singular," *Newsweek*, February 18, 1985, 81.

[6] Gilchrist, 21.

[7] Lyons, 83.

[8] "Southerner Ellen Gilchrist is the Book World's Belle," *People*, February 11, 1985, 74.

[9] *Contemporary Literary Criticism*, Volume 48, Detroit: Gale Research, 1988, 115.

[10] *Contemporary Literary Criticism*, 1988, 116.

[11] Lyle Hammons. "Writer's Style, Comments Jolt Students at Governor's School," *Little Rock Gazette*, July 23, 1984, n.p.

[12] Gilchrist, 69.

[13] *Contemporary Authors*, Volume 116. Detroit: Gale Research, 1986, 167.

[14] Leslie Myers. "Celebrated Writer Comes Home," *Jackson Clarion-Ledger*, Jackson, Miss., October 25, n.p.

## Sources

"Celebrated Writer Comes Home," *Jackson Clarion-Ledger*, Jackson, Miss., October 25, 1985, n.p.

*Contemporary Authors*, Volume 116. Detroit: Gale Research, 1986.

*Contemporary Literary Criticism*, Volume 48. Detroit: Gale Research, 1988, 114-119.

Gilchrist, Ellen. *Falling Through Space*. Boston: Little, Brown, 1987.

Goldsmith, Sarah Sue. "Learning to Love Gilchrist's Anna," *Baton Rouge Morning Advocate*, December 18, 1988, n.p.

Hammons, Lyle. "Writer's Style, Comments Jolt Students at Governor's School," *Little Rock Gazette*, July 23, 1984, n.p.

Kennedy, Joanne. "For Those Who Are Loyalists of Ellen Gilchrist," *Norfolk Virginia-Pilot*, December 4, 1988, n.p.

Lyons, Gene. "First Person Singular," *Newsweek*, February 18, 1985, 81-83.

Myers, Leslie R. "Celebrated Writer Comes Home," *Jackson Clarion-Ledger*, Jackson, Miss., October 25, 1985, n.p.

"Southerner Ellen Gilchrist is the Book World's Belle," *People*, February 11, 1985, 74, 77.

Young, Tracy. "Off the Cuff: Ellen Gilchrist," *Vogue*, September 1986, 415-418.

# Kurt Hahn

Some achievers are born achievers and never lose their touch for success. Kurt Hahn, a proponent of experiential education, is an example of staunch dedication to the ideals of individual achievement, a concept he adhered to even during his clash with Adolf Hitler. The result was a lifetime of creativity that continues to affect the lives of thousands of students.

Hahn, a stern, rugged pedagogue, began his unconventional teaching career as an idealistic and demanding German educator. By hardening bodies and toughening minds to struggle against nature and self, Hahn's Outward Bound school mushroomed into a major training center. As Hahn characterized his educational dream, "We strove to produce young people able to effect what they saw to be right, despite hardships, dangers, inner skepticism, mockery, or the emotions of the moment."[1]

Hahn's high expectations resulted in a modern-day American anomaly—an educational system that forces flabby, soft city folk, alcoholics, drug addicts, and defeatists of all stripes into the role of survivalists. Even more to the point, he strengthened self-denial and an indomitable spirit in people so that they could face all challenges and find satisfaction in benefiting society on a one-to-one basis. Today, accountants, athletes, and desk warriors leave the comforts of city life to roam the wilderness and learn how to fend for themselves according to the Kurt Hahn method of survival training.

## Early Life

Kurt Matthias Robert Martin Hahn came from a cultured Jewish background. Born in Berlin, Germany, June 5, 1886, to industrialist Oskar and Charlotte Landau Hahn, he studied at Wilhelmgymnasium in Berlin and later at Göttingen University and Christ Church, Oxford, from 1910 to 1914. He did advanced study at the universities of Berlin, Heidelberg, and Freiburg.

Hahn was neither athletic nor physically adept. He often fell because of innate clumsiness and in other ways jeopardized himself. While at Oxford, he stayed outdoors too long in extreme sunlight, suffered a sunstroke, and was forced to spend a year convalescing in a dark room in the austere climate of

Moray, Scotland. The experience inspired his entire career. From a condition that left him permanently sensitive to light and heat he evolved a personal creed: "Your disability is your opportunity."[2]

## An Eclectic Philosophy

Crucial to Hahn's creed was the undergirding of Plato's teachings, as stated in the *Republic*. Hahn believed that education must inspire compassionate action more than unactualized attitudes and opinions. He perceived responsibility as the subordination of self to the needs of others. As he summarized the connection between individualism and society, people cannot understand self until they submerge selfish goals and discover the extent of their character. It is this concept of self-discovery through self-sacrifice that made his view unique.

Hahn returned on August 1, 1914, to Germany, where World War I stymied his career plans. During the war years, he served as a lector of English newspapers for the German Foreign Office and the Supreme Command. Five years later he took the post of private secretary to Prince Max von Baden, Germany's last imperial chancellor, whom he helped to establish a coeducational boarding school for rich, aristocratic German youth at Salem Castle on Germany's Lake Constance in 1920. With von Baden's assistance, Hahn became the first headmaster of the school, which was named Salem to evoke both the castle and the Hebrew word for peace.

The structured curriculum at Salem made good use of normal student enthusiasm. Hahn helped harness youthful zest for exploration and adventure by allying them with academics and athletics. Students worked on Salem's farm and raised food for the dining hall. He also stressed long-term creative projects as well as expeditions to build endurance. Overall, he hoped to train citizens to accept the challenge of leadership and to think beyond selfish goals.

## Dealing with Opposition

Because his philosophy clashed with Hitler's concept of a master race, Hahn was arrested by the Nazis in March 1933. Colleagues took action to free him. Through the intervention of England's Prime Minister Ramsay MacDonald, who dealt directly with the German high command, Hahn gained his freedom and emigrated to Britain in July, where he later became a citizen. The ordeal dampened his spirit temporarily when he realized that he had to carry out his professional plans in exile.

Released from fears that had hampered his work in Germany, in 1934 Hahn rededicated himself to his ideal by founding Gordonstoun School, an austere educational center similar to Salem, in a decrepit stone castle in the dreary, windswept northeast quadrant of Scotland, facing the North Sea. Among the students to undergo his rigorous regimen were people of all stations, including England's Prince Philip, husband of Queen Elizabeth II, and their two sons, Charles and Andrew.

## A Unique System

From the early days of his career, Hahn was an uncompromising taskmaster to all comers, whether streetfighter or elite scion of Europe's best families. To encourage breadth in his staff, he made a practice of hiring people who did not share his philosophy. To Hahn, a constant reexamination of attitudes and philosophies was necessary both to his personal growth and to that of his school.

Hahn believed that deprivation was good for the spirit. He created a plan requiring two cold showers per day, early morning runs, a minimum of talk, no eating between meals, and high standards for physical and academic performance. His unique plan for toughening the mind and body resulted from his interest in producing strong people who could survive future world cataclysms, both natural and military.

Part of the unique system of preparing young men for physical challenge was the ingenious creation of groups dedicated to public service. The Gordonstoun school offered not only a fire service and mountain rescue teams, who scaled rocks to practice high-elevation evacuation techniques, but also coast watchers who perched in watchtowers atop Moray Firth, east of Inverness along the North Sea, to observe storms and fog. This youthful beach patrol telephoned reports to Royal Coast Guard stations to protect fishing boats and ships along the Scottish coast.

## Creating Outward Bound

More than any other aspect of his approach, the concept of self-discovery set Hahn apart from all other educational theorists. He discarded the Ionic concept that individualism is the goal of education. In like manner he rejected the Spartan notion that the individual is less worthy than the good of the state. Instead, Hahn molded his curriculum on a third principle—the ancient Platonic model that maintains that successful citizens must blend intellectual skill along with moral and physical superiority in order to discover the best they have to offer. He shored up his thinking with eclectic studies of a variety of thinkers—Max Weber, William James, Jean Jacques Rousseau, Johann Pestalozzi, Lord Baden-Powell, Johann Goethe, and Henry David Thoreau. He continued to refine this outlook throughout his career.

In 1941, Hahn's school took on a new look as a result of World War II. At the age of fifty-five, Hahn joined Lawrence Holt, a leading merchant shipper from Gordonstoun, in founding the Outward Bound Sea School. Because an excessive number of sailors died when their ships were torpedoed, Holt wanted to create a training facility to build stamina and grit in merchant seamen. He agreed to finance and staff a training center if Hahn would devise the curriculum. The school opened at Aberdovey, which lies on the estuary of the Dovey River on the west coast of Wales, and capitalized on the extremes of weather for which the area is famous.

## A Tough Regimen

Hahn's curriculum, an instant success, aimed at strengthening both the physical and mental capabilities of students to endure privation and hardships in combat convoy duty. He crammed the entire course into a single month. The experience, which resembled army boot camp, exhibited a type of benign militarism, as illustrated by the use of such terminology as reconnaissance, debriefing, and patrol.

Hahn's pupils, living in meagerly furnished dormitories and subsisting on a frugal diet, studied in small groups, which he thought best for the intensity and demand of the subject matter. The curriculum covered a broad range—athletics, small boat launching and management, cross-country orienteering, map and compass skills, and, most important, search and rescue at sea. In the end, Holt and Hahn proved their point: the students' oneness with the environment, self-discipline, self-confidence through skill, and pride in inner resources resulted in tougher seamen.

Hahn took a keen personal interest in his school. As headmaster, he set an example of hardihood and perseverance and refused to stint, even in extreme old age. In threatening weather, he climbed the metal stairs to the watchtower and took his turn against the blast of wind and rain. He walked the campus daily, troubleshooting and ferreting out individuals who needed an extra push. When a student fell into bad habits, such as stealing, Hahn woke his instructors in the middle of the night, grilled them concerning their management techniques, and forced them to pay more attention to moral development.

One of Hahn's educational innovations was "The Break," a 50-minute period four days a week when students competed against their own records in running, jumping, discus and javelin throwing, cross-country, and other standard decathlon events. He believed that this experience could help marginal students rid themselves of the "misery of unimportance."[3] Because he detested exhibitionism, Hahn rejected trophies, tournaments, and other forms of boasting and self-importance that mark ordinary team sports. Instead, he encouraged his participants to become better people rather than better athletes.

## A Modern Educational Phenomenon

In 1953, the year he retired from Gordonstoun, Hahn received accolades for his innovative programs, including an honorary doctorate from Edinburgh University. But he was far from finished with his distinguished career. Two years later, after meeting with Air Marshall Sir Lawrence Darvall, commander of the NATO Defense College in Paris, Hahn began tinkering with a non-military school for students from around the globe. The purpose, as outlined by Darvall, was to build international understanding through cooperation and character.

Utilizing committees in many countries, Hahn engineered a two-year course for high school graduates of many nationalities. By 1962, the idea became reality in Atlantic College, later called United World College of the Atlantic, in St. Donat's, Wales. The brainstorm continued to grow, spinning off the United World College of the Pacific in British Columbia, the United World College of Southeast Asia in Singapore, and the United World College of the Adriatic in Trieste.

Hahn's concept led to the foundation of thirty-two Outward Bound schools in seventeen countries. Joshua L. Miner helped establish the six U.S. schools in 1962, with headquarters in Greenwich, Connecticut. With programs in twenty states, the Outward Bound program extends to the Rocky Mountains in Colorado, the Superior Quetico Wilderness area in Minnesota, Hurricane Island off Maine, the Cascade Range in Oregon, Pisgah National Forest in North Carolina, and an urban setting in New York City.

## Outward Bound in the U.S.

The U.S. Outward Bound regimen varies little from Hahn's original plan. According to publicity releases, Outward Bound schools "help men and women discover and extend their own resources and abilities by confronting them with a series of increasingly difficult challenges, primarily in a wilderness setting."[4] The 19,000 students who participate annually complete courses from four to thirty days in length. Around a quarter of all entrants are scholarship students. Classes receive instruction in physical conditioning, technical and team training, expeditions, environmental experience, and community service. By camping, rock climbing, canoeing, sailing, rafting, cycling, kayaking, and orienteering, they develop survival skills. Additional training in emergency first aid, evacuation, and search and rescue techniques extend their awareness from recreational to practical skills.

The Outward Bound concept proves beneficial to a variety of students. Special classes for Vietnam veterans, Peace Corps volunteers, juvenile delinquents, and substance abusers strengthen mental health. In addition, over 250 schools offer adapted versions of the Outward Bound method. The schools all stress the same goal: a soundness of body and mind that ultimately leads to better citizenship and stronger international relations.

# Continuing the Quest

Hahn's interest in education did not end with Outward Bound. In 1968, at the age of 82, he toured U.S. campuses and cities and pondered the growth of racism and gang warfare from coast to coast. He continued testing his original model—a way to put youthful high spirits and competitiveness to positive use. He never stopped battling his old affliction of susceptibility to heat and light, but made his journey with resolution and hope.

The world paid attention to Hahn's accomplishments. He received prizes and distinction for his work—from Göttingen, Tubingen, and Berlin universities. In 1962 he received the Freiherr-von-Stein Prize. These honoraria came not only from educators, but also from governmental groups, which appreciated his belief that he could build better world citizens through holistic training.

In old age, Hahn remained active, despite growing weakness. In his off hours, he enjoyed walking, lawn tennis, and history. He lived alternately in Baden, Germany, and at Brown's Hotel in London until his death on December 15, 1974, in Hermannsburg, West Germany, which was hastened by injuries he received when he was struck by a car in Piccadilly Circus.

Many people have reflected over Kurt Hahn's long and productive life. John S. Holden, a lifetime trustee and former headmaster of Colorado Outward Bound school, captured his mentor's best qualities: "At times I couldn't help thinking that this was the most unlikely man to have started the Outward Bound Movement. But ... I realized that he was always moving in the same direction, always stretching himself to the limit and always demanding that same stretch in the people working with him."[5]

Holden recalled that Hahn maintained his optimism that America would grow stronger and overcome racism. He never stopped planning for the future and hoped to create a coalition of Red Cross, mountain rescue, water safety, fire-fighting, and ski patrol leaders. He armed students against fear, apathy, negativism, and self-absorption. The soul of his message was a belief that people who work together to save life are unwilling to kill.

Hahn never lost his determination to strike a balance in his pupils or in himself. He looked for evidence of their ability to harmonize the physical with the mental and for opportunities to complement weaknesses with strengths. While pitting slower performers with their superiors, he tried to instill purposeful challenge in one group, forcing the elite to pace themselves so that they could be companions and sources of inspiration to the weak. He deemed the resulting conflict a healthy condition necessary to an understanding of society's complexities.

# Notes

[1] Josua L. Miner. "My Most Unforgettable Character," *Reader's Digest*, December 1975, 129.

[2] Miner, 128.

[3] Miner, 130.

[4] *Encyclopedia of Associations.* Volume 2. 24th edition. Detroit: Gale Research, 1990, 886.

[5] Thomas James. "Sketch of a Moving Spirit: Kurt Hahn," *Journal of Experiential Education*, Spring 1980, 3.

## Sources

*Encyclopedia of Associations.* Volume 2. 24th edition. Detroit: Gale Research, 1990.

James, Thomas. "Sketch of a Moving Spirit: Kurt Hahn," *Journal of Experiential Education*, Spring 1980.

McFadden, Robert D. "Kurt Hahn, Pedagogue, Dead," *New York Times*, October 16, 1974, 36.

"Milestones," *Time*, December 30, 1974, 31.

Miner, Joshua L. "My Most Unforgettable Character," *Reader's Digest*, December 1975, 127-131.

"Transition," *Newsweek*, December 30, 1974, 37.

*Who's Who, 1970-1971.* New York: St. Martin's Press.

# Clara Hale

For at least one late achiever, drudgery has mellowed into a life of service. Mother Clara Hale, mastermind and wonder-worker of Hale House, continued to nurture babies and toddlers as she did most of her life. The one detail that set her child-care facility apart was the fact that her charges were special-needs infants, born out of Harlem's drug nightmare.

The first needy children to come under Mother Hale's care were born to heroin addicts. Sobbing uncontrollably from withdrawal pain, these under-nourished, underloved babes nestled in her lap in the well-used bentwood rocker. Without words to express their relief, they responded to her belief that, if given a chance, they could resist the bleak undertow and grow into well-adjusted, strong children.

After President Reagan honored Mother Hale with public notice and an award for selflessness, her project evolved into a child-centered receiving home for other unwanted infants. Some of "Mama Hale's children" were handicapped; some battled neglect; others suffered from AIDS. All came from Harlem, a metropolitan center seething with drug addiction and the deadly viral infection of AIDS.

Mother Hale gave these abandoned innocents what they needed—a clean, warm, accepting, and loving environment. Phrasing her hope in simple terms, she said, "They are going to turn out lovely. All my children do."[1] Her devotion to their plight brought her worldwide fame as a star mother.

## Learning to Love

From her own mother, Clara McBride Hale learned that love is the solid underpinning for human care. The youngest of four children, Hale was born on April 1, 1905, in Philadelphia. Her family suffered after her father's death when Clara was an infant. Left with few resources, her mother worked as a cook and took in boarders to make ends meet.

Poverty failed to dim Clara's enthusiasm. With her mother's guidance, she learned to take pride in self. She graduated from a Philadelphia high school and married Thomas "Sam" Hale, owner of a profitable floor-waxing, window-washing business. Proud of her American heritage, she named her first son after patriot Nathan Hale. To eke out a living for her family, she scrubbed floors and toilets at Loew's theaters.

## Hard Times

Hale recalls her worst crisis in poignant terms: "When my husband was sick and we all knew he was going to die, he made me promise I'd give the children a fine education. And I did."[2] After Sam died of cancer in 1932, she had to adapt her schedule in order to earn a living while rearing daughter Lorraine, son Nathan, and adopted son Kenneth. "There was no way under the sun that they would give you any other job except domestic jobs," she recalls. "And that meant being away all day from those poor little children who had nobody."[3]

But Clara Hale created a better way. Instead of going out to clean theaters, she remained home and opened a child-care facility. She accepted children from parents who worked out of town and superintended them until their parents returned on weekends. At her cramped Harlem flat five stories up on West 146th Street, she took in eight children at a time, treating them with the same love she lavished on her own three. By accepting foster children, Hale added a two-dollar-per-day allotment from social services. She readily filled in as a parent, even visiting the children's schools when they had classroom problems. Never one to boast, she took pride in her forty foster children, who went on to college and remained free of drug addiction and trouble with the law.

## New Needs, More Babies

In 1968, Hale, after thirty-six years of tending other people's babies, retired. The following year, her daughter, child specialist Dr. Lorraine Hale, surprised her with a new challenge. While driving through the drug-infested environs of Harlem, Lorraine saw a user nodding off on a park bench, her arms too weak to hold her infant. Lorraine feared that the baby would fall. With understanding and persistence, she thrust her mother's address into the junkie's hands and repeated instructions to take the child there for care. Out of the drug-induced fog, the mother accepted help and made her way to Hale's door.

Hale recalled that first desperate mother: "When I saw this woman at my door, I was sure that some mistake had been made. I thought my daughter didn't even know any addicts. But since she insisted, I asked her to wait while I called. When I came back, only the baby was waiting."[4] By the time Lorraine arrived at her mother's house, she found her cradling the infant and talking gently to it.

Lorraine helped her mother establish a home for other heroin addicts. Even though Hale had no experience with drugs, she knew a great deal about raising children. As she characterized the stream of needy babies, "God kept sending them, and He kept opening a way for me to make it."[5] Soon word spread through the drug underground that mothers with addicted infants could find a decent home for their babies at no cost and with no stigma. With the financial and moral support of her children, Hale jammed her tiny apartment with baby beds. Content to do her best, she worked for over a year without help from social organizations to provide for the needy infants.

## A New Start

An innovation from the beginning, Hale's receiving home became a model halfway house in New York, a city where 2,290 children needed special care in 1979 and 1980 alone. A useful adjunct to her work was a state law prohibiting hospitals from sending infants home with mothers when urine tests indicated that the children were already addicted. Mothers were willing to leave their children in her care and to submit to rehabilitation. With her assurance, they clung to the hope that one day they would reunite with their children to form a normal family.

Dr. Lorraine Hale credits her mother's success to her ability to love, even in tragic circumstances. A believer in parental bonding, Clara Hale insisted that each mother make weekly visits to keep lines of communication open while following a regimen of drug rehabilitation. To supplant the irregularity of the drug world with order, she provided each child with food, clean clothes, medical care, and individual attention. At the end of Hale's intensive nurturing, which took an average of eighteen months, most of the children reunited with their mothers. For the majority of users, drug treatment programs, along with psychological counseling, turned them into responsible parents.

## Learning the Drug Scene

With no lack of drug peddlers and users, the New York area saw the number of problem children spiral upward. At first, almost all were offspring of heroin users, themselves little more than children. The symptoms of heroin were predictable—the wracking misery of withdrawal followed by passivity. Then the mix of designer drugs and alcohol began to show up at Hale House, necessitating a new pattern of care.

Of this change in drug behavior, Lorraine Hale noted, "Now, among the babies of poly-drug users, we're seeing such a wide range of problems. Each child seems to be manifesting behaviorisms that are unique to him, yet not appropriate."[6] Their sufferings ranged from low birth weight to breathing problems, poor concentration, and learning disability. The stress of drugs and poor prenatal care was so great on developing fetuses that nearly 12 percent died before birth.

By 1971, Mother Hale's altruistic project came to the attention of Percy Sutton, a Manhattan official who wanted to rescue as many children as possible. With his assistance, she augmented handouts from her own three children with private donations and a solid base of city, state, and federal funds. One of her key donors, former Beatle John Lennon, began annual gifts of $20,000, which his widow, Yoko Ono, continued after his murder. With these generous gifts, Hale began training a staff so there would be enough love and care to go around.

## New Surroundings

In 1975, Mother Hale relieved her greatest worry by moving to Hale House, a five-story brownstone at 154 West 122nd Street. With federal grant money, she gutted the building and rebuilt from the ground up. She remodeled the facility to include a dining room, kitchen, playroom, and nursery. To remind children to think well of themselves, she lined the dining room with mirrors. As they toddled about and touched their reflections with tentative fingers, the children learned to look life in the eye and to accept themselves. Soon they were banging on the grand piano and finding reasons to smile.

On the third floor of the building, Mother Hale built her own quarters, a peaceful haven decorated in royal blue. There she weaned new arrivals from drug dependence. The tiny beds resided near her own so that she could tend them at any hour. Ministering to their self-mutilation, diarrhea, muscle spasms, runny noses, itching, and vomiting, she applied a time-honored method of soothing children—she walked them, rocked them, and sang to them until they relaxed.

The secret of Clara Hale's success became apparent to people who saw her in action. She knew how to build trust. She did not turn away from the gagging, grimacing faces and jerky, unpredictable movements. She asked no one else to clean up their vomit, change their diapers, clip their nails, warm their formula, or spoon in cereal. Clara Hale did the personal care herself.

## A Difficult Battle

In time, with steady reassurance and love, the tortured children, susceptible to emotional trauma and infections of all sorts, eventually overcame their nameless inner demons and grew strong. Most returned to their families. Only 12 of the first 500 children were put up for adoption. An additional 11 were placed in foster care. Then, with the coming of crack, a deadlier form of cocaine, Clara Hale met a more lethal adversary. For the first time in her life-long care of children, three died. Of their battle, she mourned, "Crack babies don't have a chance."[7]

After word spread that Hale House offered hope to these special infants, police officers, ministers, emergency room personnel, social workers, private citizens, and drugged mothers themselves began sending referrals to Mother Hale.

Each of the children, ranging from newborn to four years, put a heavy burden on her during the two to three weeks that they wrestled with addiction. She accepted them, refusing to continue phenobarbital and other drugs prescribed by doctors and foregoing even aspirin as a means of easing their suffering. In explanation, Mother Hale insisted, "I don't want them to get in any habits, so they go cold turkey."[8]

## In the Spotlight

Soon, the world came to know of Clara Hale's success. During Ronald Reagan's presidency, he learned of her selflessness. He admired her style of tackling a thorny, thankless task. To show his appreciation, he invited her to attend the State of the Union address on February 6, 1985. Hale at eighty was not in good health, but against doctor's orders, answered the President's summons. "I couldn't imagine that out of all the people in the world," she exulted, "the President picked me for the honor."[9]

Seated next to Nancy Reagan in the visitor's gallery of the House of Representatives, Mother Hale acknowledged a standing ovation after the President characterized her work. He said, "Go to her house some night and maybe you'll see her as she walks the floor, talking softly, soothing a child in her arms. She is an American hero."[10] Among the people applauding her were top dignitaries—members of Congress, court justices, cabinet members, and the press. The next day, she toured the White House and stopped off at the Oval Office for a more personal chat with the President.

From the attention she received, Mother Hale garnered much support for Hale House. Without currying favor, begging, or lowering her standards, she informed potential donors of her need for a larger facility so that she would not have to reject addicted children. True to her organized style, she had already selected a likely site—a roomy property at 122nd Street and Adam Clayton Powell, Jr., Boulevard.

With more space for her program, she offered a halfway house so that mother and child could get to know each other again before returning to normal life. The goal of the new facility was to assure a steadier future for the children by helping mothers find their way in society. With assistance in locating jobs, housing, and day-care, the mothers, newly rehabilitated and reacquainted with parental roles, could face life without resorting to drugs and alcohol.

With Lorraine's help, Mother Hale broadened her perspectives so that the program would continue when she became too old to superintend. Depending upon the assistance of a select cadre of social, medical, and psychological workers, Hale House expanded to other areas of the country. To assist the aging founder, Lorraine shouldered administrative responsibilities and brought in helpers who worked for a mere $175 a week.

## Answering a Need

Clara Hale surprised visitors and reporters to Hale House by her toughness. A slender, undersized woman with thinning white hair, she was nonetheless sturdy. Putting her whole self into the challenge of rescuing children from health problems, she drew outsiders into her dream of a place where childhood retained its innocence, where a safe harbor beckoned to all races and needs.

Her stalwart attitude did not go unrewarded. John Jay College of Criminal Justice awarded her an honorary doctorate in 1985. She and Lorraine, who served as president and chief executive officer of Hale House, received the Truman Award for Public Service. Five years later, at age eighty-eight, Mother Hale appeared on the "Amen" TV program, where emcee Clifton Davis praised her efforts during an annual charity revue. To raise money for Hale House, he sang "You're My Child" and ran a filmed study of the Hale House program. Other honors poured in. Talk show hosts deluged Mother Hale with requests for appearances. The National Mother's Day Committee sent an award. After the burst of interest and support for her work, she hoped to open a Hale House in Philadelphia, her hometown.

In explaining her mother's charity work, Lorraine summed up her approach to need: "Mother always thought about someone else besides herself, and certainly besides us. And if you ask me if I resented that, yes. I really, really did, because I knew we really didn't have any money and I just couldn't understand her."[11] But Lorraine has followed her mother's pattern of stretching resources for whatever needy children come her way.

The many children who have passed through Mother Hale's care remain close. Some fail to recognize the extent of her sacrifice. Others, who are fortunately a majority, keep in touch after high school and college. To them, Mother Hale is both parent and savior. Her belief in perseverance and self-actualization come through her simple philosophy: "You can have anything you want if you make up your mind. You don't have to crack nobody across the head, don't have to steal or anything. Don't have to be smart like the men up high stealing all the money. We're good people and we try."[12]

## Notes

[1] Claire Safran. "Mama Hale and Her Little Angels," *Reader's Digest*, September 1984, 50.

[2] Kathy Hacker. "Mother Hale: A Savior and Her Growing Mission," *Philadelphia Inquirer*, May 7, 1986, n.p.

[3] Brian Lanker and Maya Angelou. "I Dream a World," *National Geographic*, August 1989, 218.

[4] Lorenzo Carcaterra. "Mother Hale of Harlem Has Saved 487 Drug-Addicted Babies with an Old Miracle Cure: Love," *People*, March 5, 1984, 212.

[5] Ordinary Women of Grace: Subjects of the 'I Dream a World' Photography Exhibit," *U.S. News & World Report*, February 13, 1989, 54.

[6] Hacker, n.p.

[7] David Nimmons. "The Santa Claus Awards," *Ladies' Home Journal*, December December 1986, 168.

[8] *Current Biography*. Detroit: Gale Research, 1985, 167.

[9] Herschel Johnson. "Clara (Mother) Hale: Healing Baby 'Junkies' with Love," *Ebony*, May 1986, 59.

[10] Nimmons, 268.

[11] Susan Bidel. "When Mom's a Hard Act to Follow," *Woman's Day*, May 22, 1990, 88.

[12] *U.S. News*, 54.

## Sources

Bidel, Susan. "When Mom's a Hard Act to Follow," *Woman's Day*, May 22, 1990, 86-90.

Carcaterra, Lorenzo. "Mother Hale of Harlem Has Saved 487 Drug-Addicted Babies with an Old Miracle Cure: Love," *People*, March 5, 1984, 211-214.

"Clara Hale to Get Truman Award for Public Service," *Jet*, March 20, 1989, 23.

*Current Biography*. Detroit: Gale Research, 1985.

"$50,000 Rehab House for Cocaine-Addicted Babies," *Jet*, January 25, 1988, 23.

Hacker, Kathy. "Mother Hale: A Savior and Her Growing Mission," *Philadelphia Inquirer*, May 7, 1986, n.p.

"Hale Receives $1.1 Million to Expand Home for Babies," *Jet*, May 19, 1986, 26.

Johnson, Herschel. "Clara (Mother) Hale: Healing Baby 'Junkies' with Love," *Ebony*, May 1986, 58-61.

Lanker, Brian, and Maya Angelou. "I Dream a World," *National Geographic*, August 1989, 206-226.

"Mother Hale Appears on NBC-TV's 'Amen' Series," *Jet*, February 19, 1990, 60-61.

"Mother Hale Honored," *Jet*, July 10, 1989, 22.

"Mother Hale's Help," *Jet*, May 25, 1987, 36.

Nimmons, David. "The Santa Claus Awards," *Ladies' Home Journal*, December 1986, 122-129, 168.

"Ordinary Women of Grace: Subjects of the 'I Dream a World' Photography Exhibit," *U.S. News & World Report*, February 13, 1989, 54.

"Reagan Cites Clara Hale as a 'Hero' in Union Address," *Jet*, February 25, 1985, 6.

Safran, Claire. "Mama Hale and Her Little Angels," *Reader's Digest*, September 1984, 49-54.

Winter, Annette. "Spotlight," *Modern Maturity*, October-November 1988, 18.

# Vaclav Havel

Political achievement is a chancy affair. For a steady climber, it sometimes nets a rewarding post, but seldom the top prize. For Vaclav Havel, who has run the gamut from pampered son of a middle-class businessman to $50-per-week barrel stacker in a brewery to dissident poet to scrapper in the name of human rights to political prisoner, the presidency is the surprise of the decade. As one admirer describes his behavior during the tense early years, Havel started out a conservative hippie. His path, to say the least, was circuitous, unplanned, and anything but a sure bet.

Long before Czechoslovakia's open clash with communism, Havel, a man of uncompromising conviction, stoicism, and character, was voicing general discontent with the stumbling block of communist bureaucracy, which had enslaved his country for forty-one years. When officials closed ranks to quell his insistent voice, he kept his cool and ignored reprisals. Because followers were unsure of his goals, questions arose from all quarters as to what Havel saw as his part in Czechoslovakia's future. To an interviewer he proclaimed with characteristic honesty, "All my life I understood my role in society as that of a writer whose mission is to tell the truth."[1] Following the nation's 1989 velvet revolution, doubters had their answer—and Vaclav Havel, man of truth, was elected President.

## Notes on a Native Son

Havel, the son of Vaclav M. and Bozena Vavreckova Havel, was born on October 5, 1936, in Prague, the capital of Czechoslovakia and a manufacturing and trade center situated in the western quarter of the country on the Moldau River. His family was comfortably well off. Along the Vlatava River, his grandfather had built in 1905 the apartment building that was his home. His uncle was a successful moviemaker and owner of Barandov Studios. His father owned a restaurant and downtown real estate.

The coming of communism stripped the family of its prestige and forced them to occupy only a small portion of the building they had once called their own. Vaclav's father lost his investments and was left with a desk job; his mother worked as a tour guide. At twelve, Vaclav himself suffered the insidious spite of a bureaucratic government bent on humiliating Czechoslovakia's middle class. The stigma on the bourgeoisie left him with an indefatigable urge to fight his tormentors.

Vaclav's prospects for education and professional attainment seemed to die with his employment in a chemical factory. But by his late teens he found a way to cope—reading and studying everything from Sartre to Kafka to Carl Sandburg to past Czech heroes. He pursued higher education through night classes, which he paid for by driving a taxi. While attending technical college, he haunted theaters and cultivated the suppressed voices that once championed freedom in Czechoslovakia. At a conference of intellectuals in 1956, Havel, only nineteen years of age, spoke publicly in favor of forgotten writers, who were once the moral strength of his nation.

In 1960, his military obligation completed, Havel began to look for answers to his questions of self-worth. He found a post as stagehand and electrician for Prague's avant-garde Theater on the Balustrade. Enthralled with the writings of Franz Kafka, Samuel Beckett, and Eugène Ionesco, he started writing, beginning with critical essays, notably a monograph on Joseph Capek, and extending to verse and plays. He augmented a sketchy technical school training with two years' work at Prague's Academy of Art and worked his way up at the Balustrade from secretary and reader to manager and writer-in-residence.

## Becoming a Playwright

By the age of twenty-seven, Havel—a handsome, red-haired, blue-eyed dynamo with wiry frame, bass voice, and honest, hesitant smile—had found his medium. He satirized the absurdities of the communist regime in *Autostop* and *The Garden Party*, a four-act drama depicting the linguistic miasma of totalitarianism. Two years later, he produced *The Memorandum*, a humorous diatribe against garbled communication, which Joe Papp presented on a New York stage three years later. In 1968, he wrote *The Increased Difficulty of Concentration*, which the Lincoln Center Repertory Theatre produced during Havel's visit to the United States. The play won him an Obie.

During the stringent bureaucratic crackdown of the 1970s, which followed the Soviet invasion of Czechoslovakia in 1968, Havel smuggled his works to England and Canada for publication. In 1975, he took a more insistent stab at communism by describing his new job as a factotum in a brewery in *A Private View*, which found its way onstage in a New York theater. He also produced two didactic satires, *The Mountain Hotel* and *The Conspirators*, a one-act play from a personal perspective, *Interview*, and an adaptation of *The Beggar's Opera*.

In each of his works, Havel emphasized the frustration of lost freedoms, particularly free speech, and the dehumanization found in technological society. His allegories, set in his own times and often labeled as theater of the absurd, spoke universally to eastern Europeans and people in other areas where dissent was stifled. Some critics championed his satiric humor, comparing him to Lewis Carroll. Lee Grant, one of his admirers, describes the verisimilitude of his work: "All his plays are like personal letters—letters to the world."[2]

Ultimately, as the world focused on Czechoslovakia's struggle for an independent identity, it found a clarion prospectus in Havel's works. Not only did Havel become the darling of an elite corps of American theater-goers, he also established a name for himself in his own territory. As a result, his call for truth led to a laudable title—eastern and central Europe's greatest dramatist.

## Wins and Losses

For a time, life was promising to Havel. He readily made money off foreign royalties and at twenty-eight married Olga Splichalova, whom he had courted since her days as cloakroom attendant at the Balustrade Theater. He remarked publicly on the stability he gained from having a working class wife: "In Olga, I found exactly what I needed: Someone who could respond to my own mental instability, to offer sober criticism of my wilder ideas and to provide private support for my public adventures."[3]

To express their contempt for the deceitful communist bureaucracy, the Havels drove a Mercedes-Benz and enjoyed a country estate in addition to the Prague apartment. In 1969, Havel increased his opposition with a radio denouncement of the Soviets' illegal occupation of Czechoslovakia. That same year, he received the Austrian State Prize for European Literature, but Soviet censors, wearied of his gadfly role, banned his books from libraries and denied him access to Czech theater.

Havel, like Poland's Lech Walesa, began probing all aspects of state oppression. He toured steel plants in Ostrava and encouraged workers to join artists and writers in the fight for individual freedoms. Authorities signaled their disapproval by locking the meeting hall, but Havel spoke outside the building. He voiced his challenge unequivocally: "As long as I am invited to these meetings, I will go."[4]

Completely immersed in the struggle for personal freedom, in 1977 Havel was one of three leaders to activate Charter 77, a group of jazz musicians, writers, and church leaders. The group issued a manifesto denigrating the government for violations of civil rights and demanded human rights as outlined in the Helsinki Accord. Consequently, when the governing powers began trampling dissent and silencing protesters, they turned first to Havel, outlawed his plays, invaded his home, and dispatched him to a menial job in a brewery. For his human rights work, they incarcerated him for four months.

Subsequent harassment by communist hard-liners took many forms—intermittent jailings, perpetual wiretaps and surveillance, confiscation of his passport and personal papers, and persecution of his friends, colleagues, and even audiences who went to see his plays. Havel learned defensive strategies, including secreting his work and keeping on his person items like cigarettes, toothpaste, and razor blades for impromptu trips to jail. Although notable voices, including Saul Bellow, Tom Stoppard, Graham Greene, Joe Papp, Arthur Miller, and victims of America's McCarthy era came to his defense, Havel refused to be rescued. He rejected an offer to emigrate or to write for New York's Public Theater and continued to fight oppression in his homeland. As he phrased his outlook, "The solution to the situation does not lie in leaving.... Fourteen million people can't just go and leave Czechoslovakia."[5]

Within two years, Havel, while producing *Protest*, a one-act play about suppression, created the Committee for the Defense of the Unjustly Persecuted. This time, for thumbing his nose at an irate bureaucracy, he and five other members were arraigned for subversion of the republic. Havel was branded a traitor because he published banned writings out of the country. His sentence was four and a half years at hard labor. Authorities offered to release him if he recanted his position in a single-sentence letter, but he chose to wait them out and remain loyal to the cause of a free Czechoslovakia. This jail term, from 1979 to 1983, resulted in one minus—pneumonia with a resulting lung abscess—and one plus—hero status.

Havel's weapons were chiefly words. His poignant and reflective letters from prison were smuggled to the West and published as *Letters to Olga*. He avoided bitterness by picturing his captors as bumbling Laurel and Hardy types rather than sharp-eyed tormentors. He faced another prison sentence in 1989, but intellectuals worldwide demanded his release. By spring of that year, Havel had trounced his adversaries and become a national legend. His followers, wearing his likeness on buttons and waving his picture on posters and postage stamps, greeted him in the streets with cries of "Havel na Hrad!"—"Havel to the Castle!"[6]

## President Havel

On December 29, 1989, the parliament elected Havel Czechoslovakia's first president outside the Communist party in fifty years. He was allowed to keep the title until free elections could be organized six months later. To be elected president of a newly-emerging Czechoslovakia at the age of 53 was a sweet victory for a man who so pointedly despised his predecessors. Like the character in *Largo Desolato*, his prophetic play depicting the rise of a dissident to an influential position, Havel found himself clasping the reins of power. Whether he could maintain his control and still be as effective as he was in his earlier role remained to be seen.

In his opening appeal, Havel paved no yellow brick road for his constituents. He warned, "The state is not endangered from outside, as has happened many times in the past, but from within. We are putting it at risk by our own lack of political culture, of democratic awareness and of mutual understanding."[7] Like his Polish mirror image, Lech Walesa, President Havel, during early calls for decentralization and possible secession, had little choice but to ask that doubters take him on faith.

## Learning the Ropes

After his election, Havel continued to live much as before. He declined the official presidential suite in the castle. He and Olga, who have no children, shared the family apartment building with his brother Ivan's family. Rather than be chauffeured to work in a limousine, he drove his Renault. For meetings with counselors, most of whom had been his colleagues for years, he chose a nearby pub adjacent to St. Vitus Cathedral.

But Havel, while rejecting the trappings of power, accepted the challenge of leadership. With typical insouciance, he lessened protocol and lightened the grimness of state machinery. He even redecorated Hradcany Castle, where he met daily with dignitaries and ambassadors. Juggling so many needs and tastes at first was painful to a man who was frequently labeled a loner, yet Havel persevered, characterizing the constant entourage as "a peculiar drama, which no earthling could have written." In the shifting flow of days, he saw tragedy, absurd comedy, farce, and fairy tale. Looking back over the opening days, he concluded modestly, "I am only a second assistant to the director, or maybe one of the actors."[8]

## Alliances for Peace

At a conference in Bratislava, Slovakia, on April 9, 1990, President Havel summoned strength from neighboring nations, most of whom suffered similar oppression. In talking over mutual problems with ministers and heads of state from Poland, Hungary, Italy, Austria, and Yugoslavia, Havel inspired hope for common principles and economic agreements for reaffirming eastern Europe. Havel's visionary goal was to create a federation of lesser nations and coordinate their economic and political aims with the more privileged nations, particularly France, England, and Germany.

Without reservations, Havel expressed hope for the emerging nationalism that was creating unrest in eastern Europe. From his perspective, such a push for independence was inevitable. Nationalism and chauvinism, as he aptly phrased it, were "childhood diseases which every nation must endure before it reaches the age of reason."[9]

To questions of a resurgence of the old Austro-Hungarian Empire, Havel set minds at rest. In his words, "The principles for which we fought should become the basis of the policies of our countries. So these principles commit us to a kind of solidarity and cooperation."[10] To him, coordination was only a method of creating an Adriatic working group, not a power structure or even a buffer between Germany and the Soviet Union. Long an adversary of tyranny, Havel had no urge to create his own.

## Creating Good Feelings

A spiritual man at heart, President Havel spent some of his first days in office with religious leaders, including the Dalai Lama. He explained that humanity was facing serious threats—nuclear war, pollution, and mass starvation. To survive these menacing catastrophes, Havel declared a need for "an awakening on the part of human beings, an existential revolution, a victory of the spirit over materialism."[11] The answer to a need for spiritual growth, in his opinion, lay in participation in public life.

President Havel, not wholly comfortable as political leader of the emerging Czechoslovakian democracy, stated that he was, on the other hand, pleased to serve his country as a unifier. He acknowledged that the task was fraught was pitfalls, even the threat of assassination. But the job was worth the effort. To repeated questions about whether he could write a play about the new Havel, he expressed doubt that he could be both president and characterizer of the new era.

Unwilling to verbalize a guess at the future, Havel continued to move with the times. He viewed the breakdown of the communist state as inevitable. In the shift that brought well deserved freedom to Czechs, Havel found a niche that suited his unique talents. To the core, he expressed his Czech-ness and his oneness with the ordinary citizen. As he commented with uncommon flair and self-assurance, "Perhaps I am an actor in a play that isn't mine. But in this part, I decide the way I act. I have my role under my own control."[12]

## Notes

[1] Andrea Chambers and Toby Kahn. "Life Turns Upside Down for Vaclav Havel, Out of Jail and In As Czech President," *People Weekly*, January 22, 1990, 44.

[2] Chambers, 46.

[3] Richard Z. Chesnoff. "The Prisoner Who Took the Castle," *U.S. News and World Report*, February 26, 1990, 36.

[4] *Contemporary Authors*, Volume 104. Detroit: Gale Research, 201.

[5] Chambers, 44.

[6] Chesnoff, 37.

[7] James Walsh. "Populism on the March," *Time*, December 24, 1990, 44.

[8] Chesnoff, 37.

[9] Sonja Sinclair, interviewer. "Towards a New Europe," *Maclean's*, April 30, 1990, 26.

[10] Sinclair, 26.

[11] Sinclair, 31.

[12] Chesnoff, 37.

## Sources

Chambers, Andrea, and Toby Kahn. "Life Turns Upside Down for Vaclav Havel, Out of Jail and In As Czech President," *People Weekly*, January 22, 1990, 44-47.

Chesnoff, Richard Z. "The Prisoner Who Took the Castle," *U.S. News and World Report*, February 26, 1990, 33-37.

*Contemporary Authors*, Volume 104. Detroit: Gale Research.

Sinclair, Sonja, interviewer. "Towards a New Europe," *Maclean's*, April 30, 1990, 26-31.

Walsh, James. "Populism on the March," *Time*, December 24, 1990, 44.

# Cliff Hillegass

A foolproof idea can be the sure path to success. For Cliff Hillegass, buying college textbooks on the road and heading a wholesale book division were less than thrilling challenges. But instead of abandoning his connections with the world of students, he parlayed his skills into a unique line of classroom study guides.

Since the 1950s, Hillegass's distinctive yellow-and-black-striped logo has grown into a national phenomenon, particularly on high school, college, and university campuses. His company's product, partly because of its success and availability, has frequently sparked controversy among educators. Even though students and teachers may not recognize Mr. Hillegass by name, they all know his first name from his ubiquitous product—Cliffs Notes.

## Nebraska Beginnings

Clifton Keith Hillegass was born on April 18, 1918, sixty miles west of Omaha in Rising City, Nebraska, population 450. He was the older of two sons of Pearl Clinton Hillegass, a postal worker who believed in a sound education for his boys, and Rosena Christina Dechert Hillegass, a dedicated gardener who raised gladioli and sold them for funeral sprays. His family, natives of the small Nebraska town, were country folk at heart. They kept cows and pigs, raised a large vegetable garden, and canned food for home use. Hillegass's father covered his rural mail route by horse and buggy, cart, and sleigh. His mother influenced Cliff and brother, George, with her loyalty to the Lutheran church.

Hillegass was an eager student. He studied at home under his parents' tutelage and particularly liked to do spelling and mathematics on the family's home blackboard. While recuperating from a mastoid operation in 1925, he discovered his affinity for literary classics, which foreshadowed his success in the publishing business. He was often so wrapped up in books that his mother confiscated his three-cell flashlight to stop his reading under the covers.

Hillegass grew up in average surroundings, played sports, tootled on his clarinet, and hung out with his friends. He loved language and vocabulary and thrived under his high school Latin teacher, who encouraged his natural literary talent. For a time he served as librarian for Rising City's one-room library, where he read most of the books and all of the periodicals. His favorite authors were the popular writers, Jack Harkaway and G. A. Henty, as well as the English masters, Stevenson, Dickens, and Scott. He remarks with pride that his family had a sizeable shelf of reading material at home and usually found money for books, even during the 1930s.

Hillegass credits the conservative Midwest with inculcating in him the work ethic. To eke out a few dollars from the Depression-era economy, he tended two Jersey milk cows, sold milk products, held two paper routes, and, on his used bike, peddled *The Pictorial Review* door to door as far as the next town. To Hillegass's dismay, the local bank closed during the notorious "bank holidays," depriving him of his life savings of $714. Unfazed by his financial wipeout, he began again and soon matched the original sum.

## College and a Career

Paying his own tuition from these proceeds plus his earnings from dishwashing and stocking shelves full-time at Woolworth's dimestore, Hillegass attended Midland College, a Lutheran school of about 300 students in Fremont, Nebraska, from 1934 to 1937. He considered becoming a forester, but instead earned a B.S. in physics, geology, and meteorology. He continued scouting out good-paying jobs, even though times were hard and opportunities scarce. Later, he reflected that the education he gained from working as a maintenance man, houseboy, and camp counselor rivaled his classroom learning.

After two years of graduate work at the University of Nebraska, Hillegass met and married his first wife, Catherine, a secretary for an appraisal firm. To supplement her earnings, he took a $12-dollar-per-week job in the supply department of Long's College Bookstore, then traveled around buying college textbooks for Nebraska Book Company. At the age of twenty-four, he entered the Army Air Corps and served as a meteorological cadet. He returned to the book business after World War II and continued building his knowledge of used books by opening new territories for the company over the next ten years.

## Taking the Challenge

From his association with old friend Jack Cole, who published Coles Notes—a series of study aids—for the Book People—Canada's largest bookstore chain—Hillegass developed the idea of producing notes on individual literary titles, including novels, epics, short stories, philosophies, and plays. With Cole's blessing, Hillegass at first shared Coles Notes, then began working on his own product for distribution in the United States. One of his first colleagues in establishing a publishing firm was Lowell Boomer, manager of Boomer's Printing Company, which still prints Cliffs Notes.

Reflecting over his beginnings in the study aid business, Hillegass remarked, "At that stage, I knew probably 95 percent of the managers of college bookstores in the country by their first name."[1] Relying on his knowledge of the territory and depending on his wife's agreement and support, along with $4,000 from local bankers, in August 1958 he inaugurated his study guide business in the basement of his home at 511 Eastridge Street in Lincoln, Nebraska.

Hillegass introduced his product to friends operating bookstores via free copies of the Cliffs Notes on *Macbeth*. To lure customers, he guaranteed satisfaction and offered a toll-free order service. As a hedge, he kept his old job until he was sure of his venture. The first company to show enthusiasm was Chicago Circle Campus Bookstore, which became the first Cliffs Notes dealer. Gradually, other campus stores signed up for his racks of study guides, which lured young customers in at a steady pace.

Almost immediately, Hillegass knew he had a winner. Within six years, he was selling two million copies annually. From a small operation featuring Cliffs Notes on sixteen of Shakespeare's plays, the company expanded to cover the best in American, British, and world literature. Cliffs Notes grew to be one of Lincoln's prize homegrown businesses, with more than 90 million copies sold. The company outgrew successive quarters as Hillegass added more permanent staff and a larger sales force. The bottom line was impressive—more than $7 million per year for a handy supplemental product that Hillegass dubbed "a tutor at your elbow."[2]

## Answering a Need

From the outset, Hillegass hoped to fill an educational need. He intended to assist students in appreciating a wide range of literary classics. As he stated in his introductory letter, which appears inside the front cover of every Cliffs Notes, the notes are "intended as a supplementary aid to serious students, freeing them from interminable and distracting note-taking in class. Students may listen intelligently to what the instructor is saying, and to the class discussion, making selective notes, secure in the knowledge that they have a basic understanding of the work."[3]

The letter comments that the notes can help students prepare for tests by eliminating the need to reread a whole work and by ferreting out central themes and significance. To assure quality, Hillegass hires classroom experts to write each summary, which students turn to for analysis, review, and interpretation. The company pays its writers a small fee, ranging from $1,500 to $3,000 for each manuscript, but never lacks for applicants, some of whom have written multiple titles. One of the most famous of the 150 freelancers who have written for the company is John Gardner, noted medievalist and author of *Grendel*.

Each Cliffs Notes provides a complete overview of the information requisite to an understanding of not only the literary classic itself, but also its position in the author's literary canon as well as the whole of world literature. Each slim booklet contains a biography of the author, a short plot summary, and an annotated character list. The heart of the study guide is a detailed analysis of each chapter or act plus commentary, which is a synthesis of major critical theories. It ends with review questions and a bibliography.

To reflect changes in critical appraisal, each Cliffs Notes comes up for reevaluation and revision every ten years. More recent innovations include mention of movies, stage and television plays, operas, and other adaptations of the original work as well as chapter-by-chapter listings of difficult or foreign terms along with detailed explanations and translations. Also, the guides began featuring character genealogies in the late 1980s as a means of communicating character relationships to visual learners.

Sales of Cliffs Notes, which flagged during the 1970s when schools de-emphasized grades, burgeoned in the 1980s and continue to look promising for the 1990s. The majority of Hillegass's fans are the high school and college students who buy his products. Users write in comments and complaints. For each one who asks a question or finds an error, even a misplaced comma, a free booklet goes out promptly in the mail. Some of the strongest praise comes from teachers and other educators who visit the company's booth at national educational conventions. The brightest smiles at first sight of the familiar yellow and black stripes come from the generation of teachers who grew up on the notes. They more than others recognize the uniqueness and value of Cliffs Notes from firsthand experience.

Classroom teachers have reported that Cliffs Notes are a major aid to the better students. In their experience, students motivated to seek the best grades are more likely to consult a study guide. Teachers also comment on the suitability of the notes for reluctant readers, English-as-a-second-language classes, disabled readers, and students reading above their level of comprehension. Most of the credit for their praise belongs to Hillegass, who, from the first, aimed to publish guides that answered student needs rather than flaunting high-flown language or patronizing the reader with oversimplification.

## Covering the Market

A book lover himself, Hillegass took special interest in Shakespeare's plays. He produced individual overviews of each play, along with commentaries on the sonnets and long poems. Over a period of nearly thirty years in the study guide business, his company published more than 300 titles, with only outstanding classroom-approved works such as *The Color Purple* rating new notes among the lineup of accepted classics. The ten all-time bestsellers—the notes on *The Scarlet Letter, Macbeth, Hamlet, Huckleberry Finn, The Odyssey, Canterbury Tales, The Great Gatsby, A Tale of Two Cities, To Kill a Mockingbird,* and *The Grapes of Wrath*—remain at the top, indicating that students have not flagged in the reading and study of quality literature.

Hillegass met with competition from thirteen competitors. Early on, Monarch Notes cranked out a poor imitation of Cliffs Notes, but these fell by the wayside. In more recent times, Barron's also began publishing a line of study guides, as have textbook publishers, particularly Prentice-Hall. But these me-too efforts fail to dampen demand for the little yellow and black guides found in bookstores, department chains, and drugstores across America and in forty foreign lands.

In the 1980s, Hillegass began branching out into other areas of student needs. He first evolved a series of test preparation guides for the Scholastic Aptitude Test, Graduate Record Exam, Graduate Management Admissions Test, National Teacher's Exam, and the five areas covered by the high school equivalency exam. The test prep series proved so successful that he expanded the line with test-taking strategies, reviews, question analyses, and practice tests for a total of twenty exams, including the police sergeant examination. In addition, his firm publishes several humorous titles, cookbooks, overviews of mythology and ancient literature, complete study editions of works by Shakespeare and Chaucer, and Cliffs Teaching Portfolios, an educational product designed to assist teachers in preparation of classroom lesson plans. In 1990, an outside firm began binding 227 of the notes into a twenty-four-volume set arranged by title and a thirteen-volume set organized by author for sale to libraries.

To undergird his determination to provide the best in literary analysis for student use, Hillegass maintains a sales staff of twenty-six plus an in-house editing team composed of Gary Carey, Cliffs Notes editor, Dr. James L. Roberts, a Faulkner specialist, and Michele Spence, editor of the company's other study aids. After Hillegass accepted semi-retirement and undertook the position of CEO, he left President Richard Spellman in charge. With some well-deserved time on their hands, Hillegass and wife Mary travel, dropping in at the office several times per week when they are in town to oversee the family-owned business, root for the University of Nebraska's Cornhuskers, and hang some of the art pieces they collect on their journeys.

## A Professional Outlook

In his seventies, Cliff Hillegass maintains the charm and vivacity that earned him his place in the American publishing market. A tall, tanned man with wide smile and engaging courtesy, he disarms visitors to his new offices and 32,400-square-foot warehouse at 4851 S. 16th Street with his ebullient manner. Immaculately dressed down to string tie, he represents the spirit of Cliffs Notes.

Hillegass is proud of the fact that his firm ships 75,000 books per day to 7,000 retail stores—usually on the day the order comes in. He refuses to consider relocating his business to a more cosmopolitan area or selling his lucrative business, even for the hefty sums he has been offered. He refutes claims that students resort to the notes to avoid thinking on their own. With fervor he declares, "Frankly, I think Cliffs Notes have kept a lot of students interested in literature by making it understandable."[4]

Hillegass often remarks that he is committed to encouraging creative teaching methods to enliven literary masterpieces. To this end in 1989 he published

*Cliffs Notes in the Classroom*, a small monograph which he distributes free to educators. He claims that he can chart the ebb and flow of educational philosophy by consulting sales charts. When educators back strong, classroom-centered learning, sales are high. In contrast, during the 1970s, when students were interested in demonstrating against the Vietnam War and in searching for relevance, fewer people bought Cliffs Notes.

## Enjoying the Rewards

Cliff Hillegass finds contentment in his achievements. He is father of a son, James, and three daughters, Linda, Diane, and Kimberly. He has earned his share of notoriety and is often the subject of whimsical newspaper and magazine articles. He holds honorary degrees from Nebraska and Wesleyan universities and Kearney State College and is a board member of Bryan Memorial Hospital and Nebraska Wesleyan University. In 1967 he served on the Nebraska Centennial Commission and has received the Alumni Achievement award from Midland Lutheran College, a distinguished service award from Kearney State College, the Pathfinder award from the Fremont Area Art Association, and a Sower award from the Lincoln Foundation.

Looking over his firm's steady growth in the study aid market, Hillegass commented in a speech to the Newcomen Society: "The Notes were our single product, and we were committed to selling no less than the best study guides we could. Our product could be summed up in one word then, and that single word is still valid today: quality."[5] He added that Cliffs Notes, despite the increase in competition, remains at the top because he keeps as his primary concern the needs of the student.

## Notes

[1] Seth Kupferberg. "Keeping It Simple," *Parade Magazine*, October 20, 1985, 18.

[2] Sally S. Stich. "It's OK to Use Cliffs Notes Now," *Los Angeles Times*, n.d., B6.

[3] Mary Ellen Snodgrass. *Jane Eyre Notes*. Lincoln, Nebraska: 1988, inside front cover.

[4] Karen S. Peterson. "Paragraphs That Speak Volumes," *U.S.A. Today*, n.d., 2D.

[5] Cliff Hillegass. "Speech to the Newcomen Society," n.d., 22.

## Sources

Atkins, Norman. "Fast Food for Thought," *Rolling Stone*, March 26, 1987, 111-162.

Creager, Ellen. "Abridged Too Far?," *Detroit Free Press*, December 11, 1990, D1.

Epstein, Warren. "Summarizing for 30 Years," *The Tampa Tribune*, Tampa, Florida, 1F.

Hillegass, Cliff. "Speech to the Newcomen Society," n.d., 9-28.

Kupferberg, Seth. "Keeping It Simple," *Parade Magazine*, October 20, 1985, 18, 21.

Peterson, Karen S. "Paragraphs That Speak Volumes," *U.S.A. Today*, n.d., 1-2D.

Snodgrass, Mary Ellen. *Jane Eyre Notes.* Lincoln, Nebraska: 1988, inside front cover.

Stich, Sally S. "It's OK to Use Cliffs Notes Now," *Los Angeles Times*, n.d., B6.

Swartzlander, David. "Cliffs Notes Firm Hanging in There as No. 1 U.S. Study-Aids Publisher," *Lincoln Journal*, Lincoln, Nebraska, October 2, 1989, 10.

# Irene Hunt

People sometimes develop myriad skills through a series of lesser responsibilities, then grow into their late-in-life successes. Irene Hunt, career teacher of French, history, and English, is an example of an achiever evolving a new expression of her love for children and education. After thirty years in Illinois's public schools, she worked an additional five years in administration before retiring.

During her last years as a consultant, Irene Hunt began writing historical fiction. For many years, fearful that writing would prove too difficult, she had avoided her ambition. Then, after much classroom experience with adolescent fears and frustrations, she found that writing about young people had become easier. She published the first of eight young adult novels, some of which have been translated into German, Italian, Norwegian, Danish, and French. The outpouring of awards, critical applause, and letters from student readers proves that she mastered her second career.

## Answering a Need

The impetus for Hunt's first historical fiction was the universal complaint of her students that American history is dull. Early on, she tried to enliven history, to make it as exciting as drama. Her meticulous, creative response to student needs led to national acclaim as a writer of quality young adult literature.

*Across Five Aprils* (1964), the sole runner-up for the coveted Newbery medal in 1965, brought Irene Hunt the Charles W. Follett Award as well as an American Notable Book Award, Friends of Literature Award, the Lewis Carroll Shelf Award, the Dorothy Canfield Fisher Award, and the Clara Ingram Judson Memorial Award. Based on that initial success, critics have called her one of America's finest historical novelists. The book proved so graphic, so appealing that it was filmed. Two years later, Hunt won the Newbery Medal for *Up the Road Slowly*.

# Rural Roots

A midwesterner from the rural area around Newton in southern Illinois, Irene Hunt appreciated the forces that shaped America's heartland. She was born on May 18, 1907, one of two daughters of farmer Franklin Pierce and Sarah Land Hunt. She identified with the bucolic setting of the family ranch, which dated to earlier generations.

In an article for *Today's Education*, Hunt recalled the happiness she shared with her father as they walked down a country road. On the way, she told him the story of Goldilocks and the three bears. He listened attentively and remained silent at the end of the story. She accepted his silence and assumed that he had adult matters to consider. But he surprised her with a great compliment—he asked a question about the story. She recalled: "When I had answered, he told me a sequel to the story. But my real delight was in knowing that a beloved adult had listened, had been interested in what I had to say."[1]

Franklin Hunt died when Irene was seven. Confused and terrified when a playmate asked if she were not going to live in her old house anymore, Irene hid in a closet. In adulthood, she used the incident as the introductory scene in *Up the Road Slowly*, the story of Aggie Kilpin, who goes to live with a spinster aunt after the death of her mother.

Hunt and her sister Beulah lived for several years with her grandparents. During her years on their farm, she absorbed her grandfather's songs and impromptu fiddle playing. He also acted out scenes from Bible stories, right up to David's slingshot. In the company of such a showman, Irene, who tended to be shy, recited poetry and acted out dramatic scenes from Shakespeare's plays.

# Classroom Years

Hunt began her professional life with a well-rounded course of studies. She completed her bachelor's degree in 1939 at the University of Illinois. Seven years later she earned a master's degree in language education at the University of Minnesota. For several years she did advanced graduate research in psychology.

A career teacher in Oak Park, Illinois, from 1930 to 1945, Hunt taught French and English in public elementary schools. She served as instructor in psychology for the next four years at the University of South Dakota. She then accepted a post as history teacher at a junior high school in Cicero, Illinois, before beginning her career as a fiction writer at the age of fifty-seven. During the early stages of her second career, she also worked as a consultant in language arts in Cicero.

Upon retirement from public education, Irene Hunt made North Riverside, Illinois, her home base, from which she traveled widely. Later, she moved to St. Petersburg, Florida. Irene, whose brown hair is tinged with gray, remains slim, well-groomed, and attractive with gentle eyes that crinkle at the corners. When not immersed in research for a book, she fills her idle hours with "beautiful, well-written books and beautiful very loud music."[2] With similar flair, she enjoys refinishing old furniture.

## A Dedicated Professional

Her fellow workers at the Cicero Administration Building remember her as a helpful, energetic, and organized professional who kept her private life to herself. She demonstrated her enthusiasm for great literature and championed the understanding that readers gain from exposing themselves to the best authors. In her words, "books bring new dimensions of happiness, of confidence and enlightenment, to young people from the age of three on up."[3] From her knowledge of psychology, she evolved a philosophy that books rather than sermons are the best solace to troubled youngsters.

A nephew, Wendell Bruce Beem, wrote an article for *Horn Book* magazine about story sessions with Irene, in which she introduced him to Winnie the Pooh and Christopher Robin, among other delights. A devoted child-pleaser, she prepared her culinary specialties, sauces and condiments for him. She also shared with him a love of libraries, travel, and fine music, but sometimes feigned a delight in televised baseball and football, which did not please her.

Beem described Hunt's kitchen table as stacked with reference books, paper, typewriter, and pencils. With intensity and hard work, she crafted character and dialogue and intertwined historical event with plot. He recounted how she carefully typed manuscripts and readied them for initial rejection. Even though she realized that they might not be accepted the first time out, she was disappointed when the manuscripts were turned down.

## A Major Success

As an adult, Hunt reminisced with love as well as appreciation about her grandfather, a spellbinding teller of tales. He introduced her young mind to the Civil War era, particularly the firing on Fort Sumter and the Battle of Bull Run, which occurred when he was nine. She revered him in particular for sharing the story honestly and used her grandfather's stories as the background of *Across Five Aprils*.

To honor her grandfather, Hunt set her Civil War novel on the family farm and dedicated it to her grandfather's great-grandchildren. Even though the story of the Creighton family was fiction, she diligently researched the era and setting in family letters and other documents. To support fiction with realistic detail, she drew on "the anxiety and sorrows of the times as well as the moments of happiness in a closely knit family."[4]

## Idealism in Action

Ever the idealist, Irene Hunt clings to a strong belief in traditional values. In an article for *Writer* magazine, she concluded that children derive courage, humility, compassion, honor, and decency, not from patronizing lectures, but from their exposure to good reading. Continuing her literary contributions into her eighties, she retired to St. Petersburg, Florida, to write true-to-life fictional narratives that continued to find favor with critics, educators, and young readers. Her later works are familiar titles on school and library reading lists and include *Trail of Apple Blossoms* (1968), *No Promises in the Wind* (1970), *The Lottery Rose* (1976), *William* (1978), and *Claws of a Young Century* (1980).

Critics applauded Irene Hunt's historical fiction with positive reviews. The American Library Association Booklist praised her use of family records and stories, which the writer crafted into well-delineated narrative. In evaluating *Across Five Aprils*, the University of Chicago Center for Children's Books got to the heart of her achievement: "The realistic treatment of the intricate emotional conflicts within a border-state family is superb. The details of battles and campaigns are deftly integrated into letters and conversations, and the characters are completely convincing."[5]

## Skilled Narratives

In that story, Hunt emphasizes the sufferings of multiple layers of society, from soldier to farmer to townspeople, who live during the Civil War era. In one gripping scene, thick with the dialect of the poorly educated Creightons, a farm family, she describes a return home through the eyes of the young and impressionable central character, Jethro Creighton.

Eb, Jethro's brother, has made his way home following grim days as a soldier during the Civil War. Fearful at first to approach the younger boy, Eb, his hair matted and his clothes tattered, watches his brother from a distance:

" 'I couldn't git over it—how you've growed.'

"Then Jethro realized who it was. 'Eb,' he exclaimed in a voice hardly above a whisper. 'It's Eb, ain't it?'

"There was utter despair in the soldier's voice.

" 'Yes,' he said, 'I reckon it's Eb—what there's left of him.' "[6]

## A Sense of Purpose

Of writing in general, Hunt explained that the end product is a natural expression. She declared: "I didn't plan my first book for a certain age group. I don't want to aim at a special age of reader. I write when I have something to say, and I hope to say it as well and as gracefully as I can."[7] The method worked in her autobiography, *Up the Road Slowly*, which gained recognition for its poignant narration of a young girl's struggle against despair. The American Booksellers' Association presented the White House home library with a copy of the novel in 1970.

To foster the growth of good young adult fiction, Hunt advised that the writer must first get in touch with his or her own childhood and remember the anxieties, uncertainties, and loneliness, as well as dreams, perplexities, and joy over youthful trivialities. The sensitive writer, she insisted, must also respond to remembered tastes, smells, and colors, and to "his love of a kind hand, his fear of a harsh mouth. He must remember the imaginary companions, the wonderful secret places where he could be alone, the hoarding of nondescript material in an old box—guarding it, rearranging it, caring greatly for it without quite knowing why."[8]

In an article for *Writer* magazine in March 1970, Irene Hunt proposed that each aspiring writer answer the three questions that Goethe asked of writers:

"Do I have something to say?

"Is what I have to say worth saying?

"How best can I go about saying this thing which I consider to be worth the saying?"[9]

## Technical Skill

A believer in clarity, Irene Hunt champions a pictorial quality in literature in order to provide readers "a deeper understanding of some aspect of human behavior, of human needs, a more profound knowledge of the human heart."[10] Likewise, she believes that characters must be honestly drawn reflecting "real people who make mistakes, suffer from character flaws, and experience the gains and losses of normal human life."[11] Examples of the application of this theory abound in her works, notably in *No Promises in the Wind*, a remarkably realistic view of two young first-generation Polish-American boys growing up in Chicago during the Depression era and struggling to combat forces that stymie adults and even government leaders.

As fifteen-year-old Josh Grondowski tries to comprehend his father's growing hatred, the boy forces his gentle, sensitive mother into an either-or situation: "She looked at me steadily as I glared down at her. 'When a woman sides with her children against her husband, a marriage and a family are all in ruins, Josh. Your father is crazed with fear and terror. I'll stand by him no matter what his son says about him.' "[12] Saddened by this man-sized burden, Josh realizes that home is no place for him.

Shouldering not only his own destiny, but that of his ten-year-old brother Joey as well, Josh migrates south from Chicago through the midwest all the way to Baton Rouge, Louisiana, where he and Joey find work with Pete Harris's carnival. Five months later, giving in to circumstances that overwhelm his meager experience and wisdom, Josh returns by train to Chicago. Unsure of his reception, he strains to catch a glimpse of his family through the train window and hurries to meet his mother and sister and the father who drove him away:

"He gave a start of surprise, and then his face lighted up in recognition. With his left arm he drew Joey to him; with his right hand he clasped my hand firmly.

" 'Hello, Son,' he said. 'I'm so glad—so glad—' "[13]

## Looking Backward

Such poignant scenes are not uncommon in the prose of Irene Hunt, who maintains that any writer of children's literature must remain true not only to the delights and satisfactions of childhood, but also the pain, anger, and anxiety. She has challenged writers to recall the search for truth and beauty that characterize the teen years. She described this period as "the years which, I often think, may be described by the words which Dickens used to describe the closing years of the eighteenth century—'It was the best of times and the worst of times; it was an age of foolishness, an age of wisdom.' "[14] Apparently, her respect for the dignity and tastes of young readers bore fruit, for she has received more than 100 letters from children who identified with *Across Five Aprils*.

## A Writer of Quality

A proponent of originality, Hunt encourages aspiring writers to reach into their own wealth of talent for a blend of color and contrast as well as vigor and poetic touches. She adds that style reflects "the writer's self—his perceptions of life, his grace or lack of grace, his courage or his whining self-pity, his humility and compassion or his cynicism and arrogance."[15]

A champion of quality books for young readers, Hunt expects excellence in all areas of education. Excellence, she stresses, reflects a strong sense of values, particularly insight, compassion, and an appreciation of human behavior. In one article she advocated reading as one of life's most lasting pleasures. She believes that youngsters who listen to stories often have the urge to read the words for themselves. But if children encounter boring, repetitive reading material, they lose interest. She concludes, "In a world where the pressures of living absorb the lives of many adults, wise parents and teachers help their children find books of beauty and substance, communicate with them, and respect the opinions and individuality of the very young."[16]

## Notes

[1] Irene Hunt. "Try to Remember...," *Today's Education*, February 1973, 44.

[2] Doris DeMontreville and Donna Hill, eds. *Third Book of Junior Authors*. New York: Wilson Books, 1972, 140.

[3] DeMontreville, 139.

[4] DeMontreville, 140.

[5] Irene Hunt. *Across Five Aprils.* New York: Tempo Books, 1965, 1.

[6] *Across*, 134-135.

[7] *Contemporary Authors: New Revision Series*, Volume 8. Detroit: Gale Research, 1983, 259.

[8] *Something About the Author.* Detroit: Gale Research, 1972, 147.

[9] Irene Hunt. "Writing for Children," *The Writer*, March 1970, 17.

[10] *Writer*, 17.

[11] *Writer*, 17.

[12] Irene Hunt. *No Promises in the Wind.* New York: Tempo Books, 1970, 28-29.

[13] *No Promises*, 222-223.

[14] *Writer*, 18.

[15] *Writer*, 20.

[16] *Today's Education*, 44.

## Sources

Beem, Wendell Bruce. "Aunt Irene," *Horn Book*, June 1970, 429-433.

Chevalier, Tracy. *Third Book of Junior Authors.* Chicago: St. James Press, 1972, 139-140.

*Contemporary Authors: New Revision Series*, Volume 8. Detroit: Gale Research, 1983.

DeMontreville, Doris, and Donna Hill, eds. *Third Book of Junior Authors.* New York: Wilson Books, 1972.

Hunt, Irene. *Across Five Aprils.* New York: Tempo Books, 1965.

_____. *No Promises in the Wind.* New York: Tempo Books, 1970.

_____. "Try to Remember...," *Today's Education*, February 1973, 43-44.

_____. "Writing for Children," *The Writer*, March 1970, 17-20.

*Something About the Author.* Volume 2. Detroit: Gale Research, 1972.

# Ray Kroc

Late-in-life winners occasionally become household names, like Colonel Sanders and Grandma Moses. Others, like Raymond Kroc, may remain unfamiliar forever, but their products speak for them around the world. Ray Kroc, whose golden arches grace many superhighways, explained his achievement in one succinct statement: "We take the hamburger business more seriously than [our competitors] do."[1] That seriousness made him a billionaire.

Kroc removed the element of chance from franchising by controlling the variables in the hamburger business—from the width of the burger to the composition of bun, pickle, mustard, and catsup. He aimed foolproof instructions at teenage employees, the peers of his main customers. By maintaining strict standards, from the kitchen to the outer rim of the parking lot, he boosted sales to an impressive height, edging out older, more experienced chains. Classed with Andrew Carnegie, Henry Ford, and John D. Rockefeller, Ray Kroc maneuvered himself into very privileged and highly respected company. One Harvard Business School spokesman described Kroc as "the service sector's equivalent of Henry Ford."[2]

Combining quality ingredients and limited menu with speedy service, affordable price, and cleanliness, McDonald's, Ray Kroc's brainchild, has become a byword not only for investment success, but for the American teen years in general. In fact, when Moscow's markets opened to free trade, the establishment of a McDonald's marked the entry of American enterprise into the bastion of communism. Represented by Ronald McDonald in his two-toned clown suit, the McDonald hamburger chain, which sold its 75 billionth hamburger in 1990, epitomizes the soul of American free enterprise with a bit of whimsy for good measure.

## Getting Off to a Late Start

Born in 1902 in Oak Park, Illinois, a middle-class suburb of Chicago, to "frugal, Middle-class Bohemian stock,"[3] Raymond Albert Kroc managed to reach fifty-two without distinguishing himself, even though, when he was only four, a phrenologist predicted that he would thrive in the restaurant business. By six,

Kroc, under the tutelage of his mother, was studying classical piano. Early on he encountered greatness, attending Oak Park Elementary School with Ernest Hemingway.

Kroc was the son of a high school dropout who worked for Western Union and died of a cerebral hemorrhage during the Depression. His son deduced that the elder Kroc simply worried himself to death. He recalled: "On his desk the day he died were two pieces of paper—his last paycheck from the telegraph company and a garnishment notice for the entire amount of his wages."[4] From boyhood, Kroc vowed to do better than his father, escape the poverty cycle, and make his mark on the business world.

When World War I began, Kroc dropped out of school, lied about his age, and signed up to drive an ambulance for the Red Cross. A second brush with greatness was his friendship with army buddy Walt Disney, himself only sixteen years old. Because the war came to an end before Kroc could set any wheels in motion, he briefly returned to high school, then quit, claiming that algebra was too much for him.

Many stopgap careers lured along the way, from notions salesman to board marker for a brokerage house to playing piano in jazz bands in questionable locations and on radio. While directing a Chicago radio station, WGES, he discovered the team of Amos 'n' Andy. But music, his chosen field, proved too demanding for Kroc. He quit radio at twenty to marry and find a job with more normal working hours.

During the real estate boom of the 1920s, Kroc sold swampland near Fort Lauderdale, Florida, hit bottom when the company went broke, then returned home by Model T, sending his wife and daughter ahead by train. Back in Chicago, he sold Lily-Tulip paper products to Polish pushcart vendors who peddled sweetened, colored ices at two cents per ounce. In this last job, he rose to midwest sales manager. In 1937, enamored of Multimixer milk shake machines that could whip up five concoctions at once, he formed his own company to sell mixers to restaurants and roadside stands.

## Bad into Good

The start of 1954 found Kroc not very high on the ladder to success. The market for Multimixers was collapsing, because of the streamlining of modern drugstores and the accompanying demise of soda fountains. Ill with arthritis, diabetes, and problems with both gall bladder and thyroid, he planned to replace Multimixers as his chief source of income. He observed the drive-in style of the McDonald brothers, who bought his mixers for an efficient hamburger operation sixty miles east of Los Angeles in San Bernardino, California. Kroc linked up with their operation as business representative for future franchises. At this point, his goals were limited. As he phrased it, "If I can get the guys who run this place to open a couple more just like it, they might buy 16 more Multimixers from me."[5]

Part of the success of Dick and Maurice "Mac" McDonald was their systematic waste control, which helped hold the price of hamburgers to fifteen cents. By masterminding purchasing and storage and holding the menu to hamburgers, french fries, and milk shakes, the brothers made the most of their capital outlay. By keeping the premises clean, hiring no waitresses, and serving a prompt, simple meal at a reasonable price, they outdistanced other hamburger stands, which were beginning to crop up throughout the country.

From the beginning, Kroc's associates had little ambition or vision. They had attempted franchising on their own and discovered that branch versions of their hamburger stands seldom came up to the quality and success of the parent company. In April 1954, Kroc countered with his proposal of a better way: hiring a single trustworthy agent to oversee new franchises. Even without experience in the hamburger business, Kroc was ready to put himself on the line for the contract.

## A Package Deal

The first McDonald's franchisees got a package deal. For $950 inclusive, the licensed dealer would mimic every aspect of the owners' crowd-pleasing operation, right down to the McDonald's recipe for french fries. The agent collected 1.9 percent of the profits and passed along .5 percent to the owners. In Ray Kroc's concept of the operation, he would receive $1,400 of every $100,000; the McDonald's would get $500. But more to the point, Kroc would have an easy in to sell his mixers. Expecting his old line of goods to carry him through, he made no arrangements for a salary for several years.

From the outset, Kroc stuck with the name McDonald because of its genuine, folksy, all-American ring—just like old McDonald's farm. To maintain quality, he built into each agreement a promise of no deviations in management approach without both brothers' consent in writing by registered mail. To test his theories, he opened a Chicago branch on Lee Street in Des Plaines, Illinois, a few minutes from his house.

Rising each morning at 5:30, Kroc drove to his new business, got the day started at his restaurant, and left to sell mixers. At the end of his regular working day, he took the commuter train to the Loop and finished the day's business at his hamburger stand before returning home. The idea was neat and efficient, like most aspects of the McDonald's success story. Besides, it gave him an added perk—free parking for his car while he was out of town.

## The Fly in the Ointment

The setup lacked one key ingredient. To open his own franchise, Ray Kroc needed capital. He went into equal partnership with builder Art Jacobs, who spotted some weaknesses in the original plan. To counter differences in geography, Jacobs got telephone permission from Dick and Maurice McDonald to alter the original building so that Kroc could add a furnace and ventilation system, a necessary adjunct in the extremes of Illinois weather. The error he made was obvious: Kroc failed to obtain written permission via registered letter.

The Des Plaines McDonald's drive-in opened in April 15, 1955. From the beginning, it was a hit, but problems mounted. Kroc could not get his french fries to come out as golden and crispy as the prototypes. Conferences with the home office did not help; discussions with the Potato and Onion Association were also failures. Eventually, a foods expert discovered the internal flaw. Kroc's french fries were mushy and tasteless because he stored the potatoes in a dark basement, which altered natural sugars into starch. The McDonald brothers, on the other hand, used wire containers in a roofless shed open to the desert air. Kroc's solution was a system of electric fans to mimic the arid climate of San Bernardino.

A thornier problem supplanted Kroc's tangle with limp french fries. He discovered that the McDonald brothers had previously sold their rights in the Cook County-Chicago area for $5,000, failing to inform their new agent of the deal. This lack of communication forced Kroc to round up $25,000 to buy out the current owner's franchise. He met the price and opened three more franchises in Fresno and Reseda, California.

It was not until May of 1956 that Kroc ventured out of California again with eight more hamburger stands. The following year he went nationwide with two dozen franchises. To honor one of the founders, he inaugurated the Big Mac double burger, one of his most successful items. A major feat was that he kept the price of McDonald's original burgers at fifteen cents until 1967. With the establishment of national recognition through billboards, television advertising, and customer satisfaction, McDonald's was soon a catchword among the young as well as their parents, who approved the high standards, cleanliness, and safety of Kroc's restaurants.

## The Success Spiral

Buoyed by customer approval, Kroc began his spiral of expansion. By the end of the 1950s, he had opened 164 McDonald's. His examples brought eager investors from all quarters, including foreign countries. With a sure future ahead, he cut ties with Multimixer and developed a broader view of the hamburger market, for which he was the acknowledged expert and spokesperson.

Kroc worked out minute details, such as how high to stack hamburger patties to avoid crushing and in what size box to store them. To assure enough Idaho Russet Burbank potatoes, he bought out the entire year's output. To guarantee the right type of land for future hamburger stands, Kroc wrote up a description of the hypothetical "perfect lot" and began searching out likely matches, investing $170 million in sites. He assessed the demographics of each spot by flying over the neighborhood to note the number of schools, churches, and intersections.

Another important feature of McDonald's restaurants was its personnel, whom he hired for minimum wage. Kroc insisted on short, neat hair and no beards, mustaches, or goatees. People with decayed teeth, pimples, or tattoos were not be located at the take-out window. At first he hired only male clerks because he believed that single female employees encouraged the wrong kind of flirtatious males at hamburger stands. He eventually gave in to equal opportunity when Congress passed employment laws forbidding sex discrimination.

Another major factor in McDonald's meteoric rise was the growth of highways. Speedy service, low cost, and a simple menu, coupled with America's urge to travel fast and light, produced the legendary fast-food craze, quickly replicated by Wendy's, Jack in the Box, Burger King, and myriad other imitators. Kroc's restaurants, easily spotted by their golden arches, earned their keep because they produced no surprises. Satisfied customers could go on being satisfied, whether on Boston Common, the Continental Divide, or the outskirts of the Golden Gate Bridge.

Franchisees, who waited in line to buy into Kroc's bonanza, had to take a nineteen-day training course at the company center in Elk Grove, Illinois. Graduation came complete with a manual covering everything from how to make each fry as golden and crispy as the last to how to deal with the public. The guidebook gave practical suggestions, such as how operators could save by buying local supplies where possible. In exchange for advice and logo, franchisees paid 3 percent to the company and 8.5 percent in rent.

Early on, Kroc's obsession with plowing profits back into growth kept his cash flow at a dangerous limit. Because Kroc had made little provision for payback, he and his franchisees were realizing less return than the McDonald brothers, who did nothing to earn their cut of the profits. Upon learning that the brothers planned to retire, Kroc put himself in fiscal jeopardy by borrowing $2.7 million to buy out the brothers' share. Then he built his investment into a $500 million corporation. While making himself a billionaire, he hoisted others to the millionaire status along the way.

In 1963, Kroc elected to offer stock to the public. It opened at $22, rose to $30 by the end of the day, and quickly closed at $50. For the first time, Kroc had the cash to move confidently in the marketplace. As an added fillip, he built a competing McDonald's across from the original San Bernardino location and forced it into bankruptcy. By 1972, his restaurants boasted sales of 10 billion burgers, a fact which Kroc blazoned on every marquee.

# King of Fast Food

Kroc's McDonald's hamburger stands boosted fast food to national stardom. Although purists disagree as to whether Kroc launched the wave or merely climbed on at an opportune point in its formation, financiers hold him in high esteem for his acumen and chutzpah. He rocketed from lackluster route man to one of America's five richest people. His phenomenal growth from a single California location to 7,400 restaurants from Europe to Japan to Australia to Canada is an American fairy tale with a happy ending.

Kroc bought a 210-acre ranch in California, a grand French residence in Fort Lauderdale, Florida, and a mega-condo in the toney Lake Shore district of Chicago. His other playtoys included a 90-foot yacht, a swank Rolls Royce, and a doorbell that chimed "You deserve a break today."[6] He wanted to add the Chicago Cubs to his toy box, but failed to get the bid, so in 1974 he opted for the San Diego Padres, for which he paid $11 million. Lesser marks of his pride included daily display of his trademark golden arches on breast pocket, luggage, cuff links, tie bars, and rings.

Kroc's business reflected his philosophy of life. A comfortable host to a less-than-sophisticated crowd, he entertained guests by playing the piano. Yet Kroc, adamant that his restaurants not become hangouts, nixed music for McDonald's, along with cigarette machines and telephone booths. Rated by some as a super-patriot, he supported conservative politics and adorned his restaurants with large American flags. He supported local hospitals by founding Ronald McDonald houses to give weary, fearful parents a place to stay while their sick children received medical care.

At home at last among the moneyed class, Kroc endeared himself to Americans by giving heavily to charity through the Kroc Foundation, a custom continued by his widow, Joan Beverly Kroc, whom he married in 1969. His giving to schools was always tagged for vocational purposes. To critics who accused him of being anti-intellectual, he replied, "That's not quite right. I'm anti-phony-intellectual.... My philosophy about what education should be is best expressed right in McDonald's own Hamburger U. and Hamburger High."[7]

## Notes

[1] *Fortune*, April 4, 1983, p. 147.

[2] *Fortune*, 147.

[3] Tom Robbins, "Ray Kroc Did It All for You," *Esquire*, December 1983, p. 344.

[4] William Barry Furlong. "Ray Kroc: Burger Master," *Saturday Evening Post*, March 1981, p. 64.

[5] Furlong, 64.

[6] Robbins, 344.

[7] Robbins, 344.

# Sources

*Current Biography.* New York: H. W. Wilson, 1973.

Furlong, William Barry. "Ray Kroc: Burger Master," *Saturday Evening Post,* March 1981, 64, 69, 114-120.

*Fortune,* April 4, 1983, 147.

*Fortune,* October 22, 1990, 167, 284.

*Nation's Business,* July 1968, 71.

*New York Times Magazine,* July 4, 1971, 5.

Robbins, Tom. "Ray Kroc Did It All for You," *Esquire,* December 1983, 340-344.

*Who's Who in America,* Glenview, Ill.: Marquis' Who's Who, 1972-1973.

# Madeleine Kunin

In contrast to some people more obviously destined for success, some late achievers are longshots. The goals they set for themselves seem so out of step with their past lives and with society that attainment is doubtful. For Madeleine Kunin, the likelihood seemed slim that a female Swiss refugee who spoke no English and who escaped Hitler's SS could find safety in America and even become governor of Vermont—three times. Fortunately for Madeleine Kunin, longshots are her métier.

Bright, affable, intellectual, and engaging, Madeleine Kunin, the former governor of Vermont, maintains rapport with her state, which she loves for its natural beauty and friendly people. She performed admirable service by giving back to America some of the riches she enjoyed. Unable to sit in the stands while crucial issues such as acid rain, homelessness, bloated military budgets, diminished opportunities for the handicapped, the demise of small farms, and mediocrity in school systems plagued the nation, she made a difference, particularly in areas that affect the family.

By entering the political mainstream, Madeleine Kunin accepted each of America's struggles as personal challenges. In a reflective moment, she observed, "When your life is influenced by war, once you have the knowledge that political decisions can be a matter of life and death, then you don't want to accept those decisions passively. You want to have control and influence over them."[1]

## The Widow's Daughter

From early childhood, Madeleine Kunin was no stranger to challenge or loss. Born on September 28, 1933, in Zurich, Switzerland, she was the second child and first daughter of Renée Block May, a Swiss national, and Ferdinand May, a German-Jewish shoe merchant and importer who died in 1936. As Hitler began open oppression of Jews, the fatherless May family made a fateful decision—to escape the growing Nazi menace, which lay only twenty-odd miles north of their home, and try their luck in America. Scraping together the last of her resources, in 1940 Renée May bought tickets for herself, eleven-year-old Edgar, and Madeleine, five years his junior, on one of the last transports from Italy that Jews were allowed to board.

After their Atlantic crossing, the family accepted temporary lodging with cousins in Forest Hills, Queens, New York; Madeleine, affectionately known as Mady, set about learning English. The 1940s were traumatic times for most Jews, even a six-year-old, who realized how close her family had come to annihilation. As she later observed, she visualized herself as a doer rather than a passive victim. To demonstrate to dubious neighbors that her family was not German, she wore Swiss and American lapel flags.

As an adult, Madeleine remembers her mother's sacrifices for her two children. Renée May found work as a seamstress, governess, and French tutor and poured her energies into developing her children's talents. By 1947, the family gained their U.S. citizenship and established a permanent home in Pittsfield, Massachusetts. Madeleine finished twelfth grade, then enrolled in the University of Massachusetts, working as a waitress at Tanglewood to earn tuition. She graduated with honors in history in 1956, and followed with a master of science degree from the Columbia School of Journalism in 1957.

## A Career and a Family

Both Madeleine and her brother chose journalism as their career. On first probing the job market, however, Madeleine did not find abundant opportunities for female journalists. Interviews often led nowhere. This initial confrontation with sex prejudice later helped turn her thinking toward politics. In her words, "I wasn't exactly a conscious feminist then, but I felt the unfairness."[2] In later years, she maintained her distance from radical feminism, but refused to back down on issues that were blatantly prejudicial.

Working toward a position as a foreign correspondent, at first she wrote for the *Burlington Free Press*. She met physician Arthur S. Kunin, a kidney specialist at the University of Vermont Medical School. The couple seemed ideally suited and married on June 21, 1959. Still career-minded, Madeleine, who had wangled a "men only" post as a reporter, applied her aggressiveness and language skills to writing and producing for a Burlington television station. In 1961, she quit work before the birth of Julia, her first child. Her sons, Peter, Adam, and Daniel, followed, giving her no time for career development.

Because she liked both family life and New England, Kunin did a good job of nesting in Vermont. In 1969, the family built a roomy modern ranch house on Dunder Road in the suburbs of Burlington on the shores of Lake Champlain, just west of the Green Mountains and only 35 miles from Montpelier, the state capital. The whole family enjoyed outdoor activities, particularly cross-country skiing.

Kunin preferred informal living and decorated her home accordingly, with an inviting fireplace, photos, travel mementos, and house plants. Her husband worked as a spokesman for the dairy industry. Both of them cooked. They favored intimate meals with friends. Their typical menus featured Vermont specialties, particularly cheddar cheese, apple cider, zucchini pancakes, salmon with sorrel sauce, and blueberry pie.

## A Second Chance

Although Kunin found contentment as housewife and mother, she stayed abreast of political issues and even lobbied for Medicare. She returned to graduate studies in the late 1960s, completed a second master's degree in English literature from the University of Vermont in 1967, taught English for a year at Trinity College, and began freelance writing and public relations work.

When contact with female activists during a year-long family vacation in Switzerland in 1970 struck a responsive note, Kunin revived dormant goals to make a difference with her life. She reasoned that if a woman, who is allowed no vote in national elections in Switzerland, can rise to the position of mayor of Geneva, she could do her part in Vermont. Supporting her in these ambitions were husband Arthur and brother Edgar, himself a Pulitzer Prize-winning journalist and state senator in Vermont.

In 1972, Kunin's first bid for election as alderwoman failed by sixteen votes. Undeterred, she joined the Democratic push in 1972 and built a platform on the issues of a clean environment, better educational opportunities, and improved living conditions for the poor. To finance her campaign, she hosted wine-and-cheese parties and rang doorbells. Her husband even donned a sandwich board to advertise her candidacy. This time her liberal appeal meshed with local needs and she was elected.

By her second term, Kunin was ready for greater participation. She served on the justice committee and achieved a spot on the appropriations committee. Within two years she rose to the rank of chairwoman and chief voice in the state's budget. During this period she co-authored *The Big Green Book* and contributed articles to journals, newspapers, and magazines. Her unique style and fervor received notice from Rutgers University, which named her Outstanding State Legislator in 1975. She served three two-year terms in the state House of Representatives, the last as minority whip.

At the end of her apprenticeship, she moved up a rung on the political ladder to two terms as lieutenant governor. Defeating Republican Peter Smith by a tiny margin, she parlayed her natural courtesy, willingness to make eye contact, and self-assurance into winning assets. Within two years she made gains on her first win and swept into office with an impressive 59 percent majority.

Tall, willowy, and gray-haired, with a gracious smile and warm eyes, Kunin made her face her calling card in door-to-door campaigning, barbecues, town meetings, and rallies. She held up well under the strain of too many people, ringing telephones, and end-to-end meetings. She dressed appealingly in feminine clothes, rested when she had the opportunity, and kept herself toned with frequent workouts, favoring either jogging or laps around the pool.

Most significant to her success was her empathy, which she projected at every opportunity, even when the political heat wilted more seasoned veteran males. Her door remained open, her hand extended to all comers. She summed up her political savoir-faire in typically pragmatic terms: "I believed it was important to have personal contact with people, to show I was accessible."[3]

## On to the Governorship

Kunin's first try at the governor's post in 1982 was respectable, but short by sixteen percent. She realized that she had only a slim chance of unseating incumbent Richard Snelling; however, the experience was worth the effort. As she explained to an interviewer from *Working Woman*: "There are degrees of losing, and if you lose respectably in a tough race, you can emerge again."[4]

After the defeat, Kunin surprised adversaries by turning to other options. She debuted as radio hostess of a daily talk show over Burlington's WJOY. Using her new public voice to advantage, she challenged Vermont Democrats to rethink their position and summon new strength to beat incumbent Republicans.

By 1984, Kunin was stronger, more knowledgeable of the territory, and better able to raise funds and select issues. Running on a platform favoring fiscal responsibility, educational reform, and a cleaner environment, she defeated Attorney General John Easton—by a mere sixty votes. At the age of fifty-one, she became Vermont's first woman governor. She credited her victory more to grassroots voting power than to her own appeal. To *People* magazine she commented, "People seemed to feel a sense of history about my being the state's first woman governor. I was amazed at how deep that emotion was."[5]

Governor Kunin rejected the image of herself as a woman's candidate. Instead, she favored the view of herself as the hard-working immigrant. In her Montpelier office, she opened the office of governor to less formal trappings and more one-on-one sessions with citizens. With real élan, she balanced the budget, then faced off against the powerful ski industry and held it accountable to environmental protection laws.

To her credit, Governor Kunin stocked her cabinet with crackerjack female members. By skillful maneuvers, she increased the state outlay for schools, boosted industry, supported rape victims, and continued championing the environmental cause with a bill banning phosphate detergents. As the state's number one cheerleader, she touted local maple syrup, dairy products, lamb, beers, fashions, crafts, and art. Her support for the handicapped and her battle to halt cuts to state college and local school budgets won her many supporters.

Kunin's second election to the governorship in 1978 was a cliffhanger. The campaign, split three ways among incumbent Kunin, Republican challenger Peter Smith, and Socialist Bernard Sanders, the mayor of Burlington, threw the inconclusive vote into the legislature. There, representatives were not swayed by accusations of indecisiveness or misrepresentation against Kunin. They confirmed her leadership and returned her to office with a 9 percent margin.

## Looking Toward New Horizons

Before her third term as governor of the Green Mountain State, Madeleine Kunin was far from finished with personal aspiration. She remained active in the National Governors' Association and kept her eye on possible national-level posts. Ignoring taunts from adversaries who dubbed her straddlin' Madeleine, she kept a firm grip on her unique style. By distancing herself from male politicians and business as usual, she maintained her warmth with constituents and continued to support grass-roots objectives, particularly cleaning the environment and strengthening Vermont schools. Speaking for Americans for Democratic Action, Ann Lewis summed up Kunin's strengths from the feminine perspective: "She represents the new style of woman politician who views the values and experience of being a woman as positives—concerns for children, for education, for those in economic difficulty."[6]

## Round Three

By 1988, Kunin was an old hand at campaigning. She faced Michael Bernhardt, Londonderry's four-term state representative and House Republican leader. Her platform remained much the same as in earlier terms. She championed the environment and education against Bernhardt's support for free enterprise and big business. In the face of his accusations that she terrorized private industry, Kunin won with 54 percent of the vote and became the first woman in the nation to be elected to a third term as state governor.

Governor Kunin's third term brought new challenges, particularly child support and budget shortfalls, which plagued much of New England. She passed bills to protect groundwater and natural streams. At a meeting of governors she spoke out against federal padding of military budgets. To questions about President Ronald Reagan's effectiveness, she seemed keenly attuned to Vermont's position: "People like him as a person," she admitted, "but they do not necessarily accept what he's doing."[7] She supported her statement with direct references to military spending, lack of concern for farm families, and the aggressive stance of the U.S. in Central America.

But much of her third term was beset by difficulties. Because she called for an end to unlined landfills, she stirred up new enemies. More opposition developed to Act 200, a law that controlled land development. Her chief opponent, Richard Snelling, used the voter undercurrent as a wedge to intimidate her.

Before the end of her term of office, Madeleine Kunin, age fifty-six, capitulated and looked elsewhere for new roles. In a simple but effective statement to the press and about 200 well-wishers, she said, "It is time for me to move on to new challenges. What enabled me to arrive at this decision with a new sense of purpose was the realization that there are other ways to create change."[8] Her comments concluded with several possibilities, particularly writing a book.

## Ex-Governor Kunin

Freed from the restraints of Vermont's highest office, Madeleine Kunin has a host of options to choose from. Her staff anticipates that she will remain at the forefront of the women's movement and return to lecturing. Other possibilities include environmental activism and a cabinet post, in the event that the Democratic Party returns to power. To suggestions that she may make a good female nominee for a number of posts, she drops her characteristic Swiss reserve and replies with fervor: "The object is to be who you are. If being a woman is a factor politically, it's usually not because of a conscious bias, but because women are a novelty."[9]

Kunin has stated in interviews her belief that women have served their apprenticeship in politics and are ready for candidacy for the presidency. To *U.S. News and World Report* she said, "To sum up my thinking, I believe women get elected if they run good campaigns and if they do everything the traditional politician does."[10] Such strong advocacy of women's place in American politics leads people to believe that Madeleine Kunin sees herself as just such a candidate in future elections.

Very much a normal citizen on the streets of Burlington, Kunin does her own shopping and has lunch in public places. She keeps up friendships with neighbor women by hosting monthly coffee klatches. Her friends return the favor by being supportive. To interviewer Colette Rossant, Kunin confided, "My friends know how busy I am—some even shop for me to save me time. For my inauguration, one friend bought several dresses for me to choose from—I felt like a queen."[11]

## Notes

[1] Guy Garcia. "Ten Routes to the American Dream," *Time*, July 8, 1985, 63.

[2] Marge Runnion. "Once a Refugee from Nazi Europe, Madeleine Kunin Takes Charge as Vermont's First Woman Governor," *People Weekly*, April 1, 1985, 106.

[3] *Current Biography.* Detroit: Gale Research, 1987, 329.

[4] Nancy Day. "Madeleine Kunin," *Working Woman*, July 1986, 76.

[5] Runnion, 104.

[6] *Current Biography*, 329.

[7] "Governors Tell Washington the Word from Home," *U.S. News and World Report*, March 11, 1985, 50.

[8] Jack Hoffman. "Kunin Will Step Down," *Rutland Daily Herald*, Rutland, Vermont, April 4, 1990, n.p.

[9] Runnion, 106.

[10] "The Way Back: Ideas from Two Democrats," *U.S. News and World Report*, November 26, 1984, 33.

[11] Colette Rossant. "A Visit with Vermont's Governor," *McCall's*, January 1988, 83.

## Sources

*Current Biography*. Detroit: Gale Research, 1987.

Daley, Yvonne. "Her Long Journey to Power," *Rutland Daily Herald*, Rutland, Vermont, April 4, 1990, n.p.

Day, Nancy. "Madeleine Kunin," *Working Woman*, July 1986, 74-77.

Garcia, Guy. "Ten Routes to the American Dream," *Time*, July 8, 1985, 63.

"Governors Tell Washington the Word from Home," *U.S. News and World Report*, March 11, 1985, 49-50.

Hoffman, Jack. "Kunin Will Step Down," *Rutland Daily Herald*, Rutland, Vermont, April 4, 1990, n.p.

Rossant, Collette. "A Visit with Vermont's Governor," *McCall's*, January 1988, 82-83.

Runnion, Marge. "Once a Refugee from Nazi Europe, Madeleine Kunin Takes Charge as Vermont's First Woman Governor," *People Weekly*, April 1, 1985, 102-6.

"The Way Back: Ideas from Two Democrats," *U.S. News and World Report*, November 26, 1984, 31-35.

# Ann Landers

A late-in-life alteration in career can bring with it a new name as well as a new persona. For Eppie Lederer, life as Ann Landers has brought fame, love, esteem, and a daily following of 90 million readers, unequaled in newspaper history. The column, the most widely circulated feature worldwide, appears in 1,200 newspapers each day. The twin sister of Abigail Van Buren, herself a notable advice columnist, Ann Landers has been in the business for over three decades. In that time she has answered over 35,000 letters individually and has helped people deal with serious problems, ranging from stale marriages to infidelity, from how to find Mr. Right to how an AIDS sufferer can reveal homosexuality to parents.

A reflection of national values both in print and in person, Ann is not shy before a microphone. She speaks willingly on talk shows and campuses and at public meetings, her midwestern twang notwithstanding. Her association with politicians, priests, and other notables enables her to educate and do good on many fronts. For these and other services she has received the Albert Lasker Award for Public Service as well as awards from the National Family Service Association, National Council on Alcoholism, Lions Club, American Cancer Society, and American Medical Association. *The Women's Almanac* named her the most influential woman in America.

## Eppie Lederer

Eppie Lederer comes from Russian Jewish immigrant stock. Born Esther Pauline to A. B. "Abe" and Becky Friedman on July 4, 1918, in Sioux City, Iowa, Eppie has two older sisters, Helen and Dorothy. A brother died in infancy. In childhood, she was close to her twin sister, Pauline Esther "Popo." Both have olive skin, blue eyes, black hair, and a petite frame, although Eppie is taller, dimpled, and less chubby. In childhood, they dressed alike, studied the violin together, and exhibited boisterous creative energy. From so much togetherness, their lives intertwined.

From early times, the twins adopted their parents' habit of helping the less fortunate and bluffed their way into hospitals and the county jail, where they sang to patients and inmates. The girls managed well during the Depression. At high school, she and Popo stood out as the only wearers of civet fur coats, a gift from their doting father, who owned a chain of movie theaters. But Ann also came away with an awareness of how to avoid waste. From their father they learned social skills; from their less voluble mother they learned to dance. Within the family framework, the two girls absorbed love and generosity, which characterized their adult lives.

## Finding Husbands

Following an undistinguished high school career, especially in geometry and science, the Friedman twins remained in Sioux City to attend Morningside College, a Methodist school. Eppie, more eager to marry than graduate, accepted a ring from Lewis Dreyer; then Popo followed suit with her own announcement and the two brides-to-be dropped out of school. While shopping for her trousseau, Eppie fell under the spell of Jules "Sonny" Lederer, broke her engagement to Dreyer, shipped the ring back to the west coast, and substituted a new name under the heading of groom.

Years later, Eppie, writing from the point of view of Ann Landers, celebrated her thirtieth wedding anniversary in her column with a suitable analysis of her husband: "Thirty years with this unselfish, supportive, responsive man has enabled me to live life as few people have the opportunity to live it. Being Ann Landers' husband could pose a terrible problem, but Jules has met the challenge with dignity and incredible good humor. My husband is my best friend...."[1]

On July 2, 1939, Eppie and Popo shared their wedding ceremony and a joint honeymoon. Popo married Morton Phillips; Eppie married Jules, a high school dropout and millinery salesman who later established himself successfully in several businesses, notably as originator of Budget Rent-a-Car. In 1940, the Lederers had one daughter, Margo, who became a journalist. The wife of actor Ken Howard and mother of Eppie's three grandchildren—Abra, Adam, and Andrea—Margo lives in Connecticut and in 1982 wrote a biography of her mother.

During the early years of marriage, the Lederers moved around frequently, going wherever the work seemed more promising, whether in St. Louis, Milwaukee, or Little Rock. While living in New Orleans, Eppie worked as a volunteer at La Garde Naval Hospital. In the early 1940s, both her husband and brother-in-law were drafted. By 1944, Abe Lederer also received a call-up. As life was returning to normal near the end of the war, Eppie's mother died suddenly of a brain hemorrhage. Eppie was at her side as she took her last breath and muttered farewell in Yiddish.

## Too Much Spare Time

After the armistice, Jules returned, accepted a job selling Presto cookware, and took Eppie with him door-to-door through Los Angeles. He demonstrated pots and pans; she cut up vegetables. To utilize excess creative energy, Eppie wrote contest jingles. Eventually, Jules rose to sales manager and the family moved to Eau Claire, Wisconsin, where Eppie volunteered as a Gray Lady, a reader to the blind, and a member of the League of Women Voters and the National Council of Christians and Jews.

Becoming more aggressive in local affairs, she wrote letters to the editor of the *Eau Claire Leader & Telegram* and joined the Democratic party, adopting Eleanor Roosevelt as her personal idol. After a bitter fight, Eppie won the post of county party chairwoman. While nurturing friendship with Senator Hubert Humphrey, she learned the inner workings of Washington and made a doomed effort to unseat Joe McCarthy.

The Lederers traveled widely. In 1954, they moved to a high-rise apartment in Chicago so that Jules could leave Presto and reestablish himself at the Autopoint Corporation, a manufacturer of ballpoint pens. Unable to move her Wisconsin political clout to Illinois, Eppie cast about for a new outlet. In August 1955, she spied the "Ask Ann Landers" column in the *Sun-Times* and decided to volunteer as assistant.

## Ann the Columnist

Will Munnecke's reply surprised her: Ruth Crowley, the Ann Landers at that time, had died; a contest was under way to locate a suitable replacement. Munnecke feared that Eppie, lacking Ruth's experience as both journalist and nurse, could not handle a column syndicated in forty newspapers. Also, he warned that two of the contestants had special ins with the newspaper. However, by answering a trial letter about a walnut tree on the dividing line between two pieces of property, she impressed the editors with her resourcefulness in providing a sensible answer and beat twenty-one other contestants for the job.

Still, without every having written professionally, received a diploma, or even held a regular job, Eppie seemed destined for failure. Her daughter notes, however, that Eppie had an unusual combination of talents to bank on: "She was confident—in both her judgment and her abilities. She learned quickly, had common sense and a clear idea of right and wrong. In addition to being highly motivated, she had incredible energy and amazing chutzpah."[2] But the committee that selected her to be the third Ann Landers held out little hope that she would stick to a grueling job when she obviously did not need the money.

In his introduction to *Dear Ann Landers*, David Grossvogel notes that the mid-1950s were an auspicious time for an advice column. The country, only a decade out of a world war, felt that it was being tested by current events. In his words, "Self-confidence and optimism had carried it through previous crises to predictable and satisfactory ends, but an inclusive war in Korea and political stalemates in other parts of the world now made Americans uneasy."[3] In short, Americans were starting to question their most cherished beliefs. In place of prophet or guru, they turned to Ann Landers.

The new Ann Landers developed a credible style of no-nonsense replies couched in straightforward, conversational language. From an unimpressive desk in the back of the city room, she wrote daily columns with the help of editor and mentor Larry Fanning, who insisted that her replies to write-ins provide real information rather than merely entertain. To keep up with the overflow of letters, she worked at her desk at home, keeping secret from friends the nature of her task. In six months, she had earned the pros' respect and received a contract.

With an appearance on *What's My Line*, Landers ended the mystery surrounding her role as advice columnist. She heard from thousands of people in the television audience and almost overnight became a star. But to her, the task of advising others was never just a job. As Margo surmises: "It was, rather, a mission … a contribution to make, an identity to have. Ann Landers may have been who she was all along."[4]

## Branching Out

A unique feature of Ann Landers is the wide number of services that she supports, such as Legal Aid, Alcoholics Anonymous, Parents and Friends of Lesbians and Gays, and mental health counseling. Eventually, she added pamphlets to her credit, beginning with "Necking and Petting and How Far to Go." She devoted hours of private time to reading letters from fans and then destroyed the pages to protect the writers' privacy. Jules and Margo formed a home-based cheering section. Margo described the home scene: "Father felt Mother's new incarnation was perfect for her. He called her, with affection, 'general manager of the world.' "[5]

## Family Rivalry

For a while, Popo helped out. She filled in as secretary and learned how to shape a column. Several months later, Eppie's twin became Dear Abby for the *San Francisco Chronicle*. Abby imitated Ann's style, although critics point out that Abby relied more on comic one-liners than real advice. Their antipathy developed into a nasty public feud, but the result was an increase in sales as rival papers rushed to sign up the famous sisters.

Self-disciplined and selfless in her new role, Ann hired three secretaries to manage the mountain of mail and trained them to her specifications. Hours of travel, telephone calls, and hobnobbing with professional journalists consumed her time so that she also had to hire a housekeeper and chauffeur. She and Jules made quite a workaholic pair as they manned their IBM typewriters each evening.

## Hard Times

The schism between Ann and Abby erupted in 1957 after Abby began a demeaning game of one-upmanship. The sisters agreed to disagree and ceased all communication. *Life* magazine reported the impasse under the caption "Twin Lovelorn Advisers Torn Asunder by Success." In 1964, Ann and her sister patched up their interfamily spat and flew to Morocco to help Malcolm Forbes celebrate his birthday.

Then in 1981, the twins were again sliced apart. For no apparent reason, Abby agreed to an interview with *Ladies Home Journal* in which she downgraded her twin. This time the issues were money, facelifts, and envy, but Abby's purpose in jabbing Ann failed to influence readers. And Ann, displaying true class, refused to respond.

## Success and Then Some

During the growth years as Ann Landers, the columnist expanded her horizons. In 1959 she traveled to Russia to write and converse with the locals. Having heard Russian spoken in her childhood home, she managed with a brief brush-up at Berlitz. To gain entrance into verboten institutions, she would pose as the wife of a lawyer or a psychiatrist. Upon her return, her twelve articles captured the human situation in the USSR in typical Ann Landers fashion: "Ludmilla and Serge are in love and want to marry but they must wait at least two years for an apartment. Elina has a lecherous boss. Igor hates his mother-in-law. The problems of people are the same the world over. In Moscow they have Russian dressing."[6]

In 1967 Landers, caught up in the Vietnam War furor, visited field hospitals as a guest of the Army. After a thirty-three-hour plane ride aboard General Westmoreland's *White Whale*, she spent ten days in medical centers from Saigon to Camranh Bay. At each stop, she amazed administrators by working ten to twelve hours a day and speaking to every patient, a total of 2,500 wounded soldiers. Upon her return, she kept her promise and made personal phone calls for every soldier who had a message to relay.

## The Bottom Drops Out

At this comfortable stage in their lives, the Lederer family began taking in more money. Jules resigned his job and opened Budget Rent-a-Car, which he sold for $10 million nine years later. Margo, not wholly successful at Brandeis University, launched a marriage that produced three children, but little happiness. Landers supported her daughter through unpleasant times, even altering her own hard-nosed stand against divorce to reflect what she had learned from Margo's experiences. Landers weathered most situations with aplomb, including a talk show on which she encountered porn queen Linda Lovelace, star of *Deep Throat*. Margo characterized her mother's ability to cope: "She makes entrances and exits, attracts attention wherever she goes, and in the company of others is in control."[7]

In 1972, after Jules's sell-out of Budget Rent-a-Car, the Lederers moved to a fourteen-room Chicago apartment. Jules invested here and there, but failed to find the right outlet for his hyperactive business acumen. His wife continued to thrive as Ann Landers, breaking new ground as board member or trustee for myriad blue ribbon organizations, including the Menninger Foundation, American Cancer Society, Mayo Clinic, and Harvard Medical School. In September 1974 she even accompanied AMA officials on a tour of China. But back home, her husband was taking a tour of depression and alcoholism.

Jules's answer to his problem was to divorce his wife in favor of his mistress, an Englishwoman twenty-eight years his junior. In removing himself from the scene, he caused much family damage, not only to Ann, but also to Margo, who had known his secret for months. Ann managed the breakup amicably and turned for counseling to her old friend Father Hesburgh, president of Notre Dame University. When she was ready to face readers, she divulged her troubles.

In a precedent-setting confession, Landers relayed to her sizeable audience the misery of divorce. On July 1, 1975, she wrote, "The sad, incredible fact is that after thirty-six years of marriage Jules and I are being divorced. As I write these words, it is as if I am referring to a letter from a reader. It seems unreal that I am writing about my own marriage."[8] Part of the settlement was the stipulation that Jules get on with remarriage so that Landers could stop worrying about his welfare. Even at the nadir, she continued to shoulder someone else's misery.

## Still Working

At home on the fifteenth floor on Chicago's Lake Shore Drive, where she writes from fourteen to fifteen hours a day, Landers, in her seventies, refuses to discuss retirement. She and a staff of ten manage 2,000 pieces of mail per day, with Landers handling each letter, two-thirds of which come from women. Landers claims to stay abreast of the flow by distancing herself from sad letters. Without objectivity, she claims, she could never cope with so many confessions as well as hate mail from anti-abortion groups, the National Rifle Association, and animal-rights groups. To her critics, Ann Landers is not shy about retorting, "Anyone who has the notion that I've been writing for 35 years and not keeping up, well, *they're* not keeping up. I'm very much in touch. The readers do that for me."[9]

In truth, Landers has changed with the times. She noted in an interview, "I don't consider myself an expert. I go to the experts; I know how to get to them."[10] Among her close advisers she has consulted Supreme Court Justice William O. Douglas, Bishop Fulton J. Sheen, Father Theodore Hesburgh, and Cardinal Joseph Bernardin. Abby sums up Ann's evolution as an advice columnist: "I think she has softened quite a bit. She used to be harder, tougher.... Now she's showing more compassion. She's kinder and gentler."[11]

# Notes

[1] Margo Howard. *Eppie: The Story of Ann Landers.* New York: G. P. Putnam's Sons, 1982, 203.

[2] Howard, 105.

[3] David I. Grossvogel. *Dear Ann Landers.* Chicago: Contemporary Books, 1987, 3.

[4] Howard, 111-112.

[5] Howard, 113.

[6] Howard, 147.

[7] Howard, 194.

[8] Howard, 226.

[9] Mark McDonald, "Her Readers Are Her Teachers," *Charlotte Observer,* October 19, 1990, 2E.

[10] Nancy Hobbs, "Ann Landers Refuses to Be an 'Expert' on Anything," *Salt Lake City Tribune,* Salt Lake City, Utah, July 27, 1987, n.p.

[11] McDonald, 2E.

# Sources

Cope, Lewis. "Landers Column Pulled; Cancer Treatment Report Is Questioned," *Minneapolis Star and Tribune,* Minneapolis, Minnesota, August 26, 1987, n.p.

Grossvogel, David I. *Dear Ann Landers.* Chicago: Contemporary Books, 1987.

Hobbs, Nancy. "Ann Landers Refuses to Be an 'Expert' on Anything," *Salt Lake City Tribune,* Salt Lake City, Utah, July 27, 1987, n.p.

Howard, Margo. *Eppie: The Story of Ann Landers.* New York: G. P. Putnam's Sons, 1982.

Martin, Susan. "Dear Abby, Dear Ann," *Buffalo News,* Buffalo, New York, July 3, 1988, n.p.

McDonald, Mark. "Her Readers Are Her Teachers," *Charlotte Observer*, October 19, 1990, 2-3E.

Yim, Susan. "Dear Ann Landers...," *Honolulu Advertiser*, Honolulu, Hawaii, April 13, 1989, n.p.

Yolesias, Linda. "The Angel of Advice," *New York Daily News*, January 10, 1988, n.p.

# Gordon Liddy

Not all late achievers weather adversity unscathed. George Gordon Battle Liddy, dedicated saber rattler who served time in five federal penitentiaries for his role as mastermind of the Watergate break-ins, maintains a tarnished image in most people's minds. To some Americans, Liddy is a villain and a traitor. To others, he is a brilliant, articulate, methodical, patriotic—if amoral—hero willing to risk his reputation if such an act can strengthen his country.

Given to feats of daring to challenge his fears, Liddy stands erect, dresses well, wears his hair closely cropped, and puts forth the image of a stalwart soldier. He is loyal to the cause of conservative politics. Whatever the world may think of him, he bears it well and remains unrepentant concerning his criminal activities. To Liddy's way of thinking, no act is too heinous, no request too outlandish if it furthers the career of anyone that he supports.

In some quarters Liddy has regained stature in recent years by opening a school to teach what he knows best—security and private investigation, which he deems a must if the United States is to maintain its position among nations. He summed up the need for greater caution in a 1986 speech, "A vast majority of the people have become confused between a world as it is and what is in their minds. The world is not Beverly Hills or Palm Springs. It is a bad neighborhood. It is the South Bronx in New York at 2:30 a.m."[1] And G. Gordon Liddy is just the man to face the challenge.

## Building Up the Man

In early childhood, Gordon Liddy showed little promise of his future traits, particularly cold-blooded cunning and hawkish outlook. Born to attorney Sylvester J. and Maria Abbaticchio Liddy on November 30, 1930, in Hoboken, New Jersey, Liddy was a whiny, spindly, asthmatic child given to exaggerated fears of heights, dirigibles, fire, electricity, moths, and rats as well as his grandmother's leather strap. He recalls how he and Teresa, the Liddy family's German housekeeper, tuned in to radio broadcasts of Adolf Hitler's fiery speeches. Even though Liddy spoke no German at the time, the demagogue's delivery gave the boy courage. Taking control, Liddy determined to face and conquer each phobia.

For example, he ended his fear of heights as well as the phobia of electricity by sitting atop high-tension power poles for extended times. In another instance he cooked and ate the hindquarters of a rat.

In his best-selling 1980 autobiography, *Will*, Liddy acknowledges the role of parish priests, who encouraged him to master his weaknesses: "God gave us a free will, but to strengthen that will to meet the temptations of life required denial, 'mortification,' suffering. *Suffering*. That was the key."[2] During World War II, Liddy, while protecting his gun hand, held his left hand in a flame as a means of strengthening his resolve. He also volunteered to slaughter chickens for the neighborhood butcher so that he could face death without flinching.

In spite of his more daring exploits, Liddy was a malleable, praise-seeking child. He profited from the example of his strong-minded dock worker-turned-attorney father and also from his Uncle Ray, an FBI agent. In order to excel in their eyes, he studied hard and went out for athletic teams at St. Benedict's Preparatory School in Newark, New Jersey. Early attempts to play baseball and run track were disappointing. An average-sized boy with piercing dark eyes, he lacked the muscle and moxie to compete. To build his physique, Liddy began lifting weights and eventually did well in wrestling and cross-country by his sophomore year. His success was so complete that he won a varsity letter, developed an overweening conceit, and lorded his mastery over weaker students.

At Fordham University, a tough Jesuit school in the Bronx, Liddy maintained a B+ average and joined the Reserve Officers' Training Corps, hoping to serve in some crucial battle to defend his homeland from communist aggression. As his autobiography indicates, he cultivated visions of himself as an American version of one of Hitler's hand-picked stormtroopers, hunting out enemies and crushing them. His fantasies withered after his graduation from college in 1952, when, as a second lieutenant, he was assigned to a Brooklyn-based antiaircraft radar unit for the duration of the Korean War rather than the frontline combat he coveted.

Liddy settled back into study after the war, completing his law degree at Fordham in 1954. He again stoked reveries of civic glory during a five-year stint as agent for the Federal Bureau of Investigation in Indianapolis and Gary, Indiana, a job for which he received special training in clandestine operations. At this point in his career he married Frances Ann Purcell, a brainy computer expert and elementary school teacher, on November 9, 1957. True to his notion of Hitler's master race, Liddy selected her based on preconceived criteria of the perfect mother. He recalls with special glee that Frances tinkered with calculus problems the way ordinary people entertain themselves with crossword puzzles. He described her as a "Teuton/Celt of high intelligence, a mathematical mind, physical size, strength, and beauty, she had it all. I fell in love."[3]

Within five years, the couple, who make their home outside Washington, D.C., produced two daughters followed by three sons. The oldest son, James, later participated on a team that earned a gold medal in the pentathlon at the U.S. Olympic Festival. The two youngest children, Raymond and Thomas, became beefy, macho Marines who won their father's approval by acting tough. Alexandra, who went into nursing, and Grace, who went into computers, rated a modicum of their father's attention.

More opportunities drew Liddy away from dreams of stemming the red menace. In his father's law firm he worked as a patent attorney; then as assistant district attorney he gained notoriety in 1966 by joining a sheriff's hit team that raided the lair of drug proponent Tomothy Leary. As the racial turmoil of the late 1960s swirled to new heights, Liddy became alarmed at the menace to national order. To help stop the mayhem, he looked for a job closer to the office of the president.

## On to Washington

In an abortive attempt to run for the Republican seat in the New York congressional race, Liddy lost out to Hamilton Fish, Jr., but came to the attention of John N. Mitchell's staff and assumed a leadership role in the local Nixon camp. Through savvy dealings, Liddy maneuvered Duchess County, New York, support to an impressive high. From this position he moved on in 1969 to an anti-criminal activities post as special assistant to the secretary of the treasury, battling sky-jackers and marijuana traffickers.

During this period, Liddy honed his peculiar brand of amoral rationalization. In his words: "The nation was at war not only externally in Vietnam but internally.... I had learned long ago the maxims of Cicero that 'laws are inoperative in war' and that 'the good of the people is the chief law.' "[4] From this perspective, Liddy was mentally and emotionally prepared to accept any job that he deemed politically expedient.

With the aid of Egil Krogh, Liddy advanced to a special investigative force at the White House. Even closer to the main source of power, he worked for John D. Ehrlichman, Nixon's domestic affairs adviser, as a member of the infamous Plumbers, an ex officio gang assembled to stop leaks that might undermine government security. With the aid of E. Howard Hunt, a former CIA member, Liddy broke into the Beverly Hills office of a psychiatrist to discredit war protester Daniel Ellsberg, the man reputed to have leaked the Pentagon Papers.

Liddy's next assignment was more challenging. Under the code name Gemstone, he and Howard Hunt, along with a group of six hand-picked Cuban nationals, burglarized the Watergate, a modern apartment and office building on the Potomac River adjacent to the Kennedy Center in Washington, D.C., that housed the Democratic National Committee headquarters. The group's main purpose was to assure surveillance and to photograph crucial documents. But the overall scam involved sleazy money laundering, unprincipled political espionage, slandering public officials, and the proposed assassination of columnist Jack Anderson, all of which caused the first resignation of a U.S. president and vice president. Later accounts of the affair labeled the burglary "ill-conceived, grandiose and largely juvenile," but at the time, it was big news in the United States and abroad and ultimately served as the basis for the film *All the President's Men*, which glorifies the role of Woodward and Bernstein, neophyte muckrakers for the *Washington Post*.[5]

Liddy, realizing that the Watergate operation was in jeopardy, returned immediately to his office to shred documents and $1,300 in serial hundred dollar bills, all evidence that might incriminate him and weaken Nixon's chance for reelection. As he phrased his concern: "I was the man on the bridge when the aircraft carrier hit the reef. Damage control was my responsibility."[6] He was not arrested until the *Washington Post* broke the news of the "dirty tricks" committee, which sought to boost Nixon's chance for reelection. Liddy and cohorts were arrested and charged with multiple counts of burglary, conspiracy, and wiretapping.

## A Matter of Principle

From the beginning, Liddy refused Judge John J. Sirica's orders to acknowledge guilt for what he saw as compliance with a presidential order. He perceived the caper as a necessary evil, a method of holding on to power. As Liddy described the affair, "Watergate was anything but unique. It is the way the power of the office of the presidency is contested every time. It was simply presidential politics."[7] He later remarked, "I sought by refusing to speak about these things to preserve for however long I could the Nixon presidency, in which I believed and which cause I was seeking to advance."[8] Found guilty of both the Beverly Hills and Washington jobs, he received a twenty-one-year prison sentence, a contempt-of-Congress citation, and a fine of $40,000. President Jimmy Carter later altered Liddy's sentence to eight years. In September 1977 Liddy exited the Danbury, Connecticut, prison a free man.

## Starting Over

Although Liddy returned to domestic normalcy at his eight-room redwood home on the Potomac waterfront in Oxon Hill, Maryland, he did not resume his former professional role in society because he was a felon, precluded from full citizenship and disbarred by the legal profession. To support his family and pay off staggering legal fees, he made speeches to civic and college groups. He wrote an espionage novel, *Out of Control*, in 1979 and followed with his autobiography, which critics castigated for the author's arrogant rejection of wrongdoing. Most important, he reclaimed his role as husband and father by reestablishing home ties.

Liddy's post-prison role came to him in his fifth year behind bars: "During Watergate, I became known for trying to penetrate high-security places. I thought we could specialize in industrial counterespionage, capitalizing on my knowledge and my name."[9] In his late forties, he opened the Miami-based G. Gordon Liddy and Associates Academy of Corporate Security and Private Investigation, a mobile operation that sets up wherever the customer requests. Headed by psycholinguist and criminologist Olaf Rankis, the training school reverses

Liddy's former role of sneak thief and transforms him into an earnest pedagogue. Though it opened with only a handful of paying customers, the operation showed immediate promise.

The scope of his service ranges from detection of illegal bugs to drug investigation to recovery of hostages from foreign powers. To perform the latter function, he initiated his Hurricane Force, counterterrorist commandos trained to conduct daring rescue missions in any setting. The group's first assignments were child's play for Liddy—seizure of clothing with fake designer labels, such as Sergio Valente and Ralph Lauren.

Then Liddy moved on to training sessions. For expert advice on covert operations, students pay $1,500 for a seven-day seminar or $2,700 for a seventeen-day training course, ammunition provided. Among his protégés are lawmen, journalists, entrepreneurs, and would-be commandos, half of whom are women. Some customers admit that their main purpose in signing on with Liddy is the vicarious thrill of acting out fantasies of crime and punishment. All receive personal attention from an acknowledged master.

Liddy's lessons center on his basic philosophy: for maximum performance, reason must control emotion. To illustrate his belief in strength in the face of danger, he cites a graphic example: "Take, for example, the African jungle, the home of the cheetah. On whom does the cheetah prey? The old, the sick, the wounded, the weak, the very young, but never the strong."[10] He concludes that the survivor must identify with the strong.

## Becoming a Legend

Whereas some citizens find odious Liddy's reemergence as an expert in the very field that brought him low, others see the new Liddy as the reincarnation of a hero, on a par with Colonel Oliver North. His fans marvel at his loyalty and self-discipline in refusing to inform on cohorts during the exhaustive Watergate investigation.

To leave no impression of remorse, Liddy flaunts his criminal past with a vanity plate that reads "H2O GATE." He boasts of being under surveillance while in prison and his eight transfers to other institutions. A success in strictly monetary terms, he has paid around $346,000 in debts, drives a classic Rolls-Royce Phantom III, and owns a winter hideaway in Scottsdale, Arizona. Also, he has launched a new career as actor and entertainer with performances on "Showtime," "Super Password," "Air Wolf," and "Miami Vice."

In 1988, the Internal Revenue Service investigated his earnings from CREEP, popularized acronymn for the Committee to Reelect the President. Out of the $310,000 he received, Liddy was thought to owe over $150,000 in taxes and penalties. During the proceedings, he astounded the court by revealing information that had not come out in earlier interrogations. His description of proposed criminal activities included attempts to malign Senator Edward Kennedy with incriminating photographs, the use of prostitutes as spies on key Democrats, sabotage of the air conditioner at the Miami convention center where the Democratic caucus was to be held, and bugging of the offices of potential opponents Senator George McGovern and Senator Edmund Muskie. Liddy's candor about these plans put him in the good graces of Judge Sterrett who recognized Liddy's perversity, yet admired his honesty. The upshot of the court case was a reduced charge for Liddy.

Through an average of sixty public appearances per year at $8,000 per talk, Liddy continues to support America's strong stance overseas and to repudiate the Freedom of Information Act, which frees government documents for public perusal. He proposes standing up to terrorists, quashing organized crime, and assassinating outspoken enemies, notably Muammar Qaddafi. Liddy's gutsy approach to national politics reflects a Machiavellian view of power. As he summarizes his personal goal: "To survive means to continue to exist, and that is a terrible goal in life. To prevail means to gain the victory, the triumph, the upper hand. That is a worthy goal in life."[11]

## Notes

[1] Steve Norder. "Watergate Mastermind Says U.S. Should Walk Tall and Carry an M-16," *Shreveport Journal*, Shreveport, Louisiana, April 4, 1986, n.p.

[2] G. Gordon Liddy. *Will*. New York: St. Martin's Press, 1980, 12.

[3] Liddy, 55.

[4] Liddy, 128.

[5] David Phelps. "Watergate's Silent Man Turns Talkative in Tax Court," *Minneapolis Star and Tribune*, Minneapolis, Minnesota, August 17, 1988, n.p.

[6] Phelps, n.p.

[7] Mark Walker. "Age and Prison Haven't Mellowed Watergate Culprit," *Yakima Herald-Republic*, Yakima, Washington, October 2, 1986, n.p.

[8] Phelps, n.d.

[9] Patricia Freeman. "Breaking into New Field," *Los Angeles Herald Examiner*, March 16, 1987, n.p.

[10] James S. Kunen. "An American Samurai: Gordon Liddy," *People Weekly*, August 25, 1986, 26.

[11] Kunen, 25.

# Sources

*Current Biography.* Detroit: Gale Research, 1980.

Freeman, Patricia. "Breaking into New Field," *Los Angeles Herald Examiner*, March 16, 1987, n.p.

Kunen, James S. "An American Samurai: Gordon Liddy," *People Weekly*, August 25, 1986, 24-28.

Liddy, G. Gordon. *Will.* New York: St. Martin's Press, 1980.

Norder, Steve. "Watergate Mastermind Says U.S. Should Walk Tall and Carry an M-16," *Shreveport Journal*, Shreveport, Louisiana, April 4, 1986, n.p.

Phelps, David. "Watergate's Silent Man Turns Talkative in Tax Court," *Minneapolis Star and Tribune*, Minneapolis, Minnesota, August 17, 1988, n.p.

Walker, Mark. "Age and Prison Haven't Mellowed Watergate Culprit," *Yakima Herald-Republic*, Yakima, Washington, October 2, 1986, n.p.

# Grandma Moses

The reason for an achiever's newfound ambition is a confrontation with physical weakness, discouragement, poverty, illness, or loss. For Anna Mary Moses of Hoosick Falls, New York, the beginning of international fame was crippling arthritis, which robbed her hands of the grip and flexibility needed to pursue her hobby, embroidering pictures depicting farm life. In place of an avocation that brought pain, she compensated by taking up oil painting.

In the era from 1940 to 1961, known in art circles for the rise of abstract art, Grandma Moses defied elite trends and concentrated on the hopes and longings of Middle America. With over 1,000 simplistic, repetitive canvases to her credit, she became an unofficial spokeswoman for the appreciation and perpetuation of American values and the farms and countryside where ordinary people interacted with nature. A friend of great and humble alike, she worked at a furious speed and turned out America's foremost primitive art to the point that her name itself became an international definition of primitivism.

## Hard Work on the Farm

Anna Mary "Sissy" Robertson, whose conservative farm upbringing took its frugal philosophy from a mix of Scottish, Irish, English, French, and Indian ancestry, claimed kinship with American Revolutionary soldier Hezekiah King, who fought at Ticonderoga. One of ten children, she was born on a farm in Washington County near Greenwich, New York, to Russell King and Margaret Shanahan Robertson on September 7, 1860, shortly before the Civil War. Late in her life, she could summon memories of Lincoln's assassination and Grant's campaign songs.

In the green meadows and wild woods of the northeast, Anna Mary spent much time outdoors, even in frigid weather. Because school sessions were only three months long, she received little formal education and, like many rural children, stopped school altogether in the sixth grade. A petite five feet tall, she nonetheless moved with speed and purpose as she mastered the myriad chores common to a late-nineteenth-century farm woman—soapmaking, sewing, canning, harvesting, and candle dipping. From early times, Anna Mary competed with her brothers, and chortled: "If they'd climb up a tree, I'd climb higher. If they'd climb to the eaves of a house, I'd climb to the ridgepole."[1]

From early childhood, Mary, like her father, showed interest in art, but received no formal instruction. She recalled seeing her father paint their entire house with scenes because he could not afford wallpaper. Toddling along in his path, she painted her own expanse of wall, decorating it to her tastes with a mountain and a white house. She also painted paper dolls and drew pictures on slate or old panes of glass, coloring them with bluing and berry juice. Her mother, more practical than Mary's father, insisted that little girls needed to spend more time doing chores.

## Work and Family

At the age of twelve, Anna Mary left home and worked as a hired girl. She confided later, "Do you know, I used to do everythin'—washin' 'n' ironin' and work in the garden. I cooked three meals a day and I was only 12. Oh, I thought I was it."[2] After fifteen years as a farm laborer, she married Thomas Salmon Moses, a hireling like herself whom she remembers with warmth and affection as "a wonderful man, much better than I am."[3]

At Thomas's insistence, the couple speculated on farming prime land in the Shenandoah Valley near Staunton, Virginia. A responsible woman reminiscent of the hard-headed Yankee trader, Mary invested in a cow, which she purchased with her own savings, and developed her investment into a substantial butter-making business. Long before she set paintbrush to canvas, she earned a reputation as a cook and maker of preserves. She even made and sold homemade potato chips.

As she described her sense of self: "Always wanted to be independent. I couldn't bear the thought of sitting down and Thomas handing out the money."[4] With a stubborn head for business, Mary made the most of her cash. When Thomas borrowed from her, she charged him interest. She kept their relationship on equal monetary footing and vowed that they would work as a team. Later she said, "I had to do as much as my husband did, not like some girls, they sit down, and then somebody has to throw sugar at them."[5]

Their life together proved rich and satisfying. In Staunton they produced ten children, although only five survived infancy. When she was forty-five, Mary and Thomas moved back to Eagle Bridge, New York, not far from her birthplace, to establish a dairy farm. It remained her home for fifty-six years.

## Dreams and Ambitions

A devoted housewife and mother, Mary had simple ambitions. She worked the land, raised her children, and soaked up the culture that was an integral part of rural America. In 1927, when she was 67, her husband died. As a widow, she continued to do what she knew best: to farm and raise her family. For a time, she lived with her son Hugh and took in boarders. Then, at the age of 76, although still very much the family matriarch, she retired to the airy ranch home of her oldest daughter, Winona Fisher, in Hoosick Falls. Later, son Forrest and two of her grandsons, using a floor plan clipped from a newspaper, built her a separate dwelling across from his. There she could look out on open fields and watch the rural scenes that became the soul of her art.

In adulthood, at the request of her daughter Anna, she let needlework express her memories of life on the farm. However, in 1935, when disease made it impossible for her to manipulate worsted with a sewing needle, she had to give up embroidery. To ease the ache in stiff, balky fingers, she turned to a home remedy of several drops of turpentine in milk three times a day. To fill empty hours, she heeded her sister Celestia's suggestion and turned to her childhood love of oil painting.

## Love of Beauty

Grandma Moses had an interest in beauty, but her puritanical upbringing reminded her that, above all, she must be useful. She declared that she could never sit benignly in a rocking chair waiting for someone's help. A believer in recycling, she first painted worn canvas, pieces of board, and glass. Later, she used Masonite boards coated with white paint to set off the vitality and contrast of richly colored figures. Her idealized style fit the primitive canon in both self-taught technique and innocent point of view. But, whereas other painters of native art cluttered their landscapes with minutiae, Grandma Moses achieved a harmonious balance, furthered by a generous depth of color and illusion of space.

Ignoring the changes that sped her into the twentieth century, Grandma Moses continued to let her brush detail the contentment of bygone generations, a time of self-sufficiency and abundance. Her creative eye remained fixed on the past, when life was simpler and living full and joyous. She remarked in her autobiography, "I like to paint old-timey things, historical landmarks of long ago, bridges, mills, and hostelries, those old-time homes, there are a few left, and they are going fast. I do them all from memory, most of them are day dreams...."[6]

Like patchwork quilts and other New England folk art, the flat, naive style of Grandma Moses's paintings proved cozy, engaging, and, later, quite valuable. Along with home canned goods, she sent her first group of paintings to the county fair, where her jam won a blue ribbon, but her artwork was ignored. At the suggestion of Carolyn Thomas, she allowed her first works to be displayed at a Woman's Exchange. By that time, she had completed around 100 oils and at least 50 crewel landscapes.

In 1938, her first sales, from Thomas's drugstore in Hoosick Falls, resulted in her discovery by Louis J. Caldor, an amateur art collector on vacation from New York City. Caldor sold Otto Kallir on her work; Kallir offered her a contract and displayed the landscapes at Gimbel's Department Store, where Grandma Moses shook hands with admirers and chatted with them about recipes. In time, with Kallir's assistance, Mary's landscapes began appearing in more upscale shows and received interest in the U.S. and Europe, particularly in Paris, where critics never failed to give her an encouraging review.

Her initial works were copies of panoramic views taken from postcards and lithographs by Currier and Ives, which she first traced in pencil. Then she turned to nostalgic compositions suggested by memories of farm life in New York and Virginia. Some of the commonplace subjects among her 1,000 works include "Applebutter Making," "Catching the Thanksgiving Turkey," "Haying Time," "Out for Christmas Trees," "Taking in Laundry," "The Quilting Bee," "The Night Before Christmas," "Williamstown in Winter," "Over the River to Grandma's House," "The First Skating," and "Bringing in the Maple Sugar." The focus of her paintings was American country folk and their animals engaged in everyday responsibilities, chores, and pleasures. The most popular were unadorned snow scenes, but, in comment of their worth, Grandma Moses snorted, "People would be better off buyin' chickens."[7]

## Becoming Known

At first she demonstrated the uneven quality of most primitive artists, but she found art an easier source of money than running a boarding house. Later, as she grew accustomed to the art world and its demands, she broadened her scope to larger canvases and freer, more subjective expression. Eager for a challenge, she never hesitated to try some new approach at the suggestion of an admirer. One of her most creative ventures was the illustration of a children's book featuring Clement Moore's poem "The Night Before Christmas," published in 1962, shortly after she died.

Her work began to appear on Hallmark greeting cards, wall prints and tiles, china, textiles for home use, and art books. Entertainer Bob Hope praised her spunk that "remained fresh enough to tackle something new."[8] The upbeat subjects of her art cheered people who were weighed down by war worries and the post-war fear of nuclear annihilation. Journalists and fans who drove to her farm for interviews found a vibrant, gladsome personality reminiscent of the stereotypical grandmother—gray-haired, bustling, purposeful, and glad for news to relieve her tedium.

At times, Grandma Moses's independence surfaced in her dislike of outside interference. Of publicity, she wrote: "I have too much of it, have very little time to myself any more, have about made up my mind to go to my room and lock myself in and see no one."[9] In her letters she compared clustering journalists to chickens waiting to be fed. When her agents sold her work for exorbitant prices and sent her a share of the money, in typical outspoken style she accused them of setting "extortion prices for some of those shopworn paintings."[10]

## From Mary to Grandma Moses

Hailed as the grande dame of American primitive art, as well as America's grandmother, Mary Moses was the subject of fifteen one-woman exhibitions, numerous traveling shows, and representation in 160 U.S. exhibitions, nine American museums, the Vienna State Gallery, and the Paris Museum of Modern Art. She received two honorary doctorates, a Women's National Press Club Award, and acclaim from New York's Governor Nelson Rockefeller, who twice proclaimed "Grandma Moses Day"—on September 7, 1960 and 1961, for her 100th and 101st birthdays. She was invited to lecture to some of the most prestigious art appreciators of her day. Her paintings, praised for their individualism, freshness, and authentic homespun quality, hung in the homes of Mrs. Albert D. Lasker and IBM magnate Thomas J. Watson, Jr.

Even with all the acclaim that came her way as well as the undeniable warmth that her work generated in the public, Grandma Moses never found a stable place with art critics, particularly Americans. Some labeled her work saccharine and sentimental and her style repetitive, limited, and uninspired. Others declared that, were she not a late-in-life success and the stereotypical rural New England grandmother, she would not have ranked among the other primitivists. In rebuttal, European voices lauded Grandma Moses's spontaneity and zest for life; one critic even ranked her with Henri Rousseau. Despite these contrasting responses to the phenomenon that was Grandma Moses, the value of her work spiraled; the public never stopped clamoring for more. Until the end of her strength, she produced two canvases per week at the old kitchen table she used for an easel and complained when damp weather impeded their drying and slowed her down.

## Fans and Admirers

Mary's work was patronized by the famous, including Cole Porter, Irving Berlin, Harry Truman, and Katharine Cornell; she was interviewed on television by Edward R. Murrow. One of her paintings was a gift purchased for President Eisenhower, who was himself a "Sunday painter" of primitive art. *Time* magazine lauded Grandma Moses for dispelling "the myth that art is the province of the wealthy and the eccentric."[11] Noted actress Lillian Gish portrayed her in a TV special. Cloris Leachman, aged by stage makeup, starred in a one-woman drama of Grandma Moses's life.

At the age of ninety-two, Mary Moses produced an autobiography, *My Life's History*. Her optimism countered post-war pessimism with a fresh and wholesome belief in American values and hope for humanity. She noted that Americans, with all their prosperity and modernity, had become a nation of worriers. To counter their preoccupation with petty fears, she summarized her philosophy very simply: "Just have faith, then you won't be wasting your years with worrying."[12]

Late in her career, she noted the importance of work to longevity. She felt that painting was good for her because it helped her relax and forget her cares. She commented on President Eisenhower's hobby: "I am glad that the president paints. It must take him away from his many worries."[13] When asked to pose with folded hands, Grandma Moses refused because such a pose was unnatural from one used to daily work.

On her 100th birthday, Mary Moses, unpretentious and frail in pink and black silk outfit, accepted the world's outpouring of love. An article in *Saturday Review* proclaimed: "In effect, this elderly lady becomes the shining champion of all grandmothers, giving them hope that, without special training, both talent and fame are possible at any time in life."[14] As Grandma herself summarized her achievements, "I will say that I have did remarkable for one of my years and experience."[15]

Grandma Moses's centennial was filled with adulation. From President Dwight Eisenhower came a message honoring "the abundant fruits of your work and spirit."[16] Surrounded by important visitors and bustling relatives, including three of her thirty great-grandchildren, Richard, Christine, and Stephen, Grandma Moses sat in a place of honor on the lawn and told them stories of the past century. But the fragility of her skin kept her indoors. As she explained, "... in the sun I get those freckle spots and they make ya look kinda old."[17]

Grandma continued working up until her death. She gradually decreased from six hours' painting per day to three, resting swollen joints by reading newspapers and watching TV westerns. Slowed by a bout with pneumonia in 1960, she got weekly treatment from her doctor. On December 13, 1961, Grandma Moses died a rich woman, due mostly to the wise handling of Grandma Moses Properties, Inc. In her autobiography, she reflected on her life: "Like a good day's work, it was done and I feel satisfied with it. I was happy and contented, I knew nothing better and made the best out of what life offered. And life is what we make it, always has been, always will be."[18]

## Notes

[1] "Presents from Grandma," *Time*, December 28, 1953, 41.

[2] "100 Candles for a Gay Lady," *Life*, September 19, 1960, 110.

[3] Tom Biracree. *Grandma Moses*. New York: Chelsea House, 1989, 31.

[4] Jane Kallir. *Grandma Moses: The Artist Behind the Myth*. New York: Clarkson N. Potter, 1982, 11.

[5] *Time*, 41.

[6] Katharine Kuh, "Grandma Moses," *Saturday Review*, May 10, 1960, 17.

[7] *Life*, 106.

[8] Jane Kallir, 18.

[9] Jane Kallir, 16.

[10] Jane Kallir, 16.

[11] Jane Kallir, 17.

[12] Jane Kallir, 24.

[13] "Grandma Moses," *Look*, November 13, 1956, 50.

[14] Kuh, 16.

[15] *Time*, 38.

[16] *Life*, 105.

[17] *Life*, 109.

[18] "The Little Old Lady of Eagle Bridge, New York," *Newsweek*, September 5, 1960, 70.

## Sources

Armstrong, William H. *Barefoot in the Grass: The Story of Grandma Moses.* Garden City, New York: Doubleday, 1971.

Biracree, Tom. *Grandma Moses.* New York: Chelsea House, 1989.

"Grandma Moses," *Look*, November 13, 1956, 124-125.

"Grandma Moses," *McCall's*, May 1960, 70.

"Grandma Moses by the Yard," *Look*, July 27, 1954, 48-49.

Graves, Charles. *Grandma Moses, Favorite Painter.* Champaign, Illinois: Gerrard Publishing, 1969.

Kallir, Jane. *Grandma Moses: The Artist Behind the Myth.* New York: Clarkson N. Potter, 1982.

Kallir, Otto. *Grandma Moses*. New York: New American Library, 1975.

Kramer, Nora, ed. *The Grandma Moses Storybook*. New York: Random House, 1961.

Kuh, Katharine, "Grandma Moses," *Saturday Review*, May 10, 1960, 16-17.

"The Little Old Lady of Eagle Bridge, New York," *Newsweek*, September 5, 1960, 70-71.

Moses, Anna Mary. *Grandma Moses: My Life's History*. New York: Harper & Brothers, 1958.

"100 Candles for a Gay Lady," *Life*, September 19, 1960, 104-112.

"Presents from Grandma," *Time*, December 28, 1953, 38-42.

Thompson, Dorothy. "The World of Grandma Moses," *Ladies' Home Journal*. January 1957, 11-12, 113.

# Carry Nation

One unusual achiever made a name for herself through violent acts aimed at public betterment. Carry Nation, national temperance symbol, suffered the misery of an alcoholic husband. Her life was so unpleasant that she sprang into action upon her husband's premature death and carried the anti-liquor message into the streets.

Caricatured in press and cartoon as a stereotypical battle-ax female, Nation, supported by her second husband and numerous disciples, ignored public ridicule, armed herself with a hatchet, and strode courageously into the fray. Her jubilant cry of "Peace on earth, goodwill to men" rang out. Like a latter-day Joan of Arc, she became an emblem of activist womanhood set on a collision course with demon rum.

## Early Times

Carry Nation was born Carry Amelia Moore to George and Mary Moore in Garrard County, Kentucky, on November 25, 1846. Her homeland, deceptively idyllic in its natural beauty, was a battleground of territorial disputes between Cherokees and Iroquois. White settlers, far from peace-loving, augmented the area's reputation with deep-fought clan feuds, some resulting from minor tiffs borne to bloody climax. The local religious atmosphere, given to tent meetings and revivals, was equally emotional and supplied local sanction to the public venting of private animosities and guilt.

The Moore family, including two boys born to Mary and her first husband, William Caldwell, were abstemious people. Carry's father neither drank nor smoked and reared his daughter to follow his example. To nourish the family's religious faith, George Moore led family hymn singing, prayer, and Bible reading. Throughout her life, Carry was understandably sustained by the image of her father as stalwart, dependable, and God-fearing.

In contrast to Carry's father, Mary Moore, like her mother, sister, and brothers, exhibited manic-depressive traits, spent extravagantly, exploded in violent displays of temper, then lapsed into severe withdrawal. Her condition reached a crisis with her delusion that she served Queen Victoria as lady-in-waiting. Mary's husband humored his deranged wife by agreeing to see her by appointment only and by ordering a carriage and liveried driver to ferry her about. For Carry, however, coexistence was not so easy. Until the age of five, she was farmed out to Grandma Moore and other relatives on occasions when her mother was unable to cope with reality.

Following her grandmother's death, Carry, lonely, sensitive to criticism, and abused, took refuge with slaves. Because of her impressionable age and tenuous psychological state, she internalized many of their attitudes and behaviors. She reacted to the fundamentalist religious message of her black surrogate mothers with fear, depression, vomiting, headaches, and hallucinations of heavenly visitations.

From early times, Carry, often overlooked by adults because of her plainness, exhibited an imperious streak. Peers recall that she was brazen, stubborn, and fearless, often cooking up willful behavior to get other children in trouble. One remarked, "I especially recall the martial spirit, and how she used to delight in assuming the role of a conqueror."[1]

## Coping with Adversity

Saddened and distressed by Mary's malady, George Moore decided to escape meddlers by moving to Danville in the next county. This was the first of a series of uprootings, which formed a pattern in Carry's life. In 1855, the family auctioned their furnishings and left the ten-room log plantation house on the Dix River. The move proved therapeutic; Mary returned to normalcy and conceived Edna, her second daughter. But Mary's recovery was short-lived. Once again beset by lunacy, she forced George to move on to Woodford County, where the cycle was repeated with Mary's recovery, the birth of a son, and a return to the maelstrom of madness.

Ultimately, the family moved to Belton, Missouri, a few miles south of Kansas City. Along the way, Carry, spurned and chastised by her raving mother, contracted fever and lay physically and psychologically ill throughout the tedious move. Years later she recalled the dismal journey. Left to suffer alone, she conjured up notions that her sins would damn her utterly.

## Redemption and Release

When the family arrived at their new home, Carry's condition worsened. Lonely and fearing that she was innately doomed, she accompanied her father to a revival. She acknowledged her imagined evil and consented to being baptized in an icy river. From the experience arose a new Carry, committed to salvaging souls following the same road to perdition that she imagined in her past. Her body healed and she grew to a hefty six feet.

The family, trapped in the controversy over free states versus slave, moved to Grayson County, Texas. On the arduous journey, fifteen-year-old Carry assumed a parental role with her siblings. The move failed to restore the family's finances. Broke and discouraged, George Moore returned to Belton through Confederate lines. The military then ordered the Moores to take shelter in Kansas City. Spurred by a love of reading, Carry briefly attended a boarding school in Liberty before returning with her family to Belton and working like a hireling to keep food on the table and clean clothes on their bodies.

## Marriage and a Challenge

When Carry came in contact with her first suitor, Union Army veteran Dr. Charles Gloyd, she responded eagerly to his flirtation. Against her father's objections to Gloyd's heavy drinking, Carry married him on November 21, 1867. Even at the altar, Gloyd faced daily life through an alcoholic fog. His nightly forays to the local tavern so terrified Carry that she assailed both front and back doors with her fists and pleaded with her husband to come home. During her pregnancy, she continued the pattern of scouring the neighborhood for Charles, to the amusement of the community. She soon earned a reputation as a sharp-tongued scold.

Because her domestic situation was destroying her health, George Moore retrieved his daughter during her final weeks of confinement. After the birth of Charlien, Carry returned to Charles long enough to collect her belongings and bid him farewell. He warned her that he would not last six months without her. True to his word, he died when Charlien was six months old. Overwhelmed by self-accusation, Carry returned to his widowed mother's house to work off her guilt.

She sold her husband's medical implements, built a three-room house for herself, her child, and her mother-in-law, and rented out the original dwelling. To supplement their income, she enrolled at the Normal Institute in Warrensburg, Missouri, and taught elementary school in Holden, around twenty miles from her parents' farm, set on land that is now part of Kansas City, Missouri.

## A Second Chance

At thirty, Carry lost her job after a minor disagreement with school author-ities over her insistence on local dialect in the classroom. Apprehensive at the thought of earning a living, she met good fortune in the person of newspaperman David A. Nation, a forty-nine-year-old widower and father of eight-year-old Lola. Their union was troubled from the start. David lost his job. He weighed the most likely alternatives, law, the ministry, or farming, opted for the latter and moved his family to a 1,700-acre spread in south Texas.

Failure at farming nudged David into law, his second failure. To stave off disaster, Carry accepted a job managing the Columbia Hotel. The work was grueling, but worse, she began suffering mental torment in fits of praying and nightmares. The added onus of her feeble-minded daughter's bout with typhoid and lockjaw caused Carry to reach a momentous conclusion. She believed that her child had been marked in the womb by Gloyd's alcoholism.

At thirty-five, Carry Nation, burdened by debt from her daughter's medical treatments, invested in a hotel near Houston. Not only did she throw herself into cooking and hotel maintenance, she also undertook a local ministry, including Sunday school and aid to the poor. Her reputation for miracles spread after she claimed to summon rain during a drought and reportedly stopped a fire that threatened to engulf the town. When Reconstruction-era violence drove the Nations from town, Carry took on a new hotel in Medicine Lodge, Kansas, where her husband began preaching at the First Christian Church.

Carry involved herself wholeheartedly in David's ministry, even scouring back alleys for miscreants and chastising them with her umbrella. So vehement did she become on the subjects of sin, alcohol, and sex, that she established a dual reputation for eccentric behavior and benevolence. She battled more guilt after the deaths of her mother and Mrs. Gloyd. Following a three-day basement marathon of prayer and Bible reading, Carry emerged with an answer to her mental and spiritual turmoil. She would challenge alcohol.

## A New Frontier

Launching a one-woman campaign, fifty-three-year-old Carry Nation accosted civic leaders and saloon owners in the streets. At the request of the tearful wife of a local drunkard, Nation, garbed in black, knelt at the entrance to an illegal bar and prayed aloud, crawling about on her knees and punctuating her imprecations with wags of her poke bonnet and jabs with her umbrella. Not only did the establishment close, but the owner was reduced to penury. Nation crowed with glee.

She augmented her victory by joining the local Women's Christian Temperance Union (WCTU), which she served as jail evangelist. Spurring her on to greater contempt for alcohol was the news that her daughter had fallen prey to drink. Nation's public performances, accompanied by the Baptist minister's wife on the hand organ, included the singing of her crusade anthem, "Who Hath Sorrow? Who Hath Woe?" After trouncing the town's whiskey joints, she took on the drugstores, which were sham fronts for the sale of liquor.

Nation's physical confrontations often led to violence, but she easily countered joint owners intimidated by her size and fervor. Eventually, her prowess came to the attention of the dealers who earned their living off liquor sales. Bootleggers and vandals terrorized her campaigns with rock throwing and threats to burn down her house. Nation, undaunted, rearmed the rock cache under her navy serge cloak and fought on. By 1900 she had transformed Medicine Lodge into a dry town and set her goals for greater glory through the rescue of the whole state of Kansas.

## Into the Political Realm

Nation's political savvy grew as she recognized that political campaigns obtained major support money from the liquor industry. Alone she mounted daily assaults in new territory with well-placed rocks, then dared officials to stop her. She turned the media to her advantage, placing local officials in a bad light for their refusal to enforce anti-liquor laws. They retaliated by taking her to court. Nation welcomed the public platform.

After the WCTU ousted her over philosophical differences, she fought with renewed zeal. She delivered fiery public sermons and carried her campaign to Wichita. At the end of her one-woman foray against a luxurious bar there, she was arrested. Singing hymns, she went willingly to jail, where she endured pointed gibes and sexual harassment. From her tiny cubicle she warned, "You have put me in here a cub, but I will come out roaring like a lion, and I will make all hell howl."[2] True to her word, in 1901 she relinquished rocks and clubs and adopted the hatchet. The resulting publicity was beneficial to her cause—Nation obtained the ear of the nation.

Donations and prayers poured out on her behalf. Church wardens joined the fray. City fathers, perplexed as to how to deal with the marauding female and her "hatchetations," considered invoking martial law.[3] In Enterprise, Kansas, prostitutes and wives of rumrunners attacked her in the streets. Rather than fight back, Nation applied an old formula: she started internal warfare, then retreated to let it work. By late January 1901 she was able to move on to Topeka, where she raised funds by selling miniature hatchets to passersby.

## Refining Techniques

Wherever Nation and her female hit squad invaded, they maintained a standard method of attack. Singing doxologies or militaristic hymns, they marched in step, paused to deliver spirited prayers and Bible verses, then delivered the challenge. Since saloon owners could not or would not comply with her orders to desist, she and other temperance warriors began swinging weapons, hatcheting barrels, slicing bar tops, smashing bottles and mirrors, and soaking themselves in the free flow of whiskey. If possible, they reduced every inch to shambles before submitting peaceably to arrest.

Buoyed by the growth of prohibitionism, the jailbirds made a mockery of male-dominated court proceedings, their aim being to connect the men of the court with debauchery in the minds of voters. Nation launched a speaking tour of Iowa and Illinois. Back in Topeka, she joined forces with publisher Nick Chiles and inaugurated a newsletter, *Smasher's Mail*.

## Spreading the Message

Disciples in Boston and New York began emulating Nation's style. Forces on both sides of the issue came to open warfare. But Nation was fighting on multiple fronts. The death of her brother as well as her crumbling relationship with David led her to enter an insanity plea in a Wichita court. The collapse of a stage in Indiana injured her ankle; David's request for a divorce was more telling. Still, she refused to slow down. Advancing on New York, the chief of sin dens, she countered a threat from boxer John L. Sullivan and cowed him in his quarters. Jubilant with victory, she delivered an anti-liquor harangue at Carnegie Hall and labeled President McKinley "the Brewers' President."[4]

The tide turned against her after McKinley's death. Because newspapers reported that Carry Nation was glad that the president had died at the hands of an assassin, lynch mobs formed and defamers hooted her down. To save herself, she returned in ignominy to Medicine Lodge. When the divorce was finalized on November 27, 1901, Nation's juggernaut began to lose steam. She tried to revitalize the message by addressing youthful audiences on college campuses, yet found herself the subject of ridicule.

To maximize successes, Nation studied acting and began writing a play, *War on Drink*. For similar reasons she started composing her memoirs, entitled *The Use and Need of the Life of Carry Nation*. She appeared on the stage in character, smashing saloons, and toured more states and parts of Canada. Still battling Charlien's alcoholism, Nation planned larger speaking tours to pay hospital expenses. She took her campaign to Washington, D.C., and then to England. As a means of holding down expenses, she stopped paying fines. Often courts forced her to scrub floors in workhouses.

## End of an Era

To renew her ebbing strength, Nation built a cabin in the Ozark Mountains. She continued a daunting schedule of speeches and public appearances, but her performance wavered, sometimes causing her to halt in mid-speech. While speaking in Eureka Spring, Arkansas, on January 13, 1911, she suffered a stroke. Her final words, "I have done what I could,"[5] were the last she spoke on a public stage. She lingered for five months in the Evergreen Hospital in Leavenworth, Kansas. After her death she was buried in Belton, Missouri, alongside her mother.

## Notes

[1] Arnold Madison. *Carry Nation.* New York: Thomas Nelson, 1977, 16.

[2] Madison, 94.

[3] Nachtigal, Jerry. "Booze Basher Carry Nation Steals the Show at Museum," *The Charlotte Observer*, November 23, 1990, 30A.

[4] Madison, 128.

[5] Madison, 152.

## Sources

Beals, Carleton. *Cyclone Carry.* Philadelphia: Chilton, 1962.

Lee, Henry. *How Dry We Were—Prohibition Revisited.* Englewood Cliffs, New Jersey: Prentice-Hall, 1963.

Madison, Arnold. *Carry Nation.* New York: Thomas Nelson, 1977.

Nachtigal, Jerry. "Booze Basher Carry Nation Steals the Show at Museum," *The Charlotte Observer*, November 23, 1990, 30A.

Taylor, Robert Lewis. *Vessel of Wrath.* New York: New American Library, 1966.

# Cardinal John Henry Newman

For achievers who alter their ambitions, the change may seem minor in terms of status. But sometimes, such alterations can be far-reaching in scope and significance and can affect whole nations. Such an about-face was theologian John Henry Newman's conversion from the Anglican faith to Roman Catholicism. He achieved prominence in his early career, serving as curate at Oxford and pamphleteer for the Oxford Movement. Later, he felt the need to separate himself from the liberal church practices he abhorred.

From 1843 to 1845, Newman withdrew from organized religion as he sorted out the direction his beliefs were leading. In October 1845, he pledged his loyalties through Father Dominic Barberi to the Catholic Church. He continued battling challenges to the faith and brought honor to his name, culminating in 1879 in Pope Leo XIII's naming him a cardinal at the age of seventy-eight. By the end of his life, Newman attained respectability in several fields, particularly logic, philosophy, theology, rhetoric, literature, and education, and was proclaimed the most influential churchman of the Victorian era.

## Early Religious Leanings

One of six children of John and Jemima Fourdrinier Newman, John Henry Newman was born in London on February 21, 1801. Because his father's banking career faltered during the financial lull that followed the Napoleonic era, Newman studied first at home and then at age seven at Ealing School. Much of his learning stemmed from a thorough reading of the Bible; but, except for learning catechism, he had no formal religious instruction until his mid-teens. He recalled later that he was an imaginative reader and a believer in magical powers. During his childhood, he wished that the Arabian Knights and other fanciful stories were true. Superstitious and fearful of the dark, he made the sign of the cross himself as a talisman against beings that might harm him, even though he had never come in contact with Catholic practices.

Newman described how his companions ridiculed their French schoolmasters for believing in Catholicism. In general, his community was almost totally free from Catholic influence. People who were practicing members of the faith refrained from demonstrating their beliefs in the face of so large an Anglican population. Years later, to Newman's surprise, he turned the pages of his childhood copybooks dating to 1811 and found scribbled on the first page a solid cross surrounded by a rope of beads. His only explanation for this drawing of a rosary was that he might have derived it from reading a novel or viewing a religious picture.

While attending services with his father at the Warwick Street Chapel, Newman registered little response beyond enjoying the music and observing the altar boy swinging a censer. By age fourteen, Newman's religious consciousness began to ripen. He read deeply. He perused tracts on mature subjects, particularly those that debated the importance of the Old Testament and miracles. He copied verses from Voltaire's essays on the immortality of the soul.

In August 1816 Newman underwent a dramatic change of heart toward matters of the spirit. Filled with a sense of divine presence, he declared, "I still am more certain [of it] than that I have hands and feet.... I considered myself predestined to salvation, I thought others simply passed over, not predestined to eternal death. I only thought of the mercy to myself."[1]

Influenced by the Calvinistic teachings of evangelist Daniel Wilson, the essays of Thomas Scott, and the Reverend George Nicholas, his teacher, Newman showed intense enthusiasm for religion and scholarship and enrolled at Trinity College, Oxford. It was during this period that he was converted to Christianity, which remained firm in his spirit throughout a long and productive life.

## First Career

A serious, sensitive, frail man, Newman discarded plans to study law and devoted himself to more pious pursuits. Dr. John Hawkins, Provost of Oriel College, Oxford, showered Newman with attention. The two exchanged hot words, but Hawkins taught his protégé to think before speaking and to exercise caution over his youthful urge to rebel. To Newman's dismay, Hawkins wrote severe critiques of his early attempts at sermon-writing.

A second influence on Newman was Dr. Richard Whately, a warm-hearted man who later became Archbishop of Dublin and, in collaboration with Newman, wrote a standard text on logic. Newman, still shy and gangly, responded to his kindly tutelage and learned to rely on reason. A warm intimacy formed between them during Newman's vice-principalship of Alban Hall, but later the two grew apart in philosophy. Whately accused Newman of moving toward Arian beliefs, which maintained that Jesus was of a different substance from God the Father.

Newman regretted that the relationship ended on so negative a note, but he realized that he had to accept responsibility for his opinions, which differed markedly from the tenor of the times. In the latter portion of his life, while composing his autobiography, he acknowledged that he had indeed been growing toward intellectualism to the exclusion of morality. He was becoming a liberal and was growing cocky about his influence on others.

Newman recalled how he established a reputation after preaching his first university sermon: "Next year I was one of the public examiners for the B.A. degree. It was to me like the feeling of spring weather after winter; and, if I may so speak, I came out of my shell; I remained out of it till 1841."[2]

## Early Advancement

As a fellow of Oriel from 1822 to 1843, Newman advanced from deacon to priest, was ordained in 1824, was appointed curate of St. Clement's Church, and subsequently undertook the same post at St. Mary's Church, Oxford, in 1828. His performance in the pulpit earned him praise for a sweet voice as well as eloquence and persuasion. He carried out scholarly duties as administrator and public examiner in classics and led the ranks of liberal Anglican churchmen as spokesman and evangelist. Unfortunately, all this activity resulted in his physical collapse at the age of twenty-five.

As Newman's conversion from liberalism to high church began to influence his writings, he assumed a key position in the Oxford Movement, an effort by religious thinkers to free the church of political control and other impurities of the faith and to return it to the simple faith of medieval Christians. Newman opposed the actions of the Bishop of London, who blatantly diluted the church's strongest traditions and replaced them with worldly practices and less emphasis on scripture.

During this era, Newman, usually so strong in his faith, suffered ambivalence. He remarked, "I felt affection for my own Church, but not tenderness; I felt dismay at her prospects, anger and scorn at her do-nothing perplexity. I thought that if Liberalism once got a footing within her, it was sure of the victory in the event."[3] In place of the church's slide toward governmental control, Newman advocated an elevation of the dignity of worship, particularly an emphasis on hymns, formal liturgy, architecture, missionary work, and the study of church history. Controversy raged over his moving sermons and the publication of *The Arians of the Fourth Century* (1833).

## The Reform Movement

As a spokesman for reform, Newman demonstrated remarkable powers of rhetoric and was recognized as an outstanding master of English prose. His writings, supple and fluid, influenced the majority of his contemporaries, both religious and non-religious, with their subtlety and force. Besides ponderous sermons and thought-provoking arguments, he wrote lyrical passages, two novels, an autobiography, history, reflective essays, satire, and humor. The whole of this multifaceted canon is contained in a forty-volume work published in 1921.

On a fact-finding journey to the Mediterranean in 1832, Newman joined a colleague, Richard Hurrell Froude, who was traveling to recover his health. It was Froude who first turned Newman's thinking toward the Church of Rome. The two men visited Gibraltar, Malta, Corfu, Naples, Rome, and Sicily, where Newman was downed by a life-threatening bout of fever at Leonforte.

Three weeks of inactivity gave him time for soul-searching. As he reports, he was at a crossroads in his allegiance to the Anglican Church, though at the time he could not foresee the end result of his discontent. He grasped only an intimation that God had important work for him to do.

Eager to return to England to begin a new mission, Newman waited impatiently and visited Sicilian churches to subdue his restlessness. Finally, he booked passage on a produce boat en route to Marseilles, but was stymied for a week in the Straits of Bonifacio waiting for wind to fill the sails. The upshot of his introspection while trying to reach the continent was the composition of "Lead, Kindly Light," a poem that developed into a popular hymn. The words proved prophetic of this segment of his life: "The night is dark, and I am far from home; Lead thou me on! Keep thou my feet: I do not ask to see the distant scene; one step enough for me."[4]

Overcome by fatigue after reaching France, he had to rest for a few days at Lyons before returning to his mother's house in England. There, in mid-July 1833, Newman's fervor was sparked by John Keble, the spirited religious rebel who preached on the fallacy of a state-directed church. More influential were a series of *Tracts for the Times*, which Newman and other reformers began composing in September. In these forceful and pointed documents, he outlined his plan for a revolution in Christian worship. The publication of *Tract XC*, in which Newman labeled the Thirty-nine Articles of the Church of England as more political than religious, led to a showdown.

The Bishop of Oxford forbade Newman to publish more tracts in this controversial vein. Newman's response to censorship evolved slowly over four years. Gradually, he chose the path of Keble. Together, the two men formed the nucleus of the Oxford Movement.

## A New Beginning

Because of his past record of strong opinions on religious matters, Newman's rise to the leadership of the Oxford Movement surprised no one. Through the controversial era from 1835 to 1839, his campaign of pamphlets met with strong dissent, as did his sermons at Oxford. In response to detractors, Newman felt himself drifting irrevocably toward Roman Catholicism. He retreated to Littlemore, a chapel of Saint Mary's Church, in 1842 and lived a semi-monastic life for over a year while he contemplated alternatives. During this period, church leaders on both sides of the Atlantic awaited his decision. At the age of forty-four, he indicated his choice by preaching a sermon entitled "The Parting of Friends" and resigned his fellowship at Oriel.

Newman, abandoning the role of intellectual leader of the Church of England, began at the bottom and studied for the priesthood. To express his views of the religious world, he published *The Development of Christian Doctrine* in 1845. That same year, Newman entered the Roman Catholic Church, received a doctor of divinity degree in 1846, and was ordained in Rome a year later.

## A Slow Start

Newman's next decade of work showed little promise of success or even direction. His position as religious turncoat was marked by suspicion and doubt on both sides of the controversy. He took part in several abortive projects, including the foundation of a school for boys, a house of prayer in Edgbaston near Birmingham, England, a Catholic university in Ireland, a new translation of the Bible, and editorship of *The Rambler*. He was sued for libel by G. G. Achilli and pled his case successfully, but still had to pay a £100 fine, which contributors from several nations underwrote. To rumors from both camps that he planned to drop Catholicism and return to the Anglican faith he stated a resounding no with his pamphlet entitled *The Present Position of Catholics in England*.

During this period, Newman completed one of his most appealing works, which established him as a significant voice in the educational realm. *The Idea of a University*, begun as a series of nine lectures for Dublin Catholics and published in 1852, supported purists who maintained the liberal arts as education's prime object. He delineated the holistic goals of a university as "true enlargement of mind which is the power of viewing many things at once as one whole, of referring them severally to their true place in the universal system, of understanding their respective values, and determining their mutual dependence."[5]

Throughout the treatise, he discarded educational systems that provided partial knowledge based on frivolous or contemporary notions. Above all other pursuits, he insisted that study should lead to a greater understanding of logic itself so that it might be applied to later acquisition of knowledge. He concluded, "A university is, according to the usual designation, an Alma Mater, knowing her children one by one, not a foundry, or a mint, or a treadmill."[6]

## Facing Opposition

But even this intellectual, non-sectarian achievement did not slow his critics, particularly novelist and clergyman Charles Kingsley, who questioned Newman's honesty in an article in the January 1864 issue of *Macmillan's Magazine*. At the age of sixty-three, Newman faced and refuted Kingsley's charges against his honor. His response took the form of an eloquent seven-part position paper published each Thursday from April 21 to June 2, 1864. The collected series appeared later as Newman's intellectual autobiography, *Apologia pro Vita Sua*, which justified his move to conservatism. Without wavering from his resolve, he declared: "I have had no variations to record, and have had no anxiety of heart whatever. I have been in perfect peace and contentment; I have never had one doubt.... It was like coming into port after a rough sea; and my happiness on that score remains to this day without interruption."[7]

His good name reaffirmed, Newman moved into the most fulfilling portion of his religious and literary career. In 1865 he published a collection of verse, *The Dream of Gerontius and Other Poems*. The central poem describes Gerontius, on the verge of death, as he reflects on his life. At the age of seventy Newman assembled his essays, arguments, and histories and published them in six volumes.

In 1870, he fell out of agreement with Cardinal Henry Manning. Their dispute, based on the question of the Pope's infallibility, resulted in Newman's loss of favor with the Vatican. To establish his position, Newman published *A Grammar of Assent*. The squabble ended nine years later when Pope Leo XIII offered Newman a promotion to cardinal, which the English populace perceived as a national honor.

Even though age sapped his strength, Newman continued to write and preach and to influence Christians. The motto on his coat of arms summarizes his appeal: "Cor ad cor loquitur" or "Heart speaks to heart."[8] His late years were filled with activities which had always interested him. He followed a regimen of self-denial, which served as a steady beacon to others. He died at Edgbaston on August 11, 1890. His epitaph summarized his vindication: "Ex umbris et imaginibus in veritatem" or "Out of shadows and appearances into truth."[9] His followers on both sides of the Atlantic initiated a move to have him canonized.

## Notes

[1] William E. Buckler, ed. *Prose of the Victorian Period*. Boston: Houghton Mifflin, 1958, 227.

[2] Buckler, 235.

[3] Buckler, 245.

[4] John Henry Newman. "Lead, Kindly Light," *The Hymnal of the United Church of Christ*. Philadelphia: United Church Press, 1969, 292.

[5] Buckler, 201.

[6] Buckler, 206-207.

[7] John K. Ryan. "John Henry Newman," *Encyclopedia Americana*, Volume 20. Danbury, Connecticut: Grolier, 1987, 274.

[8] Ryan, 274.

[9] Ryan, 284.

## Sources

Buckler, William E., ed. *Prose of the Victorian Period.* Boston: Houghton Mifflin, 1958.

Newman, John Henry. "Lead, Kindly Light," *The Hymnal of the United Church of Christ.* Philadelphia: United Church Press, 1969, 292.

Ryan, John K. "John Henry Newman," *Encyclopedia Americana*, Volume 20, Danbury, Connecticut: Grolier, 1987, 274.

# John Newton

In rare cases, a late-in-life change of heart can result in spiritual rebirth. Such an about-face produced a fireworks display of ardent enthusiasm in a man bowed down by the degradation of slavery. Shamed as a dealer in human cargo, John Newton, an English sea captain, left the hellish business of fueling southern plantations and dedicated himself as a preacher and composer of God's word.

In contrast with the musty writings of Church of England bishops, Newton turned to personal experience with sin as his primary text. Perhaps the most enduring product of Newton's faith was "Amazing Grace," one of the favorite Protestant hymns of the nineteenth century, still popular today. The forthright words illustrate Newton's strength as both sailor and minister—a full-spirited, masculine creativity. Newton, who became a candid, warm-hearted Christian minister, remained true to his principles throughout thirty-seven years in the pulpit.

## Early Influences

Born on July 24, 1725, to a devout mother and a moral, somewhat distant father of Spanish upbringing, John Newton faced challenges early in his youth. His mother, a fervent member of the Dissenters, who rejected the rigid structures of the Church of England, dreamed of seeing her son ordained into the ministry. She taught him to read when he was four, emphasizing prayer books, catechism, and the Bible. Her death in 1732 was a turning point in his life.

The boy, who struggled with secret sins, was a frequent discipline problem, especially to his stepmother. She sent him to boarding school, where he received formal education, mainly in classical Latin authors such as Cicero, Livy, and Virgil. But after two years of rigid control, he left school and never returned.

At the age of eleven Newton took passage with his father, a Mediterranean sea captain. During his adolescence, he struggled to reconcile lazy, amoral ways with the religious training he received from his mother. Well suited to the life at sea, Newton came under the influence of the third Earl of Shaftesbury, an eighteenth-century moralist who wrote a plea for deism, a rational religious belief that put faith in natural morality rather than an externally motivated fear of hell and retribution. Instead of being humble or contrite, Newton became cocky and adept at blaspheming and cursing. At fifteen, he received a job offer in Alicant, Spain, but lost it because of erratic and unruly behavior.

At seventeen, Newton, while visiting friends of his mother in Maidstone, Kent, fell in love with his ideal, a fourteen-year-old girl named Mary Catlett, whom he often visited. So taken was he with Mary that he avoided a proposed trip to Jamaica by staying away from his ship for three weeks until it had sailed. Later, he served a brief stint in the British navy after being forcibly impressed on a tender in 1743.

During a period of increased tension between France and England, Newton transferred to the *Harwich*. But his first encounters with military life aboard a man-of-war did not agree with him. His father intervened in his enlistment. Unable to obtain his release, he had his son classified a midshipman.

While in officer's training, Newton deserted ship in Plymouth, England, and paid the penalty when he was caught. He was broken to the rank of common sailor and suffered a public whipping in irons, a personal catastrophe that hardened his heart. He was so low in spirits about being parted from Mary that he considered killing the captain of the ship. Instead, he was transferred to a ship bound for Guinea and lived for a time on the west coast of Africa.

## From Cadet to Slaver

Rebellious, defiant, and angry at the world, Newton responded to his humiliation by adopting an even lower form of behavior—he signed on with a white slaver off the coast of Sierra Leone, Africa. In his words, "There I could be as abandoned as I pleased without any control."[1] For fifteen months, he endured poor rations, illness, ragged clothes, and the mistreatment of the slave-ship owner's black wife. As overseer above stinking holds filled with Africans bound for the New World, John Newton prowled the upper decks, whip and pistol in hand to protect himself from revolts or treachery by the crew.

Slave vessels of the late eighteenth century were foul hellholes, not only for the human cargo, but also the crew. Holding up to 600 victims, bound hand and foot as close as they could be stored, the ships seldom reached shore with half the original number of Africans alive. Many crazed and wretched slaves leaped over-board or killed each other in savage, senseless fights. Others died of communicable disease or dehydration. Some crewmen were executed as fomenters of shipboard intrigue.

Slaving vessels like Newton's were so distasteful to other captains that they were not allowed berth in public wharves because of the stench and danger of contagion. Dealers conducted much of the slave trade at sea by night, away from witnesses and abolitionist controversy. Often, slaver captains sailed under assumed names to hide their role in the hated trade.

## A Change of Heart

Rescued by another sea captain, a family friend, Newton made a long voyage to Brazil, aboard a trader carrying precious metals, ivory, dyer's-wood, and wax. Embittered by his experiences, he pored over a Latin devotional text, *The Imitation of Christ*. The book, written in the fifteenth century and ascribed to St. Thomas à Kempis, a German theologian, gained worldwide fame for its practical advice for people who want to live by Christ's example. The book suggested some ways that Newton could shrug off worldly behavior and prepare for an afterlife. It also explained how to uphold the Christian cause and clarified how Newton could acquire sincerity and commune with Christ through prayer.

The crowning moment in John Newton's conversion came during a storm. The churning of waves and the roll of the ship threatened him and others on board with watery destruction. Ironically, Newton feared drowning because he never learned to swim. At one point, he manned the pumps from the wee hours of the morning until noon. Food spoiled or washed overboard, leaving the crew without provisions for four weeks, except for what fish they could catch. Before reaching Ireland, one man on board died from the wretched conditions.

When the storm passed, Newton realized that he had undergone a sincere religious experience. He found a room at the home of an Irish family and began attending church. He wrote to his father, who feared that John had died. The letter arrived after his father had taken a position as governor of York Fort in Hudson's Bay, Canada. John Newton and his father never saw each other again.

## New Directions

Before leaving, Newton's father gave permission for John to marry Mary. Following a second long voyage to Sierra Leone, Newton returned to England, went directly to Kent, and married his sweetheart on February 1, 1742. Throughout his sailing career, Newton wrote her regularly and mailed his letters en masse when he was in port. They adopted a daughter, Elizabeth Catlett. John and Mary remained devoted to each other until her death from breast cancer on December 15, 1790.

To occupy his restless, inquisitive mind during voyages, Newton taught himself Latin and French. He read widely, drew geometry proofs in the sand, and studied math books he bought while he was in port. He longed to be a classical scholar. Eventually, his diligence and devotion to duty were rewarded with control of his own ship, which he commanded for six years. He displayed an unusual amount of compassion toward blacks bound for auction and led his thirty-man crew in worship twice each Sunday.

In 1748, Newton knew in body and soul that he was dedicating himself to a rampant evil. Sick to the marrow and truly sorrowful for his involvement in the slave trade, he departed the old windjammer in Southampton, England, resigned his captaincy, returned to his wife, and studied for the ministry. Because of his limited formal education, such a change of profession required sixteen years of preparation. To support his family, he worked as tide surveyor for the port of Liverpool. Meanwhile, he studied Hebrew, Syriac, and Greek under John Wesley and others of the grass-roots Nonconformist movement.

During the period from 1750 to 1754, Newton kept a journal of his spiritual growth. At the urging of others to preserve his experiences as well as to express his intent for a new life, he wrote a confessional autobiography, *An Authentic Narrative*, in 1764. The work depicts the horrors of the slave trade, particularly John Newton's role in it.

## Ordained at Last

At first, the church hierarchy passed over Newton's request for a church. Then, with the aid of Lord Dartmouth, he found favor with the Bishop of Lincoln, who granted him a vicarage. At the age of forty-one, Newton received his first church in Olney, Buckinghamshire, England, a small market town southeast of Northampton. He and his wife devoted themselves to the growing revival movement, which revitalized evangelical spirit during Newton's lifetime.

This soulful, energetic era was marked by prayer meetings, pastoral visits, and preaching. Still clinging to his persona as a seafarer, Newton harangued farmer, tanner, and woodworker alike as children of God in danger of perdition. Against mockers of his emotional outpourings he wrote: "Let the world deride or pity, I will glory in Thy name."[2] Common folk flocked to hear Newton unburden himself of his wicked past. Church wardens had to add a balcony to the building to hold overflow audiences.

Not only did Newton preach in church, he also acquired a large manor from Lord Dartmouth and conducted smaller, more personal religious gatherings. He taught religion and the Bible to local children by day and to adults at night. Chief among his educational aids were hymns. When he failed to locate the exact hymn to suit his purpose, he began writing his own.

Six years after establishing residency and learning how to manage congregational needs, Newton sent for his neighbor, William Cowper, famed English poet, and Mrs. Mary Susannah Unwin, widow of Morley Unwin, an elderly Evangelical pastor. Cowper befriended Mrs. Unwin and moved her family to Orchard Side, his home near the Market Place in Olney, which is today a public garden and museum. There he participated in the evangelical center that Newton had founded.

Newton had his most productive years at Olney. He published *Sermons* (1760), *Omicron* (1762), *Narrative* (1767), *Review of Ecclesiastical History* (1769), *Omicron's Letters* (1774), and *Cardiphonia* (1781). The latter work attests to his close friendships with other Dissenters and his dedication to letter-writing as a means of uplifting their spirits and guiding their paths. He collaborated with Cowper on a major endeavor, *Olney Hymns* (1779), a book of instructional revival hymns published when Newton was fifty-four.

## "Amazing Grace"

Of these hymns, sixty-eight resulted from the poetic genius of Cowper, a revolutionary forerunner of the English romantic school of writers. Notable among them are "God Moves in a Mysterious Way" and "O, For a Closer Walk with God." The verses emphasize the need for atonement and realignment with godliness. Newton opened with a preface dedicating the hymnal to religious education. He added his own touches, including "Glorious Things of Thee Are Spoken," "How Sweet the Name of Jesus Sounds," and a memorable benediction, "May the Grace of Christ, Our Saviour."

But the jewel of the collection was John Newton's four-stanza hymn "Amazing Grace," now a Protestant staple. It reflects much of the writer's self-abnegation as a result of his part in slavery. Like his emotional, first-person sermons, the hymn relies on Newton's experiences for its sincere message. Beginning with a verse about his wretchedness prior to conversion, the hymn lauds grace as a relief from fear. The concluding stanza remarks on Newton's belief that his state of grace was eternal. He exulted: "We've no less days to sing God's praise/Than when we first begun."[3]

In all, 281 hymns are credited to Newton. Because of Cowper's mental breakdown, Newton completed the work alone, thereby emphasizing his own religious agenda over Cowper's. He divided the book into three parts. Part I centers on scriptural texts used to end a sermon or illustrate talks about characters from the Bible. Part II responds to seasonal needs, such as Lent, Advent, and Pentecost. Part III, the most emotional of the sections, features the individual's struggle to find and maintain faith.

The subjects of these noble, dignified hymns touch on familiar themes in Christian religion—mercy, conflict, the Gospels, Holy Communion, confidence, belief, forgiveness, redemption, prayer, and peace. Most are written from the first person point of view. All demonstrate an intimate knowledge and understanding of biblical teachings. They were repeatedly published and extracted in England and America for hundreds of years. In time, most of Christendom knew of the Olney hymns and incorporated them in worship and Christian education.

## Later Evangelism

Cowper assisted Newton with his Sunday School and joined in parish work. The relationship between Cowper and Newton was made more reciprocal by the help that Newton rendered to his mentor. When Cowper fell ill with depression and mental instability, Newton moved him to the rectory. Newton reassured Cowper that God would accept his confessions and pleas for forgiveness. He convinced Cowper that he was not doomed to a fiery afterlife in hell. After Cowper recovered his sanity and began caring for himself, he rejoined Newton's parish outreach.

Newton held his post as curate at Olney until 1780. For the next twenty-seven years, he served as vicar of the united parishes of St. Mary Woolnoth on King William Street and St. Mary Woolchurch Haw on Lombard Street, London, a wealthy neighborhood quite different from Olney's country congregation. He cut an impressive figure with his captain's uniform and cane as he strode about the pulpit, read from his Bible, and admonished his parishioners about the state of their souls. A significant portion of his sermons he devoted to the spiritual nature of humankind, particularly the interpretation of dreams.

Newton's texts were narrow and his judgments harsh. At one point, he castigated Handel for basing his *Messiah* on scriptural passages. Another sore point with Newton was the deathbed confessions of sinners who had led profligate lives. Against such eleventh-hour conversions he railed: "Tell me not how the man died, but how he lived."[4] Two years before the end of his career, friends pressured him to retire because of blindness and failing hearing and memory. To them he roared, "What, shall the old African blasphemer stop while he can speak!"[5]

Still in service to the Anglican Church at the age of eighty-two, Newton died on December 21, 1807. That year also marked the end of slavery in the British Empire through a bill initiated by William Wilberforce, one of Newton's converts. Newton was buried alongside his wife at St. Mary Woolnoth. In 1893, his body was removed to the Olney church on the banks of the Ouse River, where a memorial still stands summarizing his achievements. In London, a simple inscription in St. Mary Woolnoth Church memorializes the services of John Newton, Clerk. The dedication reads: "Once an infidel and libertine; a servant of slaves in Africa was by the rich mercy of our Lord and Saviour Jesus Christ, preserved, restored, pardoned, and appointed to preach the faith he had long laboured to destroy."[6]

## Notes

[1] Albert Edward Bailey. *The Gospel in Hymns.* New York: Charles Scribner's Sons, 1950, 124.

[2] Cecil Northcott. *Hymns We Love.* Philadelphia: Westminster Press, 1954, 118.

[3] Clint Bonner. *A Hymn Is Born.* Chicago: Wilcox & Follett, 1952, 19.

[4] Northcott, 118.

[5] John Julian. *A Dictionary of Hymnology.* New York: Dover, 1957, 803.

[6] Bailey, 127.

## Sources

Bailey, Albert Edward. *The Gospel in Hymns.* New York: Charles Scribner's Sons, 1950, 123-130.

Bonner, Clint. *A Hymn Is Born.* Chicago: Wilcox & Follett, 1952, 18-19.

Demaray, Donald E. *The Innovation of John Newton, 1725-1807: Synergism of Word and Music in Eighteenth Century Evangelism.* Lewiston, New York: E. Mellen, 1988.

Guerlac, Henry. *Newton on the Continent.* Ithaca, New York: Cornell University Press, 1981.

Julian, John. *A Dictionary of Hymnology.* New York: Dover, 1957.

Newton, John. *Letters of a Slave Trader,* paraphrased by Dick Bohrer. Chicago: Moody Press, 1983.

Northcott, Cecil. *Hymns We Love.* Philadelphia: Westminster Press, 1954, 116-119.

Pollock, John. *Amazing Grace: The Dramatic Life Story of John Newton.* New York: Harper & Row, 1983.

# Ronald Wilson Reagan

Ronald Reagan, unlike other late achievers, was never a genuine under-achiever. Rather, he is a model of achievement heaped upon achievement. From sports, acting, and radio to governor of California to two-term president of the United States, he advanced along the trail of accomplishment. But it was his blend of talents turned to new uses that placed him among other late achievers. As the oldest contender and first actor to win the American presidency, he set two precedents at once.

Critics were at first kind to Reagan, a congenial, non-threatening personality whom the media named the "Great Communicator" and lauded for his affability and charm. At his height, he garnered two-thirds of the vote in popularity polls. On the down side, after his departure from the White House, his eight years in Washington, when viewed in retrospect, proved less than admirable. But overall, Americans professed love and respect for their fortieth President, who retired with honor and remained relatively free from scandal throughout his political career.

## Typical American Beginnings

Ronald Reagan can claim one of the standard American ancestries—genea-logical linkage to poorly educated working class grandparents, Scotch-Irish immigrants who farmed their plot in the Midwest. The second son of John Edward "Jack" and Nelle Wilson Reagan, Ronald was born on February 6, 1911, in Tampico, Illinois. He enjoyed a normal boyhood and was a constant com-panion to his brother Neil.

Of his family's social status, Reagan says, "We didn't live on the wrong side of the tracks, but we lived so close to them we could hear the whistle real loud."[1] The Reagans resided above Pitney Store, a variety store on Main Street where his father clerked and sold shoes. Reagan was influenced by his parents' small-town ideology, his father's tippling, and his mother's cheer, encouragement, and religious faith. A familiar scene to the two Reagan boys was the return of Jack Reagan from a speakeasy and his mother's efforts to get him to bed without degrading the man before his sons.

Reagan, nicknamed "Dutch" by his father because he resembled a chubby Dutchman, drew upon the example set by his mother, who incorporated charity into her daily affairs as naturally as cooking or sewing. From her he learned self-reliance, faith in democracy, and a belief in the work ethic. The family, relying on Jack Reagan's search for a way to make a living, never acquired middle-class comforts. At age two, Ronald moved with his family to Chicago; when he was nine, the Reagans moved to Dixon, Illinois, where he attended Dixon High School, immersed himself in sports, took part in plays, and served as art editor of the yearbook and student body president. Outside school he earned spending money by lifeguarding.

He chose Eureka, a small Christian liberal arts college, to prepare him for a career and earned a $180-a-year athletic scholarship to help pay expenses. Other jobs included dishwashing at the Tau Kappa Epsilon house and teaching swimming. Not scholarly by nature, Reagan did well in school, played football, and served as class president. At nineteen, he demonstrated an interest in politics for the first time while leading a protest against school budget cuts. His major accomplishments were in theater, where he earned an award for his role as a shepherd in Edna St. Vincent Millay's *Aria Da Capo*, presented at an annual Northwestern University drama festival.

## Hard Times

While Ronald and Neil attended college, the Depression put strains on the Reagan family. After losing Reagan's Fashion Boot Shop, Jack Reagan slid into unemployment from a series of economic disasters. By 1931, Ronald and his mother were supporting the family with his campus jobs and her $14 per week earned by making alterations in a dress shop. Jack, who never gave up, took any temporary work he could find.

Reagan willingly shouldered any jobs that would keep his family afloat financially and bring him closer to graduation, which he achieved after eight years of working and going to classes. He also wangled a deal with college officials to accept Neil without tuition, which he agreed to pay after graduation. During these difficult years, Reagan championed the recovery efforts of his hero, President Franklin D. Roosevelt, who buoyed flagging spirits across the nation during his regular radio "Fireside Chats." Mugging from an early age, Reagan gave believable imitations of FDR, complete with cigarette holder. In his later speeches, analysts found strong traces of FDR in Reagan's tone, style, and content.

Reagan's former drama coach, B. J. Frazier, urged him to follow his star. He moved from radio sportscaster at WOC in Davenport, Iowa, to discovery by Warner Brothers in 1937 during a stint in Catalina. This led to his first film role in *Love Is On the Air*. His discoverer labeled him another Robert Taylor; Reagan more modestly called himself the "Errol Flynn of the B's."[2] After parts in *Brother Rat* and *Dark Victory*, he achieved memorable successes as George Gipp in *Knute Rockne—All American* in 1940 and Drake McHugh in *Kings Row* the next year.

# Mr. Average

Reagan's personal and professional life followed a respectable course. He thought of himself as average and even adopted the soubriquet of Mr. Norm. He married actress Jane Wyman on January 26, 1940. Their marriage produced daughter Maureen Elizabeth in 1941. The prosperous little family built an eight-room house outside Hollywood; in 1945, after failing to conceive more children, Ron and Jane adopted son Michael Edward in 1947. That same year, a second pregnancy produced another daughter who died the day of her birth.

The idyllic marriage ended in divorce in 1949, in part because of Jane's success with the movie *Johnny Belinda* and her objection to Ron's increased political involvement. The couple parted amicably. Jane received custody of the children as well as visitation rights to their Northridge horse farm, "Yearling Row."

Reagan had served in the U.S. cavalry reserve from 1942 to 1945, making training films. He was kept out of combat because of poor vision. He returned to the commercial screen in *The Voice of the Turtle, The Winning Team, Bedtime for Bonzo, Hellcats of the Navy,* and *The Killers,* a Universal picture adapted from Ernest Hemingway's short story. By the end of this acting career, he had played in fifty-two films and served as chairman of the Motion Picture Industry Council.

Some observers credit much of Reagan's later success to Nancy Davis, a former costar whom he married on March 4, 1952. Their marriage produced two children—Patricia Ann (Patti), a writer who goes by her mother's maiden surname, in 1952, and Ronald Prescott (Ron), Jr., a professional dancer, in 1958. Later criticism about Nancy Reagan's manipulation of his career through a fortuneteller cast doubt that Reagan was as strong a leader as his public image conveyed.

# A Shift of Values

Between the late 1940s and 1960, while serving six terms as president of the Screen Actors' Guild, Reagan experienced a complete shift in his political thinking. Influenced from childhood by his mother's altruism as well as FDR's public works projects, he had strongly championed the Democratic point of view. Then a reevaluation of the free enterprise system while conducting union negotiations led him toward conservative politics. As a collaborator in the blacklisting of communists in the film industry, and as representative of General Electric on their weekly television show, he began to speak out for the free market system and against communism. He opposed the income tax and controls on business.

During a three-year position as host of *Death Valley Days* on television, he formally allied himself with the Republican party and gave persuasive speeches for Barry Goldwater. His political career, undergirded by years at the microphone, stints of memorizing scripts, and the savvy that comes from connecting with audiences, took off in the mid-1960s with the "Friends of Ronald Reagan" movement to elect Reagan governor of California.

Pitted against a complacent liberal incumbent, Governor Edmund "Pat" Brown, Reagan seemed destined for defeat. Brown, who underestimated his opponent's charisma, dismissed him as an over-the-hill actor too inexperienced in politics to be a threat. Reagan, sure of himself and his ideals, pumped energy and personal dynamism into a one-note campaign pegged on a return to patriotism. The ploy worked, netting him a million more votes than his adversary. In four years, he did it again, this time against Jesse Unruh.

Reagan surprised even his backers. Confronted by the obstinacy of a Democratic legislature, he applied logic to political compromise and made real inroads against anarchy at state colleges and universities during the height of the anti-war movement. He trimmed back phenomenal costs that were threatening to engulf California's budget. By the early 1970s, the tidy coffers that he had filled with tax monies, along with restraint in public spending, resulted in hefty tax savings for his constituents. By reforming the grotesquely swollen California welfare system, he lopped thousands of so-called cheaters off welfare rolls, channeling the savings to people he termed the "truly needy."

## Bigger and Better Things

The road to the White House was long for Reagan. The post-Watergate years slowed his progress, as did two unsuccessful attempts to gain his party's nomination, but by 1980, his skillful, painstaking preparation paid off. Part of the success Reagan owed to his choices of William Casey and Edwin Meese as campaign organizers and George Bush as running mate. Another factor was Reagan's deft wooing of independents, conservative students, and right-wing religious groups.

That year, Reagan was virtually unopposed by other members of the Republican party and ran on a tightly conservative platform. His public appearances netted him a consistently favorable showing, owing to his rugged good looks, softly persuasive voice, and positive pragmatism. From the beginning, his hard line on civil preparedness, women's rights, abortion, school desegregation, and welfare alienated him from liberal elements and the press. But the times were right for his message. Voters identified with his get-tough stance and gladly threw over Jimmy Carter, giving Reagan 51 percent of the popular vote.

Swiftly moving to the aid of big business, Reagan earned a reputation for featherbedding the economy in favor of his millionaire friends. On the other hand, for the average American, his "Reaganomics" stood for lower taxes and interest rates and lessened involvement at the federal level.

With the return of American hostages from Iran shortly after his inauguration, Reagan moved into the people's hearts. Throughout his presidency, even in dark times, Reagan maintained his popularity. He manipulated the economy heavily on the supply side and attempted to balance the budget within four years, but his hard-nosed support of the Pentagon, the "Star Wars" missile defense system, and a militaristic stance against communism kept him in the red.

## A Chance Encounter

Then came the unexpected events of March 30, 1981. Reagan was shot by John W. Hinckley, Jr., a crazed gunman, and fell to the sidewalk outside the Washington Hilton Hotel. But the bullet wound in his lung healed cleanly, leaving Reagan strong not only physically but politically, for the public embraced him upon his return to the Oval Office on April 28.

Vigorous and ebullient in the face of concern for his advancing years, Reagan at seventy-three took on Walter Mondale in a second bid for the presidency. In this phase of his career, Reagan found the times in his favor. His popularity—and the economy—held firm for an even larger victory at the polls than his first election. With 525 electoral votes, he swept into his second term as the presidential candidate with the greatest support in American history.

Reagan's budget was less successful. Unemployment rose as recession gripped the economy. To set money matters back in order, Reagan opted for elevated taxes and more budget cuts, particularly in Medicare. His conservative stance found favor with one of his chief international supporters, Margaret Thatcher, the "iron lady" Prime Minister of England. He furthered his conservative purpose by trouncing a strike by air traffic controllers, yet offset a negative image with feminists by selecting Sandra Day O'Connor as the first woman to serve the Supreme Court. On the home front, he suffered embarrassment when his daughter Maureen sparred with his conservatism by supporting feminist issues, but carping by the press failed to deflate him.

In the foreign arena, Reagan traveled, shook hands, smiled, ate jelly beans, and gave photo opportunities. In the background, however, he remained tough on the nations he perceived as America's enemies. Never wishy-washy on matters of philosophy, he supported right-wing politics in El Salvador, tried to bring peace to the Mideast, and sent Marines to quell armed aggression in Lebanon. His pre-dawn invasion of Grenada in October 1983 brought cheers from hawkish supporters, but jeers from doves who insisted that such deployment was egregious grandstanding.

On the other hand, the public sided with his stiffened policies against the terrorism of Libyan strong man Muammar Qaddafi. Following the hijacking of a TWA flight and murder aboard the Italian cruiseship *Achille Lauro*, Reagan indicated to the Mideast world that he had had enough. In April 1986 he sent Air Force jets on a deadly strike at Qaddafi's Tripoli headquarters.

## Winding Down

The last years of Reagan's presidency brought the usual shifting of loyalties, cabinet changes, and realignment of ideology. White House support for old friend Ferdinand Marcos created difficult choices. After elections ended his regime, Marcos, under Reagan's protection, flew to a permanent residence in Hawaii. Apartheid required a firmer American response. Reagan, loath to interfere in business, gave grudging order to impose sanctions against racist white control.

To stave off fatigue, Reagan repaired often to his Rancho del Cielo in Santa Barbara, California, where he rode horseback and enjoyed a rustic lifestyle. He continued reading the popular conservative press, speaking directly to the American public through his weekly radio addresses, and smiling for the cameras. Always at his side was his wife, a necessary adjunct to his image as family man.

At the end of his second term, Reagan made a graceful exit. He earned praise from liberals by switching his stance on the AIDS issue and making a televised appeal for public support of AIDS research. Still popular with his fans, he avoided too strong a link with the Oliver North and savings-and-loan scandals by pleading diminished memory. However, so long as his impressive six-foot-one frame remained trim and agile, Americans refused to believe that he was succumbing to advancing age, even when with much hoopla he celebrated his eightieth birthday.

## A Memorable Figure

Reagan achieved for himself a memorable spot in the lineup of American presidents. Even though he miscalculated many details, his creation of a decentralized, scaled-down bureaucracy and a lessened tax burden brought him immense popularity. His identification with home and church issues made him the darling of conservative religious groups. His laid-back "aw shucks" style furthered general acceptance, even from his enemies. During his meetings with Russian President Mikhail Gorbachev he created the illusion that President Reagan could do no political wrong.

Reagan departed the White House and blended back into public life as pleasantly as he had emerged from it. His follower, President George Bush, kept the legend alive with continued adulation for Reagan's accomplishments. People no longer thought of him as an actor-turned-President. To most Americans, he represented firmness abroad and control at home, the perfect blend of pragmatic leader and ideal citizen.

## Notes

[1] Lou Cannon. *Reagan.* New York: G. P. Putnam's Sons, 1982, 22.

[2] Cannon, 52.

## Sources

Auth, Tony. *Lost in Space: The Reagan Years.* New York: Andrews & McMeel, 1988.

Boyarsky, Bill. *The Rise of Ronald Reagan.* New York: Random House, 1968.

Cannon, Lou. *Reagan.* New York: G. P. Putnam's Sons, 1982.

*Current Biography.* Detroit: Gale Research, 1982.

Powell, Dwane. *The Reagan Chronicles: A Cartoon Carnival.* New York: Algonquin Books, 1987.

Speakes, Larry, and Robert Pack. *Speaking Out: The Reagan Presidency from Inside the White House.* New York: Scribner, 1988.

# J. I. Rodale

Steeped in the elements of their respective milieus, some achievers experience visions of things to come. One of these, counterculturist and organic food evangelist Jerome Irving Rodale, suffered the ridicule of people with less awareness of the future until he began convincing people that what he foresaw was indeed taking place. According to Rodale, humanity was violating nature when it would do well to study and emulate her methods.

Called by *Newsweek* the "Don Quixote of the compost heap," Rodale founded an organization dedicated to natural farming methods, improvement of the environment, and betterment of health.[1] He added the term "organic food" to the language, meaning food—whether meat, fish, vegetable, grain or fruit—raised or produced without poisonous inorganic chemicals. His best-selling magazines, *Prevention* and *Organic Gardening*, have surpassed the million mark in circulation and have influenced the diets, gardening methods, and outlooks of millions of people worldwide.

As a propagandist, Rodale, pictured frequently in his publications with professorial beard, conservative suit, graying hair, and glasses, turned the world's attention to encroachment of pollution and its resultant poisoning of the environment. Rodale Press, his publishing firm, produced a cascade of brochures, pamphlets, books, and newsletters, from "How to Eat for a Healthy Heart" to "Pure Air Can Be Found—in Bottles," from *The Complete Book of Composting* to *Happy People Rarely Get Cancer*. Riding the crest of earth consciousness and the move back to nature and communal living, his cult quickly expanded into a viable audience. Unlike most philosophers, Rodale capitalized on his public image, sold organic products by mail, carried his message to foreign shores, and created a mini-empire dedicated to the strengthening of humanity primarily through the production of untainted food.

## City Boy

Rodale's background gives little hint of his later specialization in gardens and the production of pure food. The son of Michael and Bertha Rouda Cohen, he was born on August 16, 1898, in an established Polish-Jewish neighborhood near

196

Norfolk and Grand Streets on New York City's Lower East Side, where his father was a grocer. The area's street language and self-denigrating humor remained with him throughout his life and emerged in his retelling of anecdotes and funny stories.

His background was a mix of old country mores and New World enthusiasms. He grew up in a tenement and, even though he familiarized himself with fresh produce, he had little contact with the farmland on which it was grown. His only contact with gardening was a meager collection of plants in clay pots on the fire escape outside his window.

Jerome was the smallest and least promising of eight children. Overmothered by a woman who insisted on nursing her son well past the toddler stage, he was a weakling from an early age and suffered a plague of hypochondriacal ailments, including colds, vertigo, nightmares, and headaches. He was severely nearsighted and never excelled in the physical activities common to boys his age. When he was seven, he entered a Jewish school, where the schoolmaster whipped him to encourage his Hebrew and Talmudic studies. From this era of religious orthodoxy he absorbed the stringent dietary laws that later colored his attitudes toward food and purity.

As a teenager, Jerome was far removed from the alfalfa sprouts, herb tea, brown rice, and soybeans of his mature years. He developed more predictable adolescent vices. He kept late hours, visited honky-tonks with his pals, and smoked cigars. To build up his physique, he ordered body-building aids through the mail.

He studied accounting in night school at New York and Columbia universities and landed a job as an auditor for the Internal Revenue Service in 1919. The next year he joined Robertson, Furman, and Murphy, an accounting firm, which made him a partner. About that time he altered his last name from Cohen to Rodale. In 1923 he and his brother Joe opened a factory making electrical wiring devices. The business barely weathered the onset of the Depression. In 1930, Rodale saved it from extinction by moving the operation to the lush, fertile highlands outside Emmaus, Pennsylvania.

To Rodale's dismay, the entrepreneurial realm failed to excite his imagination, which secretly longed for public expression through writing, humor, and the theater. For a time he entertained the notion of going into vaudeville or writing plays for a living. He tackled the problem of diction and produced the *Verb-Finder*, which in a later edition was named *The Word-Finder*. In 1930, while still maintaining the electronic business, he began publishing two magazines, *Fact Digest* and *Health Guide*.

## An Awakening

In 1941, Rodale came under the influence of the writings of Sir Albert Howard, British agriculturist and soil biologist who championed the cause of natural farming methods, particularly composting. Rodale established a correspondence with his mentor, then launched an American version of Howard's dynamic crusade. Rodale railed against soil laced with chemical fertilizers and also attacked the dangers of fluoridation, food additives, pesticides, herbicides, smog, tea, coffee, refined sugar, wheat flour, tobacco smoke, aspirin, plastic, aluminum, as well as certain forms of food packaging and processing.

Applying the concept of returning natural goodness to the soil, Rodale bought a farm and ran it by unprecedented pioneer methods. The work was labor-intensive, but his vegetable plots and orchards proved him right by producing ample, oversized crops. The results so encouraged him that he decided to share them with others. "I felt I had to share this information with the rest of the country," he proclaimed. "It would not be fair to know this and say nothing about it, considering that I owned printing presses and was a publisher."[2]

## A Public Platform

To spread the word, Rodale wrote *Pay Dirt*. Then, at the age of forty-four, he unveiled *Organic Farming and Gardening*. At first, his ingenuous, populist philosophy mixed with genuine altruism fell on deaf ears among conservative farmers and ranchers. The magazine convinced only one group—home gardeners—of his sincerity. The whole enterprise languished for sixteen years before moving into the black.

More and more converts swore off their dependence on chemistry and turned to natural garden builders and manageable predators, such as earthworms, crickets, praying mantises, toads, lizards, beneficial bacteria, and ladybugs. Some were less enthusiastic about the back-breaking chore of composting, which involves stacking kitchen wastes, grass clippings, and leaves alternately with soil and lime, dampening and turning with a pitchfork, and sifting the results through fine mesh to produce a rich humus additive.

On the other hand, veteran gardeners were pleased to see the finished product turn compacted clay and hardpan into friable soil. As Rodale demonstrated to a skeptical audience, loosened soil produced greater yields because plant roots reach farther down and supply each plant with more nutrients and water. Another important aspect of organic gardening is the improvement of cultivation and control of the rate at which plants absorb nutrients. Whatever the challenge, Rodale's converts were happy to exchange outworn methods for anything that would net them the bumper crops that are typical of organic methods.

The gospel according to Rodale quickly passed from fringe kooks to legitimate agronomists. With the aid of his multimillion dollar organization, colleges added organic gardening courses to their lineup. Small, immaculately tended organic gardens cropped up from the New England hills to the plains of the Southwest. Moreover, disparate groups—from vegetarians to members of La Leche to utopian dreamers—clustered under his banner. Not all agreed with every tenet, but their acceptance of his basic credo—that nature has its own wisdom—kept them in the fold.

## From Gardens to Health

In 1950 Rodale turned to his second area of interest, *Prevention* magazine, which surpassed *Organic Gardening* in influence and readership. Devoted to health and nutrition, *Prevention* evolved a regimen that avoids sugar, salt, dairy products, bread, citrus fruit, animal fat, canned and processed foods, stimulants, drugs, and tobacco. He touted the nutritive and rejuvenating powers of organically grown fruits and vegetables, seeds, and natural vitamins and minerals. To spread the word, he traveled and published in South America and Europe.

Some voices labeled as quackery and monomania Rodale's stringent naysaying to commonly accepted foodstuffs. Chief among the critics were food producers themselves, who stood to lose millions should Rodale's philosophy permeate too large a portion of the food-buying public. The American Medical Association, eager to debunk Rodale's quirky theories, labeled him the "merchant of menace" and claimed that his message appealed only to nutrition neurotics.[3] He was particularly lambasted for his eccentric notion that human beings lose electricity from their bodies through insulation and overhead steel girders.

Rodale ran afoul of the Federal Trade Commission with his 928-page book *The Health Finder*, which purports to tell people how to avoid illness. He was charged with false and deceptive advertisement, even though his work was based on articles in medical journals and broad-based university research. At first, he seemed like the lone wolf bayed about by hounds. Then he found support from Commissioner Philip Elman and the American Civil Liberties Union, which proclaimed his right to draw conclusions about health from his readings in nutrition.

Rodale refused to be swayed in the buffeting he received from the federal government. Supported by adequate money to pursue what he perceived to be a noble cause, he vowed to carry the fight to the Supreme Court. He drew upon his commercial successes in other investments to underwrite expenses. Ultimately, the Circuit Court of Appeals found in his favor.

## The Stage and the Lectern

*Organic Gardening* and *Prevention* were on their way. Meanwhile, his less popular publications—*Fitness for Living*, a compendium of tips on exercise; *Compost Science*, an overview of recycling methods; *Theatre Crafts*, concerning dramatic productions; *Quinto Lingo*, an educational magazine written in English plus five other languages; and *Rodale's New York*, a philosophical grab bag filled with varied writings—brought him less profit but fulfilled his urge to actualize his talents.

But publishing was not Rodale's only outlet. In 1962, he opened his own theater in the Bowery. The antique building featured an open stage with surrounding seats. A notorious self-promoter, Rodale wrote his own material in longhand, although the rambling, plotless productions bore little likeness to normal theatrics. Along the line of morality plays, his "happenings," such as *The Hairy Falsetto*, a play about Little Red Riding Hood, typically portray some danger to health along with a white-hatted solution, which swoops down to rescue humanity from perdition.

Because of his outspoken philosophies, Rodale opened himself to criticism along many fronts. He despised big business, particularly advertising, and feared that it would corrupt government. He rejected all advertisers who did not espouse his personal belief in organic living. He sought to promote health, reduce genetic deficiencies, and lower cancer rates by stabilizing ecology. Notable among his adversaries were companies producing DDT, cyclamates, monosodium glutamate, and phosphate detergent.

Rodale kept the world wondering what dragons he would slay next. Through an organized local campaign, he defeated plans to fluoridate water in Emmaus. He denounced grants from chemical companies to agricultural institutions. Later, he gave expert testimony at Congressional hearings concerning adulterated agricultural products.

## Family Man

Readers, enamored of Rodale's old-fashioned values, such as the example set by his forty-year marriage to wife Anna Andrews, wrote letters testifying to their own applications of his theories and their gratitude for his advice. His son Robert, who followed his father's example, took over Rodale Press, developed world awareness of organic farming methods until his death in a car accident in Russia in the fall of 1990, and was a source of pride for J. I., as he preferred to be called.

Content on his rural fifty-acre experimental farm outside Emmaus in the Lehigh Valley near Allentown, Pennsylvania, J. I. lived close to his son and two daughters and their families. The architecture of his stone and wood farmhouse and barn was Pennsylvania Dutch. The chicken houses were odorless and stocked with fowl that knew neither artificial hormones nor antibiotics. The surrounding animal lots boasted black Persian sheep and Hereford and Angus cows, free of steroids and other artificial bolstering agents.

Rodale's interests extended to all realms of farm life, particularly his greenhouse and orchard, as well as to a number of extraneous topics, such as posture, rare books, teaching gimmicks, an improved European trash can, manhole covers, composting toilets, a dictionary of cliches, and plaques for doors. Near the end of his life, he was assembling data to be used as background for plays on women's liberation, Russian lifestyles, early U.S. history, and Christmas. An author of thirty-three plays, he had contemplated but never opened a comedy theater for Allentown.

Rodale's daily schedule included time to himself followed by hourly exercise, inspection of his fields, and a strict diet supplemented by vitamins. Of his vitamin intake he noted: "Nature wants me to be a dull individual. By increasing the potencies, I can beat nature."[4] He was an inveterate note-taker and passed on myriad requests for information to his staff. One employee remarked: "It takes him ten seconds to write something down and it takes you six weeks to get the information he wants. Little yellow slips, that's his trademark."[5]

Rodale came to depend more and more on his son and son-in-law, who shouldered responsibility for the electrical factory. Still, he maintained an interest in his magazines, continued to crank out articles, and searched for innovations in electrical devices. His three-story factory, offices, and press provided work for local people. He undergirded his patriarchal concern for the families employed in his empire with wise business practices, notably solid wages and frequent raises. "We keep paying them more," he commented, "but our volume goes up. I've stopped worrying."[6]

## Sticking to His Guns

A dependable trooper, Rodale, whether gadfly or genius, persisted in his pursuits and maintained that his followers, too, benefitted from "a little gleam of something that is missing [from commercially-produced food]."[7] Ultimately, his theories caught the attention of powerful people, who were beginning to listen to his warnings about pollution, particularly the poisoning of the soil through chemical compounds. More ecology groups were resorting to slow-release soil enrichment to halt nitrate pollution, which was beginning to show up in bodies of water as large as the Great Lakes. Likewise, youth groups such as the Boy Scouts applied his techniques to their own experimental plots of ground.

An honest iconoclast, Rodale admitted that he could not account for the difference between organic and inorganic additives, but he clung to the notion that artificialization of the soil debilitated the modern diet. His regimen included seventy-odd nutritional supplements, although he admitted to indulging in an occasional pizza and his downfall, ice cream, particularly while residing in his New York apartment. On June 8, 1971, while taping an interview for the "Dick

Cavett Show," seventy-two-year-old J. I. Rodale suffered a heart attack and died. A proponent of dolomitic lime, manure, sunflower seeds, rose hips, and kelp, he had looked forward to a long, productive life. He reached his goal and then some.

## Notes

[1] "Death of a Salesman," *Newsweek*, June 21, 1971, 69.

[2] Eleanor Perenye. "Apostle of the Compost Heap," *Saturday Evening Post*, July 16, 1966, 33.

[3] Perenye, 30.

[4] Perenye, 32.

[5] Wade Greene. "Guru of the Organic Food Cult," *New York Times Magazine*, June 6, 1971, 54.

[6] Perenye, 31.

[7] Greene, 56.

## Sources

"Catching Up to Rodale Press," *Time*, March 22, 1971, 51.

"Death of a Salesman," *Newsweek*, June 21, 1971, 69.

Greene, Wade. "Guru of the Organic Food Cult," *New York Times Magazine*, June 6, 1971, 30-69.

Perenye, Eleanor. "Apostle of the Compost Heap," *Saturday Evening Post*, July 16, 1966, 30-33.

# Dr. Peter Mark Roget

Some late successes leave one purposeful career and advance to another that is equally useful, although more apt to receive public notoriety or critical acclaim. Such is the case with Dr. Peter Mark Roget, the precise and orderly man who distinguished himself as physician, researcher, lecturer, writer for *Encyclopedia Britannica*, and senior secretary to the Royal Society during his first career. Then, in retirement, he turned to an interest that remained with him from youth and invented the thesaurus. The concept of a thesaurus was the outgrowth of the elderly Englishman's infatuation with words.

## Early Loss

Dr. Roget, a mild-mannered, somewhat fussy London-born professor of physiology, was born in 1779 in Soho, London, the son of the Rev. Jean Roget, a French Protestant minister from Geneva, Switzerland, and Catherine Romilly Roget, daughter of a noted attorney. The Roget family dated their ancestry from feudal records of the mid-1300s. Both Dr. Roget's grandfathers were mechanically minded, one a jeweler and the other a Swiss clockmaker.

Roget's family, which moved to Lausanne, Switzerland, in hopes of bettering Rev. Roget's delicate health, was deeply immersed in politics, in particular the outcomes of the American and French revolutions. The boy, who grew up in the shadow of the gothic spires of Notre Dame Cathedral near the Flon River, was five years old when his father died of tuberculosis. Roget's mother returned first to Marylebone to reside with her parents, then wandered here and there through Europe, looking for the perfect spot on which to settle and raise two fatherless children.

At her brother Chauvet's suggestion, Catherine Roget decided to develop Peter's considerable talents for mathematical calculation and scientific research. Because of the reputation of its schools, Catherine chose Scotland as their new home. Ultimately, she moved her family to Edinburgh in 1793, where she, Peter, and his sister Nanette settled in a third-floor apartment in Rose Street, New Town, northwest of Edinburgh Castle. At 14 Peter entered medical school at the University of Edinburgh.

In the company of the venerable Humphry Davy and James Watt, the young Roget distinguished himself at Dr. Thomas Beddoes's Pneumatic Institution in his research on lung ailments and the use of nitrous oxide or laughing gas as an anesthetic for minor surgery. Completing his medical degree at the age of 19, he set up medical practice in Bristol, England, in 1799. For more than twenty years Dr. Roget associated with the Royal Society of London for the Improvement of Natural Knowledge and enjoyed philosophical pursuits, particularly the classification of words.

## Roget's Brush with Napoleon

At the age of twenty-three, Roget employed his hobby during a year's virtual imprisonment in Geneva after he was caught, during an extended vacation, in the hostilities between the Swiss government and Napoleon's regime. After Napoleon issued orders for the detainment of Englishmen over age eighteen, Roget began to plot some safe way out of Switzerland. He found, to his dismay, that the authorities had cut off most avenues of escape.

Upon the publication of a general arrest warrant, Roget asked for exemption on the grounds that he was a medical doctor. As the noose tightened, he attempted to evade a local spy network. Warned by the notorious Madame de Staël, keeper of Paris' wittiest salon, he left disguised in a nightshirt, dirty vest, greatcoat, hat, stick, dark pants, and red handkerchief.

To assure safe passage, Roget emphasized that he was the son of a Genevan and therefore a French citizen. While watching fellow Englishmen in similar straits, he enjoyed an uneasy truce with authorities, who still regarded him with suspicion. Upon reaching the Rhine River, he was thrilled to walk on friendly soil. The escape seemed like the end of a nightmare.

During the roundup of English sympathizers, who were incarcerated at the Castle of Montmelian in Savoy, Roget remained in Geneva and passed the time with word games. Acquainted with the *Amarakosha* or treasury of Amara, a Sanskrit word book compiled by the grammarian Amara Sinh around 650 A.D., as well as with the *Pasigraphie*, a French version of the word book published in 1797, Roget refined the techniques of these earlier versions by grouping words according to ideas, such as time, space, number, matter, sensation, and affections. Eventually he gained his freedom and abandoned his word listing.

## Dedication and Philanthropy

By 1804 Dr. Roget advanced to a respected position at the Public Infirmary of Manchester, England, where he distinguished himself as a medical lecturer at the Great Windmill Street School in Soho and a researcher in the area of animal physiology. Motivated by sincere humanitarianism, he lived in the Bloomsbury section of London from 1808 to 1843, where he founded and donated his services to a charity clinic for eighteen years. Roget was also instrumental in the establishment of the University of London and served on its governing board.

As was common in his day, Roget delayed marriage until age forty-five, when he wed twenty-nine-year-old Mary Taylor Hobson of Liverpool. His courtship, like other aspects of his life, was low-key, almost clandestine. In Mary's journal and letters are glimpses of Roget's conservative existence. Both she and her husband were affectionate, idealistic, and unfailingly restrained and upright in their public behavior. Roget took great delight in his family, as evidenced in his joy at the birth of Catherine Mary in 1825.

During the years before and after the birth of John, who arrived in 1828, Mary developed a tumor and declined in health. Roget wrote to her brother Sam of his mental torture over her impairment, but shielded his feelings from Mary. He feared not only for himself, but even more for his children. Mary died of cancer in 1833 at the age of thirty-eight.

Once more immersed in scholarly endeavors, Roget made numerous contributions to science. He developed a frigidarium or facility for cold storage. Even before the discovery of bacteria as the prime means by which water is contaminated, his studies for the London water department led to the Public Health Act of 1875, which substituted sand filtration for more primitive methods of purifying water.

## The Inventive Spirit

A clever, insightful thinker, Roget was affiliated with fifteen scientific societies. In a paper delivered in 1824 at one of these gatherings, he introduced the idea of the movie camera. From his one-man observations came the kaleidoscope, which influenced Michael Faraday and others engaged in studies that eventually led to the invention of motion pictures. A fourth contribution was the underlying principle of the slide rule. Roget deduced that computation could be simplified through a device commonly called a log-scale. However, he rated these accomplishments well below a favorite but rather insignificant treatise known as "Animal and Vegetable Physiology Considered with Reference to Natural Theology."

Roget retired from practice in 1840 at the age of sixty-one and devoted his remaining twenty-nine years to scholarly pursuits, including editing a surgical journal for the Medical and Chirurgical Society, writing medical articles for the *Encyclopedia Britannica*, and, his major avocation, studying motion. A lifelong chess player, he invented a pocket chessboard and calculator and wrote a two-volume work on phrenology, the study of how the shape of the human skull relates to behavior.

Following a difference of opinion with the Royal Society, Roget withdrew from membership and, in order to stave off depression over the debacle, busied himself composing his thesaurus. Biographers have commented on the paradox of an aged physician compiling this valuable word compendium when any of hundreds of London's literati were better equipped to undertake the herculean tour de force.

## The Birth of the Thesaurus

Roget was not particularly skilled with words. He read Latin, German, and Italian and, owing to his heritage, could be considered bilingual in English and French. His prose style was utilitarian, lacking the elegance, energy, and grace of a poet or wordsmith. No portion of his scholarly training or experience touched on philology, etymology, or linguistics. Yet in his preface to the first edition of his thesaurus, he claims to have worked on his volume of related words from 1805, that is, over most of his adult life.

From the beginning, Roget demonstrated a scientist's joy in order and classification. He clearly stated at the outset that his purpose was not to define words but to classify and arrange them according to usage. The work divided human knowledge into a thousand categories, for example, teacher/instructor, resemblance/similarity, supposition/hypothesis, beginning/commencement. Within these categories he listed 15,000 synonyms. This meticulous task was published in 1852, when Roget was seventy-three.

The work was beset by difficulties. After settling the matter of how to classify, Roget had to decide what to do with words that have vastly opposite meanings, such as *cleave, let, ravel,* and *priceless.* He separated from common proverbs the idiomatic phrases he intended to include. Also, he dealt with the matter of prefixes like dis-, un-, il-, ir-, and non-, which reverse the meanings of words.

In addition, Roget wisely avoided discriminating among synonyms. As he explained, such a differentiation would have overtaxed him. He summed up succinctly that the thesaurus was merely an arrangement of like words. The selection of individual terms remained the province of the user.

Roget was particularly open-minded on the subject of new words, especially those arising from scientific and artistic endeavor. With surefooted understanding of the literary world, he commented that these additions to a growing language were perfectly legitimate and beneficial in that they introduced the gradual changes that all languages undergo.

## A Late-in-Life Success

Roget's *Thesaurus of English Words and Phrases Classified and Arranged so as to Facilitate the Expression of Ideas and Assist in Literary Composition* was an immediate success—not among philosophers, as Roget had expected, but among editors, scholars, students, and writers. In the preface to the first edition, Dr. Roget, a modest man, stated that he offered only the knowledge that his skills allowed. He understood the difficulty that writers faced as they put words on paper and intended his *Thesaurus* as a reference.

Roget's compilation was in no way similar to a dictionary. Its primary purpose is to list word relationships. Because a single word may have multiple meanings, thesaurus entries are divided into groups of synonyms with frequent cross-references to draw attention to other possible relationships. For example, *mean* can be a synonym of *middle, median,* or *average* in its noun form; of *common, base, malicious, narrow-minded, humble,* or *ignoble* as an adjective; of *augur, imply, signify, split the difference,* or *pair off* as a verb; and of *on the average* or *in the long run* as an adverb. A colloquial alternative to *mean* is *fence-sitting*; possible antonyms include *inferiority, superiority, beginning, exalted, dignified, essential,* and *end.* In like manner, Roget demonstrated how a single word quickly branches out into multiple meanings, which create a problem for a writer looking for just the right word. In addition to providing synonyms, Roget's word book allowed the writer to replace tired or overused terms, convey a complex idea in a single explicit word, and inject vigor and freshness into writing.

At first, reviewers were perplexed about how to characterize and utilize the hundred-page penny notebook. Instead, they concentrated their praise on the cataloguer himself. Roget's work presented a particular challenge for American lexicographers. Their versions of American words and meanings required some careful delineations, some of which met with stiff challenges from readers and reviewers. At times, sensitivity to social and political issues resulted in the removal of certain synonyms, such as unflattering words referring to Jews.

In 1913, the birth of the crossword puzzle craze provided a boost to sales. By the 1920s, public enthusiasm for puzzles spread to England and reached its height in 1925. During this frenzy for word lists, booksellers could not keep adequate supplies of the *Thesaurus.* The *New York Times Magazine* lauded the work in 1925 and proclaimed Roget the saint of crossword puzzles. One wag noted that the *Thesaurus* resided next to the Bible in some homes.

## A Well-Ordered Life

Roget lived to the age of ninety. Much of his adult life was spent in a brick residence on Bernard Street near Russell Square in London. To his dismay, his wife and friends died before him. To withstand increasing isolation, he poured himself into the first editions and printings of his book. His obituary notes that he continued adding words to his thesaurus up to his last day.

As a diversion, Roget enjoyed frequent walks, the tender attentions of his unmarried daughter Kate, collecting and classifying humorous epigrams, and reading from his sizeable library. He expressed his piquant sense of humor in a poetic journal entry. Aside from deafness, he enjoyed good health up until the last weeks, when he succumbed during a heat wave while visiting the hills of West Malvern.

Roget's book went through twenty-eight printings during his lifetime. After his death, his son, lawyer John Lewis Roget, and grandson, engineer Samuel Romilly Roget, took charge of the immensely profitable family business. They watched Roget's first receipts of £150 grow to more than £1,000 per year. By 1947, Samuel was receiving more than £3,750 annually. They revised the initial text, produced updated versions by expanding the original, removed obsolete and archaic words, and added more recent terminology.

Essential to the utility of the volume was Roget's heirs' decision to alter the categorical arrangement to alphabetic dictionary form. In 1950, Samuel sold out the family rights to his grandfather's work to Longmans, Green for £4,500. Because of the family's dedication to the cataloguing of words, subsequent editions still bear the Roget name and the original designation of *thesaurus* in honor of the man who conceived the idea.

## Sources

Emblen, D. L. *Peter Mark Roget: The Word and the Man.* New York: Thomas Y. Crowell, 1970.

Roget, Peter Mark. *Roget's International Thesaurus.* Foreword by Robert L. Chapman. New York: Harper & Row, 1977.

# Harland Sanders

A very few late achievers, like Grandma Moses, achieve stardom and become national symbols. Harland Sanders, known to most American chicken lovers by the antebellum title of "the Colonel," arrived at that pinnacle through hard work and financial wizardry. In 1956, at the age of sixty-six, he amplified a one-man operation into Kentucky Fried Chicken, a billion-dollar fast-food success. At its height, the company, composed of 5,300 stores, had spread to thirty-nine countries. By 1967, the Colonel's franchise ranked sixth against fast-food competitors, far ahead of Dairy Queen, McDonald's, and Chicken Delight.

Daily, Kentucky Fried Chicken sells almost a million chickens in the United States, amounting to seven percent of the federally inspected broilers sold here. During its peak years—1964 to 1971—125 of the Colonel's employees became millionaires through investment in Kentucky Fried Chicken. And crowning it all—buckets, boxes, napkins, and billboards—is the convivial smile of the Colonel himself, one of the few men honored in his lifetime with his own museum.

## Early Life

Sanders, born to Wilbert D. and Margaret Ann Dunlevy Sanders on a farm three miles from Henryville, Indiana, on September 9, 1890, is more often associated with his later home, Louisville, Kentucky, the heart and soul of bluegrass country and motherland of thoroughbreds. In the land where acres of pasture are lined with pristine white fences and cooking is as much a part of tradition as last names and heirloom silver, Colonel Sanders has become part of the local folklore.

Sanders's father was a butcher. He died at twenty-nine, when the boy was six, leaving Harland, the oldest of three children, to tend Clarence and Catherine when his mother left each day to peel tomatoes at the Henryville canning factory or sew for neighbors. She was often gone for days at a time. "We didn't have any babysitter, but we got along fine," he comments on these motherless, unsupervised times. "We knowed enough not to burn the house down.... We was already firmly disciplined. Mom didn't spare the rod if we disobeyed her.... Whatever Mom said went."[1] By the age of eight, young Harland was an accomplished cook and produced a varied menu for his younger brother and sister.

## Moral Training

From his mother, Sanders derived a strong constitution as well as a dislike for liquor, tobacco, and gambling. She taught him self-respect and insisted that he be strong and God-fearing. Of this time he reminisces, "On Sunday we wasn't even allowed to whistle. I don't hardly know one card from another to this day. Cards were as poison to me as alcohol or cigarettes. I never drank coffee until the last four or five years, because Mom always taught us it was bad for us."[2] Throughout his life, he continued to follow her strictures, allowing himself only an occasional sip of table wine.

One factor that his mother apparently failed to mention was swearing, which colored her son's rhetorical streams during his adult years, to the chagrin of less profane opponents. He tried to curb his urge to mention the Lord's name in vain, but never quite got a firm hold on the bridle. Fans forgave the Colonel his failing, choosing to laugh at his riotous sense of humor, which he often directed at his own shortcomings.

## Casting About for a Trade

Harland and his brother left home with the arrival of a stepfather, William Broaddus, who had no fondness for children. His brother lived with an aunt in Alabama. Blaming algebra for ending his enthusiasm for higher education, Harland quit school in the seventh grade and boarded out on Charlie Norris's farm in nearby Greenwood as a $2-a-month laborer, a job he soon lost for wasting time and accomplishing no work. His mother shamed him for being unreliable.

Sanders tried numerous trades—farmhand, streetcar fare collector in New Albany, soldier in Cuba, blacksmith's helper, and railroad fireman. He was fired from the last job and blacklisted from holding other railroad jobs. At age eighteen, he married his first wife, Josephine King, and fathered three children, Margaret, Harland, Jr., and Mildred. The marriage was stormy because of Sanders' inability to hold a job but lasted until 1947.

After military service, more careers came and went, including section hand; claims adjuster; Prudential Insurance salesman in Kentucky and Indiana; steamboat ferryman between Jeffersonville, Indiana, and Louisville, Kentucky; gaslight manufacturer; secretary of the Chamber of Commerce in Columbus, Indiana; and tire salesman. For a time, Sanders studied law by correspondence course and practiced at the justice-of-the-peace level in Little Rock, Arkansas. His exit from the courts stemmed from a fight with a client and Sanders's arrest for assault and battery.

At the age of forty, Sanders worked as a roadside service station operator in Nicholasville and Corbin, Kentucky. The Depression years were painful ones. First his son died of a blood clot following a tonsillectomy. Shortly afterward, Sanders was involved in a shooting incident and charged with wounding a disgruntled competitor. But Sanders recovered and began extending his gasoline profits by concocting homemade blue plate specials, which rocketed him to local acclaim. He explains, "We'd fix dinner—dinner was the noon meal then, you see—for the family, and if nobody came, we'd eat it."[3] His devoted following, wearied of greasy take-out food, couldn't get enough of real, unpretentious southern fare.

Sanders's menus derived from whatever he was cooking for the family in their back-room kitchen—chicken, country ham, green beans, okra, cole slaw, apple pie, or gravy and biscuits. His only advertising was word-of-mouth endorsements by satisfied customers. By the late 1930s, his name was echoing up and down the highway and was listed in Duncan Hines's *Adventures in Good Eating*.

## Where There's a Will

Eventually, Sanders gave up pumping gas and camped out permanently in the kitchen, from which he derived the most profit and satisfaction. To reduce the time needed to fry chicken, he employed a unique method—pressure cooking—which also sealed in natural juices. In 1939 he bought an oversized cooker and reduced frying time for chicken from a half hour to eight minutes. He hit on the name Kentucky Fried Chicken to differentiate his recipe from mere southern fried chicken, which he claimed was a far inferior product. At the height of his fame, envious wags knocked the name down to its barest minimum—KFC, an abbreviation now used by the corporation.

The Colonel's venture grew from a mundane truck stop to Sanders Court & Café, seating 142. The property alone rose in value to $164,000. The event that brought him to national acclaim was a blessing disguised as a catastrophe—the construction of two new highways, which forced him into bankruptcy by directing the lion's share of traffic away from his roadside eatery. In despair, he sold his property at auction. Faced at the age of sixty-six with the choice of living on $105 per month in Social Security or striking out in new directions, he chose the latter. The rest is history.

## Spreading the Word

Traveling for ten years in a 1947 Ford with fifty pounds of his secret seasoning and the essential ingredient, his pressure cooker, Sanders toured the countryside, knocking on doors and setting up more than 700 restaurant managers with his special recipe in exchange for four cents in royalty on every chicken they sold.

The method took its toll; Sanders accepted free meals with friends along the way and slept on the back seat of his Ford. But it soon paid off.

In the first four years, his idea expanded into 400 franchises throughout the United States and Canada. With the help of his second wife, Claudia, Sanders took control of his growing interests. He kept the books; she mixed and packaged spices and herbs. Using his one-on-one sales technique, he traveled to likely spots and chose with utmost care the restaurants he wanted to represent his idea.

With glee, Sanders reflected on the short-sightedness of some restaurateurs who rejected his humble process: "That bird out in Portland who turned me down is still sittin' downtown in his restaurant talking about the fifty-thousand-dollar chandelier he's got in his cocktail room. But the fellow who took my chicken there, he'll do seven million dollars in volume this year."[4]

## Details, Details

Sanders knew his product. He could recite the background information that kept his fried chicken at the forefront of American tastebuds. KFC birds are typically eight weeks old, weigh two-and-a-half pounds, and are severed into nine pieces, then served as three portions. Cooking takes place in a pot designed by the Colonel himself. Each chicken chunk is coated with a soft-wheat grade of flour from Texas and Illinois and seasoned with his personal formulation of eleven herbs and spices, which he evolved after years of tinkering. The secret recipe for the coating is known only to two of his most trusted associates.

To maintain quality, Sanders remained close to the product through the final cooking stage. His vigilance paid off in a reputation that remains unchallenged by lesser fast-food franchisees. Not overburdened with modesty, the Colonel lauded his peripheral goods, that is cole slaw, biscuits, and gravy, claiming that the gravy itself is worth the price of the meal.

## The Good Years

During this period, Sanders unwittingly selected the costume that marked his style—a white Palm Beach suit, which continues as the visual representation of the man, the region, and his product. By 1964, Colonel Sanders, a national symbol, commanded 638 restaurants and pulled in $37 million a year.

The success scared him a little. He commented that "this danged business is beginning to run right over me."[5] When the necessity of locating a successor loomed before him, he bucked the notion of retiring or handing over the reins to somebody who might tamper with his product, but agreed that the future of KFC deserved serious consideration.

## Moving On

To ease the burden of work and provide for retirement in 1964, the Colonel sold out most of his rights, along with patents and trademarks (except in Florida, Utah, Montana, England, and Canada, where they had already been sold), to attorney John Young Brown, Jr., financier Jack Massey, and former franchisee Leon W. Harman for $2 million. Unwilling to lose all contact with his brainchild, Sanders agreed to stay on the payroll as goodwill ambassador. Part of the deal included a lifetime annual salary of $125,000 and control of quality.

His successors, who credit the Colonel with clever PR, were soon rolling in profit. Part of their success stemmed from Sanders's expertise in customer and dealer relations. After his departure, the new owners encouraged him to visit late-night talk shows and other sources of exposure to exploit his image in the New York area, which he had left untapped. Another lucrative idea to bolster the already popular product was the creation of a red-and-white-striped prefab building different from a sit-down restaurant and dedicated primarily to the take-out trade.

To assure success for franchisees, Brown, Massey, and Harmon provided on-site training at their Louisville center, affectionately known as KFC University. For day-to-day reminders of the company's goals, they produced *Bucket* magazine. At sellout time they relinquished their share to Heublein in 1971 for over $70 million. Sanders agreed to the deal, but kept his options open.

## Spending the Profits

A wealthy man at last, the Colonel enjoyed his late-in-life money. In the early 1970s, Sanders, who preferred his own culinary talents to those of upscale, nouvelle cuisine chefs, started a restaurant in Shelbyville, Kentucky, to honor his gentle-natured wife and partner, "Miss Claudia." He called it the Colonel's Lady Dinner House and zeroed in on four crowd favorites—steak, roast beef, ham, and lobster.

In the meantime, the marriage of KFC and Heublein proved rocky. Sanders, who could be cantankerous when the situation called for it, brought a $122 million suit against the conglomerate in 1974 for promoting pastries, dairy products, and other goods without his approval. But more to the point, he demanded rights to the new restaurant, which Heublein claimed as an infringement. Heublein accused the Colonel of having second thoughts about the original sale and challenged his suit as harassment.

In high Old South dudgeon, Sanders fired his retort. He admitted selling his image, but denied that it applied to anything but fast-food restaurants. He declared ungentlemanly the conglomerate's under-the-table pressures against potential franchisers of his new Miss Claudia restaurants. In a courtly rejoinder, he declared that he was merely taking up for his wife, as any well-brought-up southern male would do in similar circumstances.

## The Image and the Man

In addition to new business pursuits, Sanders supported numerous foundations, schools, hospitals, and churches. He and Claudia shared a modest two-story, ten-room house in Shelbyville, thirty miles east of Louisville, and purchased a second place in Toronto. He kept up his workaholic ways, rising at five A.M., conditioning arthritic hands in a diathermy machine, and hitting the trail at six. He traveled over 200,000 miles per year, during which he represented the spirit of KFC in the flesh.

In addition to globe-trotting for the company, the Colonel was a regular at parades, conventions, and festivals. He appeared on television commercials and accepted cameo roles in movies. His fans collected wherever he appeared to savor his gentle humor. He rewarded their loyalty by posing for photos, signing autographs, and admiring their children.

To relieve work stress, he tended a greenhouse and walked. In reply to questions about such a demanding regimen at his age, he snapped, "Work never hurt anyone. More people rust out than wear out. But not me. I'll be damned if I'll *ever* rust out."[6]

Designated an honorary colonel in the 1930s by a Kentucky governor for "contributions to the state's cuisine," Harland Sanders was an alert, quick-witted man who stood over six feet in height and weighed 200 pounds. An interviewer for *Louisville Magazine* described him in his white-suited best as looking like a "benign polar bear."[7] By the end of his life, which came in Louisville on December 16, 1980, he suffered from a host of maladies, diabetes, leukemia, arthritis, and pneumonia among them.

## Public Image

Renowned as a jolly, benevolent, but shrewd Santa Claus, Harland Sanders sported tousled white hair, mustache, and goatee along with pristine linen double-breasted suit, gold-headed cane, black string tie, and black shoes. His bespectacled face crinkled into easy laughter. During the height of his company's hold on American fast-food eating habits, he established a $50-million-per-year advertising budget to keep that familiar face and form in the public eye, and wore out eight suits in the process.

He remained testy and cantankerous to the end of his days. Long associated with quality and uniformity, Colonel Sanders applied his skill as taster in impromptu visits to franchisees. When he found samples that failed to meet his discriminating taste, he was known to grow red in the jowls, bang his cane on the counter, and demand an explanation. He described himself as "a-lickin' and a-tastin' and never bein' satisfied. Whether I'm in Cedar Rapids, Iowa, or Tokyo, Japan, I want my chicken to taste the way I prepare it with my own hands."[8]

# Notes

[1] W. Whitworth. "Profiles: Kentucky Fried," *New Yorker*, February 14, 1970, 42.

[2] Whitworth, 42.

[3] John Ed Pearce. *The Colonel.* Garden City, New York: Doubleday, 1982, 56.

[4] Whitworth, 43.

[5] James Stewart-Gordon. "Saga of the 'Chicken' Colonel," *Reader's Digest*, February 1975, 144.

[6] Stewart-Gordon, 146.

[7] Stewart-Gordon, 144.

[8] Stewart-Gordon, 146.

# Sources

"A Centennial Celebration for the Colonel," *Travel South*, Fall/Winter 1990, 5.

"The Colonel's Lady," *Newsweek*, January 28, 1974, 63.

"Cooking Up Profits, Southern Style," *Business Week*, June 24, 1967, 176-180.

"How to Make a Million After You're 64," *Saturday Evening Post*, March 1977, 46-47.

Pearce, John Ed. *The Colonel.* Garden City, New York: Doubleday, 1982.

Stewart-Gordon, James. "Saga of the 'Chicken' Colonel," *Reader's Digest*, February 1975, 143-146.

Whittingham, A. "Home to Roost," *Macleans*, December 29, 1980, 37.

Whitworth, W. "Profiles: Kentucky Fried," *New Yorker*, February 14, 1970, 40-52.

# Albert Schweitzer

Far from lacking achievement in their early lives, many late achievers accentuate a new aspect of greatness in their late careers. Albert Schweitzer is a prime example of such multi-talented people. Gifted in music, theology, philosophy, and medicine, he developed a noteworthy career, then abruptly altered his goals. From a life of preaching, teaching, administering a college, writing scholarly treatises, designing pipe organs, and performing the works of Bach, he changed directions and moved toward humanitarian endeavors.

Committed to aiding Africans, he left his home and established a benevolent healing ministry at the Schweitzer Hospital in French Equatorial Africa. His guiding principles, reverence for life and an abhorrence of violence, received much attention from his admirers in the outside world. One philanthropist, Larimer Mellon, emulated Schweitzer's faith in goodness, studied medicine, and set up a sister hospital in Haiti.

Schweitzer, known among the people he served as "le grand docteur," metaphorically described humanitarianism: "Sometimes our light goes out but is blown again into flame by an encounter with another human being. Each of us owes the deepest thanks to those who have rekindled this inner light."[1] In such fashion did he touch other lives. Soon the rest of the world began rewarding his humanitarian efforts. He received the 1952 Nobel Peace Prize for furthering world brotherhood.

## Developing the Mind

No family member doubted that young Albert Schweitzer would do great things. Born on January 14, 1875, in Kaysersberg, Alsace, which is now a part of France along the German border, he was the eldest son of five children and the grandson of two organists, one also a schoolmaster. When Albert was an infant, his father, Pastor Louis Schweitzer, accepted an ecumenical pastorate in an Evangelical Lutheran church in Gunsbach, where he led both Protestant and Catholic worship. Schweitzer learned early the pressures and expectations that affect a minister's son, particularly the need to curb an argumentative streak.

From childhood, Schweitzer was a musical prodigy. At age eight he began studying organ, substituting for the regular church organist, and giving public recitals. He displayed a gift for sight reading and improvisation. At age nine, Schweitzer went to live with his great-uncle Louis and great-aunt Sophia in Mulhouse in northeastern France so that he could attend the school Louis directed. While living under the frugal, puritanical rule of his uncle, the boy continued to study music and developed interests in politics and religion. His teachers remarked upon his gifted interpretive renditions at the pipe organ and encouraged his study of Bach's mystical power.

## Success at Strasbourg

During his university days at Strasbourg, his father's alma mater, Schweitzer lived at No. 36 Old Fish Pier, where the poet Goethe had lived as a student. Adopting Goethe as his hero and idol, Schweitzer applied himself intently to his studies, which formed the nucleus of his writings on Christianity and its importance to humanity. For his diligence he was awarded a Goll Scholarship in theology. In 1899 he wrote his doctoral thesis on philosopher Immanuel Kant.

At the suggestion of one of his professors, Schweitzer transferred to the Sorbonne in Paris for a greater concentration on philosophy, then studied New Testament doctrine at the University of Berlin. He graduated *magna cum laude* with a second doctorate in theology in 1900, and accepted a post as lecturer and administrator at the Theological College of Saint Thomas. In addition, he preached at St. Nicholas's Church while pursuing his avocation of organ construction and serving as organist of the Paris Bach Society.

## On to the Mission Field

In 1904, Schweitzer happened upon a copy of the *Paris Missionary Society* magazine. His readings into the needs of Congo natives made an abrupt change in his thinking. On January 5, 1905, he preached a sermon announcing his call to the mission field. To the surprise and dismay of his colleagues, particularly his organ teacher, he re-enrolled as a medical student so that he could help the sick in the African Congo. In reply to naysayers, he stated his credo: "Anyone who proposes to do good must not expect people to roll stones out of his way, but must accept his lot calmly if they roll a few more upon it."[2] To support himself he gave organ recitals and lived off the royalties of his biography of Bach, which he published in both French and German in 1905, and *The Quest of the Historical Jesus*, an influential text completed the following year.

His family labeled the whole dream a bit of youthful foolishness. In the face of family and friends' shallow commitment to Christianity, he persevered, shored up by one voice, that of Helene Bresslau, a Jewish historian's daughter and quiet scholar who did social work among prostitutes, a shocking specialty in conservative German society. Also, he battled a second obstacle, the refusal of the Paris

Missionary Society to support his mission because of differences in philosophy. Undeterred, Schweitzer joined Helene in raising private funds to underwrite the expedition.

Shortly before setting out for Africa, Schweitzer married Helene, who matched his altruistic zeal with her own desire to serve as a nurse among Africa's poor. On March 26, 1913, following Schweitzer's investiture as an MD, he and his bride sailed from Bordeaux, France, down the western coast of Africa to Lambaréné in Gabon forty miles below the equator on the Ogooué River. The presence of monkeys, hippopotami, snakes, and crocodiles assured him that he was indeed in Africa.

## The Realities of Mission Work

Problems abounded from the moment of his arrival. The promised interpreter was not to be found. Patients, learning that a doctor was arriving to care for them, crowded around. With calm assurance, Schweitzer established a triage, questioned patients who spoke French, worked through a French-speaking native to talk with the rest of the sick, and promised to help them all as soon as the next boat arrived. In the meantime, he treated the critically ill in a nearby chicken coop. Three weeks later, he unloaded seventy packing crates of medical supplies and equipment and, with the help of natives, began setting up a hospital.

Within a year's time, he had treated 2,000 patients for ordinary maladies and accidents as well as typical jungle diseases—leprosy, fever, malaria, amoebic dysentery, sleeping sickness, elephantiasis. His compound, containing a dining area, convalescent ward, dispensary, and surgery, welcomed natives alongside Caucasian tradespeople and government workers. Many arrived by water in pirogues; others were carried by litter through the jungle.

Often, Dr. Schweitzer battled not only disease but malnutrition, superstition, and ignorance, all contributory causes to the high mortality rate in Africa. In cases where litter-bearers refused to ferry people or rejected blood from members of a different tribe, he modeled a humanitarian example and did the work they rejected. On other occasions, he delivered impromptu sermons about human brotherhood.

To support his effort, Schweitzer at first managed expenses from his earnings from books, recordings, lectures, prizes, and concerts, then from gifts and support from foundations around the world. He pinched pennies to make the most of his investment, even building furniture from his original packing crates and establishing a garden to supply needed vegetables. Volunteers washed bandages, baked bread, and performed menial chores. Native tom-toms beat out messages to neighboring villages. His missionary hospital became a blend of early twentieth-century technology and native know-how.

# Diversified Efforts

The compound at Lambaréné developed into both a church and teaching facility. Each Sunday Dr. Schweitzer delivered a sermon in French, which was translated into native dialects. Native children studied French under his tutelage, using wood slabs for tablets and leaves for erasers. In addition to medical and religious endeavors, Dr. Schweitzer pursued an interest in native animals, which he tended and bred on the premises. To protect young animals from harm, he whispered a nighttime prayer that they be kept safe from evil.

Schweitzer pondered the myriad roles of doctor, minister, teacher, and veterinarian in serving world needs. In *The Hymn of the Universe*, a reflective treatise, he set himself a lifetime role as humanitarian. In his words, "As far as I can, because I am a priest I would henceforth be the first to become aware of what the world loves, pursues, suffers, I would be the first to seek, to sympathize, to toil; the first in self-fulfillment, the first in self-denial."[3] Lambaréné was the actualization of those roles.

Dr. Schweitzer recognized that his multi-purpose compound was not large enough to accomplish his goals. Space was in such short supply that attendants slept under patient beds and displaced students from the boys' dormitory. His sixteen-bed hospital, beset by frequent epidemics, required at least twenty-four more beds. As he assessed the native response to his mission, he realized that the future would always be in a state of flux, that his plans would forever be stretching and growing to suit his changing role in the Congo. Often, he built whatever was needed with his own hands.

# Swept Up by War

The outbreak of world war threatened Dr. Schweitzer's entire operation. On August 5, 1914, his idealistic endeavor ground to a halt with the couple's house arrest in their residence as enemy aliens. Native patients, encamped about the house, wondered at a political situation that would deny their adored doctor the use of his own hospital.

As a result of the experience he wrote *Philosophy of Civilization* (1923), a two-volume work that expressed his concern for human survival. In his view, humanity could be saved by the creation of a moral commitment to life. The book contrasted harshly with the reality of armed guards posted outside his door. Within three months, the French commandant recognized the absurdity of the situation and allowed Dr. Schweitzer, an obvious noncombatant, to return to community service.

In 1917 the Schweitzers were deported to a concentration camp, an ancient stone monastery with a walled-in garden at Saint-Remy-de-Provence in the Pyrenees, where Van Gogh had spent his last days. Not one to waste time, Schweitzer used his imprisonment as an opportunity to practice organ technique, even though his keyboard was a table and his pedals were imaginary. As part of a prisoner exchange the following year, authorities allowed the Schweitzers to return to Alsace.

Soon after, Schweitzer suffered personal grief when his mother, Adele Schillinger Schweitzer, was trampled to death by German cavalry while walking along a road in Gunsbach. Louis Schweitzer, devastated by the loss of his wife, lost the will to live. Sick and discouraged, Albert Schweitzer worked at a Strasbourg hospital and resumed his former pastorate in order to remain solvent. He gave recitals and lectures in Switzerland, Spain, Czechoslovakia, Sweden, Denmark, and England. To revive his body, he undertook the rebuilding of old pipe organs. To strengthen his spirit, he agreed to psychoanalysis. In 1923, he returned alone to Africa, determined to improve his initial mission. Helene, also ill from her prison experience, stayed behind to care for their daughter Rhena, born in 1919.

## A Bigger and Better Hospital

At age forty-seven, Schweitzer, no longer young, but still committed to his dream, returned to Lambaréné. He found the compound overgrown with vines. Together with native assistants he rebuilt his 500-bed hospital two miles upriver and added a facility for lepers. Word of his kindness spread over ten tribes, whose sick filled the hospital wards with a babble of languages.

Soon Dr. Schweitzer was performing surgery daily and battling epidemics and famine. In spare hours he worked as a day laborer on additions to the complex and as supervisor of cargo shipments. While performing herculean tasks on a daily basis, he learned that he had received an honorary degree from the University of Prague and the Goethe Prize, awarded by the city of Frankfurt. More exciting, perhaps, was the news of the arrival of his first registered nurse, who greatly relieved him of drudgery.

## Growth of a Dream

As World War II became inevitable, Dr. Schweitzer chose to wait out the clash in Africa. Part of his decision was based on his debilitating experience during World War I. A major factor was the fact that Helene was Jewish and a natural target of Nazi oppression. The doctor's decision to remain at Lambaréné proved challenging because of the difficulty in receiving supplies. But the negative aspects were matched by one miraculous positive: by 1943, the arrival of sulfa drugs, underwritten by the Albert Schweitzer Fellowship in New York, increased Dr. Schweitzer's effectiveness against leprosy. The lepers, arriving daily, swelled his hospital population to overflowing. With a new source of glasses, shoes, rubber gloves, and other essentials, the hospital was back in business.

## Later Years of Service

The post-war years at Lambaréné brought the harvest of Dr. Schweitzer's patient, optimistic sowing. In 1952, the Nobel Prize money provided 300 more beds. In 1950, Dr. Emeric Percy joined Schweitzer to study tropical diseases. Donors throughout the United States and Europe responded to the need. On Dr. Schweitzer's eightieth birthday, admirers bombarded the aging physician with letters and remembrances. Among them was a tribute from his old friend, Albert Einstein: "He did not preach and did not warn and did not dream that his example would be an ideal and a comfort to innumerable people. He simply acted out of inner necessity."[4]

In the late 1950s, Rhena Schweitzer-Eckert studied laboratory technology so that she could assist her father with his work. By 1963, the medical facility included a staff of thirty-six doctors plus nurses and native assistants.

## Later Writings

While devoting the lion's share of his energies to the hospital, Schweitzer continued to do scholarly research and writing. He published *Memoirs of Childhood and Youth* (1924), *The Mysticism of Paul the Apostle* (1931), *Out of My Life and Thought* (1933), and *Peace or Atomic War?* (1958), a philosophical work gleaned from a series of Oslo radio broadcasts. When funds ran low, he made more recordings and initiated more musical tours.

Dr. Schweitzer continued to influence world opinion throughout his later years. He made keen observations on the decay of European institutions, particularly the church. A strong-willed activist, he decried the savagery of world war, the cynicism and greed of colonialism, and the madness of atomic armaments. A friend to all elements working for peace, he strove to end repressive governments, protect nature from human encroachment, and halt military technology from overrunning humanity.

After Helene's death in 1957, Schweitzer remained active well into old age and died at Lambaréné on September 4, 1965. He was buried in a simple grave beside his wife at the jungle compound. Idealistic to the end, he challenged his followers with simple wisdom: "Grow into your ideals, so that life can never rob you of them."[5]

## Notes

[1] Erica Anderson. *The World of Albert Schweitzer*. New York: Harper & Row, 1955, unpaginated book.

[2] Anderson, n.p.

[3] George Marshall and David Poling. *Schweitzer: A Biography.* Garden City, New York: Doubleday, 1971, 53.

[4] Marshall, 239.

[5] Anderson, n.p.

## Sources

Anderson, Erica. *Albert Schweitzer's Gift of Friendship.* New York: Harper & Row, 1964.

_____. *The World of Albert Schweitzer.* New York: Harper & Row, 1955.

Berrill, Jacquelyn. *Albert Schweitzer: Man of Mercy.* New York: Dodd, Mead, 1956.

Marshall, George, and David Poling. *Schweitzer: A Biography.* Garden City, New York: Doubleday, 1971.

Schweitzer, Albert. *Out of My Life and Thought.* New York: Henry Holt, 1933.

# Billy Sunday

In some instances, one career may supplant another but the underlying skill remains the same. For Billy Sunday, baseball and evangelism were disparate outlets for the same talent—the ability to entertain huge and diverse audiences with dramatic displays. From humble beginnings, he honed his athletic prowess on the baseball diamond, then dropped his career, worked for the Young Men's Christian Association (YMCA), and moved inexorably toward a personal, individualized ministry, which came to be called the "sawdust trail."

After developing a keen instinct for oral delivery and crowd manipulation, Sunday burst onto the American scene with extensive revivals, each calculated to touch the emotions of thousands. He thumped the lectern, stamped the floor, pointed his finger at the audience, and raced about the platform in whatever style suited his evangelism. His zeal hit the mark, striking the unrighteous in vulnerable spots and convincing them to take up clean living.

By the end of his life, Billy Sunday claimed converts in the millions and became the best known fundamentalist evangelist of his day. *American Magazine* named him the eighth greatest man in America. In his own modest fashion, he sidestepped efforts to lionize him: "I have just gone along," he said, "entering doors that the Lord has opened one after another."[1]

He touched the lives of derelicts, society debutantes, newspaper editors, politicians, ministers, convicts, gamblers, church deacons, and saloon keepers. He conducted more than 300 formal revivals and accepted more than a million dollars in offerings. With his Christian outreach, he inspired an estimated 100 million people and remained in the pulpit until his death in Chicago, Illinois, on November 6, 1935.

## Early Beginnings

A native of Ames, Iowa, William Ashley Sunday, offshoot of pioneer stock, was born on November 19, 1862. He had two older brothers, Roy and Edward, and lived in a two-room log cabin. His father, Private William Sunday, fought on the Union side of the Civil War for the Twenty-third Iowa Infantry Volunteers from July 1862 until his death in Patterson, Missouri, December 22, 1862.

Consequently, he never saw the third son who carried his name. Billy's grandfather, Kentuckian Squire Corey, served as surrogate father and provider. Still, the family suffered wretched poverty. Eventually, Billy's mother was no longer able to cope with the demands of caring for her children.

At age twelve, Billy accompanied brother Ed on a train first to the Soldiers' Orphanage in Glenwood, Iowa, then later transferred to the Davenport Orphanage. Of his two years away from his mother he lamented: "Mother knew; she knew that for years she wouldn't see her boys."[2] After his return to the homeplace, he walked the trail once more to hunt squirrels with a favorite dog.

Billy supported himself through school, first as a school janitor, then as an undertaker's assistant in Nevada, Iowa; he never graduated from high school. Later, he created endless sermon material from his understanding of what it means to toil for a living. In later years, he came to regret his limited education and tried to compensate with an assortment of college classes. In 1883, after a brief period at Northwestern University, he was scouted by A. C. "Pop" Anson in Marshalltown, Iowa, and signed up to play professional baseball for the Chicago White Stockings.

## Billy in Limelight

Even though he was never a star hitter and didn't develop the keen judgment of a baseball whiz, Sunday quickly earned a reputation for speedy base running, hard throws, and daring steals. He became the first player to run the bases in fourteen seconds. Sunday was a crowd pleaser and later moved to two other National League teams, Pittsburgh and Philadelphia, but at the end of his eight-year career, he turned down a $500-per-month contract in order to go into the Christian ministry.

In 1887, while Sunday was still earning a living as an athlete, the leader of a group of street singers from the Pacific Garden Rescue Mission persuaded him to become a Christian. From that time to the end of his life, he poured his enthusiasm into religious meetings, evangelism, and meditation. He joined the Park Presbyterian Church, attended prayer meetings, and took part in Christian social activities. At one of these sessions he met Helen A. Thompson, whose father objected to her dating a baseball player. The following September they were married and honeymooned on the circuit with Billy's team. The Sundays had four children—Helen, George, William, and Paul—and made their home in Mount Hood, Winona Lake, Indiana.

## Learning to Be a Speaker

Sunday developed his physical talents almost exclusively over his intellect and never gave much thought to training for public speaking. However, he impressed others with his one-on-one sincerity. He rejected an offer to serve as physical director for the Young Men's Christian Association. Instead, he served as secretary from 1891 to 1895. Later, as assistant to Rev. J. Wilbur Chapman, Sunday learned the rudiments of organization, including securing speakers, raising funds, selling songbooks, hammering tent pegs, organizing choirs, administration, visitation, and following-up on likely candidates for conversion.

In 1896, Rev. Chapman's path parted from Sunday's. Sunday was without a job and unsure of which way to turn until a summons from Garner, Iowa, led him to conduct eight sermons. From that time until the end of his career, he never canvassed for work. Instead, he waited for Providence to tell him where to go. In his thirties, influenced by his idol, Dr. Dwight L. Moody, he slowly evolved the high-powered delivery, acrobatics, and pressure tactics that led to hundreds of thousands of converts. In 1905, at the age of forty-three, he was ordained a Presbyterian minister in Chicago.

## Speaking to the Masses

Skeptics doubted that Sunday's midwestern experience would be repeated in higher-toned eastern settings. His successes proved them wrong. A master of everyday language, Sunday relied on the common vernacular as his means of communicating with the masses. As his biographer described his orations: "He talks religion as he talked baseball. His words smack of the street corners, the shop, the athletic field, the crowd of men. That this speech is loose, extravagant and undignified may be freely granted: but it is understandable."[3]

Sunday's attack on sin was ruthless and unremitting. He ferreted out hypocrisy and denounced wrongdoing. No two-faced minister, no backsliding Christian was immune from his chastisement. He made no apologies for his down-to-earth style: "I want people to know what I mean," he declared vociferously, "and that's why I try to get down where they live. What do I care if some puff-eyed, dainty little dibbly-dibbly preacher goes tibbly-tibbling around because I use plain Anglo-Saxon words."[4]

## A Style of His Own

Sunday's fans accused the press of misconstruing his unorthodox methods. Because print could not carry the import of his gestures and demonstrative delivery, newspapers could not completely represent his impact. Supporters fell back on a single proof of his efficacy—the bottom line, the number of converts who answered his call. For them, Sunday was the champion of righteousness, the church's paladin in wicked times.

Sunday made no claim to be either theologian or original thinker. He fell back on former teachers and mentors as well as the writings of noted church fathers. He kept a black leather notebook of ideas and carried them to his lectern for handy reference. His words, transcribed from shorthand notes, appeared in local papers after every revival. All bear the same earmarks—an open assault on sin in the most forthright language, some even shocking to more refined ears.

Sunday undergirded his homespun approach with the slick public relations methods of his cadre of revival specialists and the soulful music of choir director Homer A. Rodeheaver. Together, they pulled audiences into auditoriums from the Tenderloin of New York to the mills of Pittsburgh to the Barbary Coast in San Francisco. A cross section of Americans—college students, mechanics, farmers, businessmen—thrilled to his powerful images. Swept up in the rush of emotions, they were borne along toward a catharsis of confession and complete acceptance of his message. From January 3 to March 21, 1915, his revival campaign received nationwide attention. This single episode in his career produced $118,000 in collections and 41,724 convert signatures.

## Developing Campaigns

During the uncertain years of World War I, Sunday wowed audiences in major U.S. cities with energetic sensationalism. Newspapers devoted whole sections to his words. Many who responded to his emotional message were the uprooted, dispossessed rural Americans who felt trapped and overwhelmed by metropolises, where alcohol, gambling, sex, and crime lured the unwary to their doom. Sunday's sermons, set off by large orchestras and choirs, tapped into the American scene and poured out hot condemnations of sin and alcohol. As he castigated wickedness, his message was unequivocal: "I believe that cards and dancing are doing more to damn the spiritual life of the Church than the grog-shops—though you can't accuse me of being a friend of that stinking, dirty, rotten, hell-soaked business."[5]

Sunday served as initiator of each revival, but tried to prevent the campaign from being a one-man show. His advance committee insisted that local religious groups pay his expenses. Thus, he never became dependent on the rich. Instead, he put greater responsibility on local church members, who took shares in the proceeds and accepted a receipt as pay. Because the campaigns were overwhelmingly successful, no guarantor had to underwrite Sunday's work. Collections were always more than adequate.

## A Suitable Setting

To facilitate his orations, Billy Sunday insisted that a huge tabernacle be erected for each campaign. These raw lumber edifices resembled turtle-shell barns. By designing his own buildings, Billy controlled acoustics as well as the crowd. He needed a single-floor dwelling with sawdust floor so that converts could move soundlessly to the front without disturbing his delivery. He maintained quiet by stopping when people coughed or became unruly. To assure himself that no member of the audience could be trampled in a general panic, he had a door placed at the end of each aisle.

Each board of the tabernacle was held by no more than two nails so that a quick kick could release it. Around the perimeter were fire extinguishers, firemen, and guards. But the choir's platform and the pulpit area were sturdily constructed to support Sunday's gymnasium antics. To augment each word of his sermons, Sunday had a shell-shaped sounding board suspended over a battered wooden lectern before a simple wooden chair.

His staff of ushers was a polished drill team, skilled in crowd control and commissioned to head off problems before they could escalate, particularly insistent overflow crowds. These assistants honed their collection of offerings so that they could canvass 8,000 people in three minutes. For most of each campaign half the money collected went to local benevolences and expenses, the other half to Sunday's staff. Only on the last day did he accept a freewill offering to cover his personal needs. In Pittsburgh alone, Sunday received $44,000—a generous sum in his day. To his critics, he refused to discuss money and claimed that his income was a private matter.

## Shepherding Converts

While Sunday greeted converts at the front, his choir sang emotional hymns. Among the most touching were "Almost Persuaded," "Where Is My Wandering Boy Tonight?," "I Am Coming Home," "I Love to Tell the Story," and "Ring the Bells of Heaven." He swooped down to welcome his public and lavished energy and enthusiasm on them. His face, pale and dripping, registered the exertion of his evangelism.

At the rear of the tabernacle was a nerve center. Here Sunday collected and organized names of converts to be sent to local pastors so that fledgling Christians could receive steady support in developing their faith. Alongside this room were a nursery and first aid room staffed with child-care workers and a nurse. The overall effect of such organization was unquestionable. He knew how to run a thorough campaign.

Following the acceptance of converts, the Sunday organization sent out support materials. One small tract, meant to be kept with a Bible, defined Christianity and asked the convert pointed questions about commitment. Then the pamphlet outlined seven steps to remaining committed. They included Bible study, prayer, evangelism, keeping good company, joining a church, benevolent giving, and a positive outlook.

## Self-Renewal

At the end of his workday, Sunday did not stay in hotels. He insisted that private accommodations were better for him, his family, and his staff. His bodyguards whisked him away from the furor of well-wishers to a makeshift home away from home. In the privacy of four walls, he could maintain a semblance of normalcy. In this way, he avoided star status and kept himself humble.

At least four to six weeks per year, Sunday recuperated from his intense exertions on the sawdust circuit. He devoted Mondays to setting up campaigns in new cities. Averaging two speeches per day, he taxed his body and voice to the limit. To spare himself the tedium of everyday details, he turned to "Mother Sunday," as his wife was known among the staff, to manage the wardrobe, meals, and luggage.

## Prohibition Effort

In addition to spreading Christianity, Sunday was a dynamo on behalf of prohibition. In 1917 in New York City, he joined the grassroots movement to halt alcohol consumption while battalions of police held back throngs. He earned a reputation as the "most effective foe of the liquor business in America."[6] Because of his work, eleven out of fifteen towns in Illinois joined the "dries." Similar successes followed in Pennsylvania and West Virginia. Sunday's rallying cry was the refrain "De Brewer's Big Hosses Can't Run Over Me!," sung along with whistles and imitations of escaping steam.

## Skeptics and Admirers

Critics were divided as to Billy Sunday's sincerity. His enemies included the obvious—newspapers and companies with a vested interest in alcohol and gambling. Some ministers were also dead set against Sunday's evangelistic techniques. Some portrayed him as a cynical, barely literate opportunist who reveled in the news that thousands were turned away for lack of space. Others, noting his influence on evangelical churches and dedicated laypersons, declared him a truly gifted preacher of God's word.

Among Sunday's supporters were powerful people. Notable among them was William Jennings Bryan, secretary of state, who advised in a personal letter: "Do not allow yourself to be disturbed by criticism. God is giving you souls for your hire and that is a sufficient answer.... No man can do good without making enemies, but yours as a rule will be among those who do not hear you."[7] By 1914, Billy Sunday achieved the height of his fame. He was honored by Princeton and greeted on a first-name basis by national leaders, including the president himself.

## Notes

[1] Fern Neal Stockes. *Billy Sunday: Baseball Preacher.* Chicago: Moody Press, 1985, 141.

[2] William T. Ellis. *Billy Sunday.* Swarthmore, Pennsylvania: L. T. Meyers, 1914, 25.

[3] Ellis, 70.

[4] Ellis, 71.

[5] Ellis, 73.

[6] Ellis, 80.

[7] Ellis, 5.

## Sources

Ellis, William T. *Billy Sunday.* Swarthmore, Pennsylvania: L. T. Meyers, 1914.

Stockes, Fern Neal. *Billy Sunday: Baseball Preacher.* Chicago: Moody Press, 1985.

# Corrie ten Boom

History often catapults people from comfortable, but obscure niches into public notice by unforeseen and sometimes catastrophic circumstances. In 1937, Cornelia "Corrie" ten Boom, a meek forty-five-year-old spinster and watchmaker, with the aid of her fifty-two-year-old sister Betsie, took care of their aged father. Secure in the ten Boom family's strong religious faith, Corrie enjoyed a pleasant, but demanding life. Within months, however, her responsibilities increased tenfold after Nazi forces captured the Netherlands and imposed impossible rules on Jewish residents.

Most influential in shaping ten Boom's view of her changing world was her older brother Willem, a minister in the Dutch Reformed Church. With his help, ten Boom became instrumental in the rescue and resettlement of a growing stream of Jewish refugees fleeing the German SS. By the end of World War II, Corrie was transformed into a twentieth-century heroine.

## A Strong Family Background

Born April 15, 1892, in Bloemendaal, Holland, to clockmaker Casper ten Boom and his wife, Corrie lived half her life on a village street alongside craftsmen and shopkeepers. Quietly keeping the books and repairing watches in her father's shop in Haarlem, Corrie formed warm, lasting friendships with neighbors and opened a church school for retarded children. Surrounded by two sisters, a brother, three aunts, and numerous nieces and nephews during the bleak 1930s, she relied on family support, especially after her mother's death from a cerebral hemorrhage.

From early childhood, Corrie relied on the strength and wisdom of her father. In her autobiography, *The Hiding Place*, she quotes his comforting words to her at a particularly dismal point in her life—the age at which she realized the finality of death: "When the time comes that some of us will have to die, you will look into your heart and find the strength you need—just in time."[1]

# A Firm Commitment

Times grew hard in Holland for Jews and Gentiles both after the queen's departure. Eventually, the country was forced to surrender to the Nazis. Curfew and rationing inhibited Willem's underground resettlement work until Corrie and other assistants offered backup. They risked discovery and pedaled their bikes to meetings, where fellow rescuers took the generic name of Smit to lessen chances of arrest. As Jewish neighbors began to disappear from Haarlem, hiding places for them became scarce.

In 1942, two years after the fall of Holland, ten Boom committed her family to a program of concealing refugees behind her bed in a secret room built by a sympathetic architect. To provide necessary food, she used stolen ration cards, which were delivered by Fred Koornstra, who posed as a meter reader. With Fred's help, she saved over 700 lives.

To protect their operation, the family resorted to secrecy, regular drills, a hidden buzzer, and a window signal, but were betrayed by Jan Vogel, a Dutch informer. As Corrie lay in bed with flu on the morning of February 28, 1944, SS officers arrested a total of 35 people, including Corrie, Betsie, and Casper. Corrie, at age 52, was identified as ring leader. The Gestapo discovered their hidden radio, but failed to locate the false wall. With the aid of Rolf, a sympathetic local police officer, Corrie managed to shred and flush down the toilet incriminating documents.

On the evening of their arrest, the group, accustomed to sharing prayers and scripture readings with Casper, clustered around him for solace. From memory, he quoted: "Thou art my hiding place and my shield: I hope in thy word.... Hold thou me up, and I shall be safe...."[2] From this stirring recitation Corrie took the title of her autobiographical account of the ten Boom family's capture and imprisonment.

# In Enemy Hands

At the first hearing, Casper reaffirmed the family's ministry to "any man in need who knocks."[3] He and his daughters parted at police headquarters. The old man failed to survive the first ten days of incarceration and died in the hallway of The Hague. At Scheveningen, a seaside penitentiary, Betsie and Corrie were separated. Still, they communicated whenever possible.

Prison was made bearable by smuggled amenities—two bars of soap, a package of safety pins, and four Gospels of a Bible, which Corrie kept in a bag around her neck. Ten Boom at first had cellmates, then was taken to a solitary chamber, "six steps long, two wide, a single cot at the back."[4] Even communication with prison guards was forbidden.

Ten Boom struggled to maintain sanity and keep well in the face of bitter cold and loneliness. She fashioned a knife from a corset stay and scratched a calendar. On it she recorded important dates—arrest, transport to Scheveningen, beginning of solitary confinement, and her birthday. To celebrate, she began singing, then was cut short by an authoritative voice. To steady herself, she read the Bible and made friends with an ant.

Messages from home brought hope to ten Boom, who contracted pleurisy and the early stages of tuberculosis. She learned of relatives and friends who had been released from custody. A package containing a sweater, cookies, vitamins, needle and thread, and a red towel arrived. Beneath the stamp on the package was a concealed sentence—the Jews left behind during the raid were safe. Ten Boom wept with relief.

In May, she received a letter telling of her father's death. Lieutenant Rahms, ten Boom's interrogator, tried to extract information about her smuggling operation and refugee way station. Impressed by her staunch faith and her determination to help downtrodden people, Rahms, who despised his work, responded to her evangelism. In mid-June 1944, he reunited her with Willem and other members of her family for the reading of Casper's will, which awarded the Haarlem home and shop jointly to Betsie and Corrie.

## Evacuation to a Work Camp

As the Allies brought pressure against the Nazis, Corrie was evacuated by train south to Vught, a concentration camp for political prisoners near Brabant. Disembarking onto a muddy path, she, Betsie, and other female prisoners marched for over a mile to a wooden barracks surrounded by barbed wire. Her room contained bare tables and benches that served as beds.

The guards intimidated prisoners who made trouble, threatening to wedge them into locker-sized bunkers and tie their hands over their heads until they were adequately punished. In the face of grim surroundings, Betsie, anemic and weak, took hope and announced her plan to spread Christian love among prisoners and guards alike. She surprised her sister by declaring, "Corrie, if people can be taught to hate, they can be taught to love! We must find the way, you and I, no matter how long it takes."[5]

Because of her background as a watchmaker, Corrie was assigned to assemble tiny parts at the Phillips radio factory. Her role was to measure glass rods and arrange them by size. The monotony of the work was relieved by the kindness of Moorman, the foreman and a fellow prisoner, who taught her how to sabotage radios as a means of deterring the Nazis.

Next, Corrie and Betsie were transported for four days with a group of eighty women aboard a single waste-fouled rail car to Ravensbruck, Germany, site of a notorious women's extermination camp. The gray walls were posted with skull and crossbones to warn of electrified wiring along the top. Huge iron gates opened to admit arrivals. In place of barracks, Corrie and the others were assigned to a canvas pavilion. Inside, the straw-covered ground, their only bed, teemed with lice and later was soaked with rain.

The two sisters, assigned to Barracks 8, within earshot of the punishment center, stayed their fears with hymn-singing and prayer. Following weeks of quarantine, in October they moved to permanent quarters. The foul stench of women stacked three layers high on wooden platforms caused constant claustrophobia. The babble of voices was a tapestry of languages representing many nationalities.

## Hard Work and Sickness

Corrie and Betsie plodded to grueling eleven-hour work details at the Siemens factory, where they pushed a handcart and unloaded metal plates from a boxcar. Each Friday, the prisoners submitted to the humiliation of physical examinations. As winter set in, the Siemens factory closed and the two women were assigned to road work near the camp wall.

A week before Christmas, Betsie, who had been coughing up blood, suffered paralysis in her limbs. As she was loaded onto a stretcher, she muttered, "Must tell people that there is no pit so deep that He is not deeper still. They will listen to us, Corrie, because we have been there."[6]

Corrie found a way to visit her sister, who later died in the camp infirmary. As the time approached for discharge from the prison camp, Corrie remained in the hospital until swelling in her legs receded. After Christmas, her legs returned to normal. She was outfitted in decent clothes and new shoes and forced to sign release papers stating that her treatment at Ravensbruck had been good.

## Back to Holland

On New Year's Day 1945, ten Boom traveled by train to a bomb-gutted terminal in Berlin. On the way, her bread and ration coupons were stolen. She wandered fitfully from station to station, trying to bargain for food. In the coffee bar at the Uelzen station, ten Boom fell asleep and was beaten on the ear for vagrancy. A kindly station worker who spoke Dutch helped her onto the right train, which took her back to Holland.

At Groningen, where the sabotaged rail lines ended, ten Boom limped toward a hospital. There, a kind nurse recognized the symptoms of malnutrition, fed her tea and rusks, and treated her to a hot bath, a bed with sheets, and pillows on which to prop her swollen legs. Ten Boom, her skin encrusted with scabs, reveled in the woman's kind treatment.

She drew back in alarm at the pristine tablecloth and polished silver. To ten Boom, the table indicated that the hospital staff was having a party. In her words, "Like a savage watching his first civilized meal I copied the leisurely gestures of the others as they passed bread and cheese and unhurriedly stirred their coffee."[7]

Following ten days of recuperation, Corrie telephoned Willem, who was by then gravely ill with tuberculosis. Climbing aboard a food truck, she traveled illegally by night without headlights to a rendezvous at Willem's nursing home in Hilversum. She rejoiced in being held and loved by family members once more. With heavy emotion in her voice, she told them about Betsie's ministry in the prison, work camp, and extermination camp and of her bravery in the face of death.

Because of limitations on travel, Corrie had to wait for the return trip to Haarlem. Willem arranged for a long black limousine with official government plates and curtained windows. When Corrie climbed inside, she recognized an old friend whom she had last seen, bruised and bleeding, in a prison bus at The Hague. From him she learned that all but one of the Jews who had been in the hiding place when she was arrested had survived.

## A New Mission

As life returned to normal at the watch repair shop, ten Boom began taking in feebleminded residents of Haarlem, whom family members hid to save them from extermination by the Nazis. The work busied her hands, but did not still her restless mind. She filled the windowsills with plants and hired repairmen for the shop, but was unable to relax in her old home. To quell discontent, she returned to underground work and delivered falsified release papers to the police station.

Back home on quaking knees, she thought over the situation. Ten Boom refused to credit her skill at deception to natural talent. Always, she thanked God for being with her in difficult situations. Then the reason for her restlessness became clear. She missed her sister, who had stood beside her during hard times and given her courage. Accepting the fact that Betsie was gone forever, she repeated her sister's commitment: "We must tell people, Corrie. We must tell them what we learned."[8]

As the war wound down in the spring of 1945, ten Boom began spreading the news of her prison experiences and the need for a home to aid victims of the war. As she bumped down cobbled streets on her bicycle, she found the place vastly changed. No familiar tulips bloomed that spring. Hungry people had eaten them. Ten Boom found the landscape cheerless, but she discovered love and commitment in the hearts of people who came to hear her speak.

Corrie shouldered the task she and Betsie had begun in prison—turning hate into love. With the aid of a Dutch aristocrat, Mrs. Bierens de Haan, she opened a center for war victims in a fifty-six-room mansion in Bloemendaal. Work in the surrounding gardens proved therapeutic and eased the mental torment of inmates. In May 1945 the Allies liberated Holland from the Nazis. Dutch flags flew once more from the windows and the "Wilhelmus," the Dutch national anthem, sounded day and night. Canadian donors rushed food to the cities.

By June, hundreds of victims began pouring in to the center. Each required care. By 1947, the flood peaked a second time with survivors of Japanese prison camps in Indonesia. Ten Boom, absorbed in mission work, donated her own residence to the most despised of the war victims—members of the NSB or Dutch collaborators, who crept about the streets with shaved heads and furtive eyes. Eventually she saw signs of their repatriation among vengeful countrymen. "As flowers bloomed or vegetables ripened," she wrote, "talk was less of the bitter past, more of tomorrow's weather."[9]

## A Full Life

Corrie ten Boom's post-war activities included the establishment of a refuge for Dutch war victims at Darmstadt in 1946 and years of touring the world to spread her evangelistic message. Her home stayed in use for war victims until 1950, when it was enlarged to welcome other invalids for rehabilitation.

One night at a church service in Munich, Germany, ten Boom met a personal enemy, the SS guard who had herded naked women prisoners to the showers at Ravensbruck. He greeted her warmly and shook her hand. Paralyzed by her own pain-wracked memories, she recalls the feeling of his touch: "From my shoulder along my arm and through my hand a current seemed to pass from me to him, while into my heart sprang a love for this stranger that almost overwhelmed me."[10] Her own healing had begun.

As age took its toll, ten Boom turned from hands-on missions to the printed word. Among her numerous books are *A Prisoner and Yet* (1954); *Amazing Love* (1959); *Plenty for Everyone* (1967); a bestseller, *The Hiding Place* (1971); *Tramp for the Lord* (1974); *Corrie ten Boom's Prison Letters* (1975); *In My Father's House* (1976); and *This Day Is the Lord's* (1979).

In 1959, ten Boom returned to Ravensbruck Prison to honor its 96,000 female victims. She learned from camp records that her release had been a mistake. Had she remained, she would have gone with others her age to the gas chamber. Heartened by her luck, she took up Betsie's evangelistic mission as a memorial to her sister and best friend.

The founder of Christians, Incorporated, Corrie supported missions with the proceeds of her books. She visited oppressed people in Cuban sugar fields, African schools, British prisons, factories in Uzbek, and parts of the communist bloc. Her personal outreach included the adoption of a Vietnam refugee, Do Van Nguyen. After a heart ailment and several strokes slowed her evangelistic activities, she settled with friends in Placentia, California, where she died on her birthday in 1983 at the age of 91.

Corrie ten Boom wrote her most important work, her autobiography, with the aid of John and Elizabeth Sherrill, both editors for *Guideposts* magazine. The work was the basis for the World Wide Pictures movie of the same name, starring Julie Harris as Betsie and Jeannette Clift as Corrie. Corrie ten Boom's vita contains no accolades or honorary doctorates. Her reward lies in the number of readers who turn to her autobiography for an account of one Dutch woman's spiritual development and struggle against Nazi tyranny.

# Notes

1 Corrie Ten Boom. *The Hiding Place.* New York: Bantam Books, 1971, 25.

2 Ten Boom, 135.

3 Ten Boom, 138.

4 Ten Boom, 147.

5 Ten Boom, 175.

6 Ten Boom, 217.

7 Ten Boom, 229.

8 Ten Boom, 234.

9 Ten Boom, 237.

10 Ten Boom, 238.

# Sources

Ten Boom, Corrie. *The Hiding Place.* Bantam Books, 1971.

# Lech Walesa

To move from skilled laborer to president of an emerging nation is more than an accomplishment—it's a miracle. Lech Walesa, Poland's president, like Abraham Lincoln, rose from simple origins to man of the hour. Also like Lincoln, Walesa carried with him an almost mythic stance among his countrymen. Like his pious, industrious ancestor, Mateusz, Lech, a devout Catholic and father of nine, spoke the rough vernacular of the semi-literate worker. But the gist of his words left no doubt of the dissident's heartfelt call for a new day in Poland.

An ordinary man in size and appearance with neatly groomed mustache, curling reddish-brown hair, and rosy Saint Nicholas cheeks, he carries his five-foot-six-inch frame with pride. He has a feel for the land and its promise. A man of bravura and humor, he understands how the media can carry his message of liberty to working people throughout Poland. By making the most of his charisma and Poland's drive to end Communist domination, he has served his country well.

## Early Times

Lech Walesa has not known a life of luxury. He was born in 1943 in Popowo, Poland, the fourth of seven children. His village lay to the south of Gdansk on the banks of the Vistula River. His simple home was situated on seven acres of swampland. His father, Boleslaw, worked as a carpenter and married Fela Kaminska, a local girl who was well-read, but had only four years' education.

Times were not propitious for Lech's birth. Because of the German occupation of Poland, which began in June 1941, Poles went without necessities. In the months before Lech's birth, his father hid from conscription in dense forest before being arrested and imprisoned in Chalin. He was forced to labor near Lipno, a grueling assignment which broke his health. Two months after his return in 1945, he died of lung disease. As Boleslaw directed in his final moments, Lech's mother married Boleslaw's brother Stanislaw, a lumberman and builder. The couple had three sons.

Lech's childhood was marked by devotion to two stabilizing influences: his family and the church. Like most farm boys, he played soccer, swam, and chopped hay for the stock. He took seriously the example he set for the younger children. For his self-confidence and goodwill, his older sister, Izabela, nick-named him the "village mayor."

Lech studied farm machinery at a state school in Lipno, where his performance was average and his behavior at times rowdy. In an attempt to better his lot, he worked for the POM (State Agricultural Depot) and learned to repair a wide range of items, including farm machinery, televisions, motorbikes, and washing machines. With a sound reputation as a competent mechanic, he at first found satisfaction in his life.

## A Taste of Discontent

At twenty-four, Walesa suffered minor discontent when a love affair soured and his job grew stale and unchallenging. He left the POM in 1967 and settled in Gdansk, a seaport on the Gulf of Danzig on the Baltic Sea. As a naval electrician he laid and spliced cable on fishing boats in the Lenin Shipyard. Accustomed to some variety in his former job as a general repairman, he disliked intense speciali-zation, but stuck with his job choice anyway.

Walesa was particularly dismayed at the poor working conditions. There were no facilities to dry rain-soaked work clothes and no cafeterias. The work week was long and the pay barely adequate. Workers, lacking homogeneity, vied for places in a complicated caste system that lacked an even-handed reward system. Walesa recalls the dreariness and lack of autonomy in his career: "Even though most of us realized we were being manipulated and this knowledge gave us a certain superiority over the directors of the shipyard, the fact was we were shuffled about in a way which left us with little control over our destinies."[1]

## A Man with Responsibilities

After meeting dark-haired, brown-eyed Miroslawa Danuta at a flower stall in 1969, Walesa married her in a few months. He and his new wife, whom he affectionately called Danka, settled in a hostel, a four-story tenement, on Klono-wicza Street. Surrounding the building was a littered vacant lot. The interior, similar to a dormitory, was bleak, with a kitchen and bathroom at the end of each hall. The stresses of work, fights, and drinking dominated family existence, so as soon as they could afford to, the Walesas moved to an attic over a beauty salon.

Work became more grueling as new policies changed the basis for wages. With a ploy which fooled no one, political economists recommended more work for a meager amount of zlotys. Safety measures, also inadequate, led to needless deaths as teams pressed for the finish of each ship. In 1968, twenty welders died in a fire fueled by tanks filled early in a foolish cost-cutting measure. As Walesa observed these reckless management blunders, he commented, "The money saved, at our expense, and which didn't benefit the engineer in any way, served to aggravate the mutual distrust between labor and management."[2] A labor leader in the making, he began fighting worker oppression.

## The Beginnings of Revolt

When a rise in food prices provoked a unanimous outcry in December 1970, Lech witnessed spontaneous revolt. Workers, united as never before, sang the Polish national anthem and the "Internationale," a spirited workers' anthem. Walesa joined with 4,000 other shipyard workers in a confused scene. The uproar concluded in the militia's massacre of 55 strikers during a four-day clash. The resignation of Wladyslaw Gomulka and the instatement of Edward Gierek as Communist party leader benefitted laborers, to whom Gierek made concessions.

Lech's first attempts at organization were disappointing. Unable to sit by while his country suffered at the hands of corrupt, incompetent officials, he organized a strike. The officials labeled him a troublemaker. After the revolt failed, he was arrested, interrogated, and forced to sign an oath of loyalty to the Communist government. A change in the labor policy at top bureaucratic levels brought some concessions and promises of lower prices, but the workers' situation soon returned to an intolerable state. In the spring of 1976, Walesa's leadership role led to hard times after he received his official dismissal from the shipyard because of attempts to organize workers.

## Forced to Take Action

While immersed in the business of raising a growing family—with a new baby arriving about every other year—Walesa found a job as a mechanic in Stogi, but remained attuned to the political situation, particularly through reading editorials in *Robotnik*, a workers' newsletter. He actively followed the progress of fledgling independent unions, even though secret police maintained discreet surveillance, and continued to meet with secret committees and distribute leaflets, some of which he printed in his crowded quarters. His activism led to unemployment and frequent unexplained jailings. His children often went hungry.

Walesa, a moderate, joined forces with KOR, the Committee for Social Self-Defense. Even though the group professed radical aims, it was useful to the growing workers' union, which still lacked its own educational and communications systems. The church, a mainstay of Polish peasants from early times, also served as a bolster. In 1976, church officials responded to urgent needs by pushing for amnesty and human rights. In June 1979, the first Polish Pope, John Paul II, came to Gdansk and met with Walesa. The meeting raised spirits and helped solidify patriotism among Poles.

In January 1979, Walesa, buoyed by worker commitment, initiated *The Worker of the Coast*, a bimonthly newsletter to inform laborers of developments in their movement. He likewise supported the twenty-one demands of workers, which called for free speech, an eight-hour work day, a voice in discussions of workers' rights, better job and safety conditions, and a reasonable wage. At this point in the push for freedom, the workers were beginning to sound like a viable force.

## Creating *Solidarnosc*

1980 became the landmark year of Polish activism. Because anti-union opposition reached a stalemate in Warsaw, the workers stepped into the void with their own organization, a free trade union called *Solidarnosc* with Walesa at its helm. For the first time, Polish citizens found a cause that united worker, farm laborer, and college graduate in the first free labor union in the history of communism. Overnight, world leaders began paying heed and lending support.

Late in the summer, the doubling of meat prices caused a nationwide strike, beginning with the workers' seizure of the Lenin Shipyard on August 14. Spokespersons demanded that Walesa be reinstated in his old position there. By August 31, government officials, cognizant of the threat they faced, reached a workable settlement with *Solidarnosc*. In a precedent-setting accord, Poland's workers gained major rights in both the workplace and religion.

The plan did not go unchallenged. In October, Walesa led a minor strike to counter delays in action. A second test occurred in November and ended with a moratorium on strikes. January saw a repeat clash of wills as Walesa forced the issue of free Saturdays. Via more confrontations, workers showed their determination not to back down to government niggling and intimidation. By September 1981, *Solidarnosc* was strong enough to demand free political elections and to urge the spread of free unions to other Communist countries.

## The Creation of a Leader

The next month, Walesa, not without his political adversaries, but the strongest voice among many, was reelected head of the movement. More power plays produced a November summit of three principals—Wojiech Jaruzelski, the Polish premier, Lech Walesa, and Archbishop Jozef Glemp. Walesa refused to be backed into a corner on political issues. Clinging firmly to the sole issue of workers' rights, he declined the role of anti-socialist.

On December 13, 1981, after 500 days of the *Solidarnosc* plan, Walesa was again arrested and martial law was established in Gdansk. He endured eleven months' confinement, which cost him vigor and youth and denied him close association with comrades, supporters, and fellow workers. In March 1983 he gained a tiny victory by returning to the shipyard offices after the end of martial law, although he was assigned to isolated work in a repair hut rather than daily association with his supporters, the rank-and-file workers.

By that time, life had improved for Walesa and his family. He wore a better grade of clothing for public appearances and moved his family from their two-room apartment to one three times larger. With Danuta's support, he continued his hectic lifestyle of travel and meetings, always surrounded by bodyguards.

The reward for his commitment to Polish workers' rights was the 1983 Nobel Peace Prize, a fitting tribute to his self-denial and fortitude. Fearful that Communist apologists would demand his ouster, he delegated Danuta to Oslo as his proxy. At home, he listened to the radio broadcast praising him as "one of the great spokesmen in the world today for the longing for freedom that can never be silenced."[3]

His reward from the Communists was typical—temporary exile from the shipyards. Their underhanded tactics included media broadcasts of personal slurs and accusations of collaboration with western powers as well as warnings from Warsaw that "political gatherings against the existing order" were not going to be tolerated.[4]

As Communism tottered in other parts of the bloc, Walesa evolved into a symbol. When Poland's government began to crumble, he was ready to step into the void to avert anarchy. A non-threatening (to the people), familiar figure, he worked tirelessly to bolster courage. He jeopardized his coalition by calling for "a president with an axe—decisive, tough, straightforward."[5] But he assured fearful voters that he did not want a dictator—only a man impervious to residual Communism.

On December 9, 1990, his long years of struggle reached a pinnacle. At the age of forty-seven, he defeated challenger Stanislaw Tyminski, a Polish-born Canadian entrepreneur, and was elected president of Poland's first post-Communist government by a landslide vote of 75 percent. He and Danuta were at last leaving tenements for the Belvedere Palace.

## An Oath to the People

Standing alongside his wife before both houses of Parliament on December 22, Lech Walesa took oath: "I solemnly swear to the Polish people that I will be faithful to constitutional decisions. I will protect the dignity of the nation, the sovereignty and security of the state.... So help me God." His first promise was to end Russian influence in internal political matters. He vowed to make Poland "an element of peaceful order in Europe."[6] However, President Walesa's promises were not without their warnings of increased responsibility. The people, he said, must continue to believe in themselves and their economy. He admonished them that passivity and apathy were the greatest stumbling blocks in Poland's future.

In a mild gesture of revenge toward Jaruzelski, who harrassed Walesa in his rise to power with frequent jailings, President Walesa ignored the former premier and refused to invite him to the inauguration. Taking the reins from the government-in-exile, which had subsisted in London since the rise of Nazism in 1939, he revived popular control in ceremonies held at the Royal Castle, where Poland produced its first democratic constitution in 1791. He consecrated his presidency with the blessing of Poland's Catholic head, Cardinal Jozef Glemp and announced triumphantly, "Since we defeated the system without one gunshot or one drop of blood, we can dare to build a new system."[7]

## Counting the Cost

President Walesa's rise from electrician and mechanic to cult leader of a revitalized democracy in central Europe was not without cost. One of his earliest formal acts was paying homage to workers machine-gunned in the 1970 strike. A fitting tribute—three tall metal crosses raised by local welders—now stands in the yard. Walesa promised to remember their intent as he worked to improve life for the working classes of Poland. He also pledged to push for a free market while lowering prices and unemployment.

Looking over the twenty-year struggle, Walesa admitted that internal strife had taken its toll. The nation owed $49 billion in foreign debt. Communist hangers-on continued to fill important roles that could not be delegated to working-class Poles. His personal life exhibited its own travail—in 1973, his mother died in a highway accident while visiting the United States. Her husband, Walesa's uncle and stepfather, took up residence in Jersey City, New Jersey, leaving Walesa without the familiar support he had always depended on. His body, too, rebelled against long hours and short rations with stomach ulcers and an aggravated heart condition.

As he examined the shreds of governmental machinery that remained, Walesa found a need to reshape factories and markets. Of the large factories, he waggishly proposed to turn them "into bakeries or museums of Marxism and Leninism."[8] But Walesa, a purposeful common man capable of panache, demonstrated early in his administration that dramatic quick fixes were not an option and that hard work was the order of the day. For Poland, the road to private enterprise and an end to austerity covered ground similar to Walesa's journeys twenty years earlier. It demanded more sacrifices, more dedication. Fortunately for Poland, Lech Walesa knew the way.

## Notes

[1] Lech Walesa. *A Way of Hope.* New York: Henry Holt, 1987, 51.

[2] Walesa, 51.

[3] Sue Masterman. "Walesa's Tumultuous Life," *Maclean's*, December 19, 1983, 21.

[4] Masterman, 22.

[5] Nemeth, Mary. "A Lesson for Walesa," *Maclean's*, February 24, 1990, 16.

[6] "Walesa Sworn in as President of Poland," *Hickory Daily Record*, December 22, 1990, 6D.

[7] James Walsh. "Populism on the March," *Time*, December 24, 1990, 44.

[8] Victoria Pope and Christopher Bobinski. "Weimar Poland?: The Authoritarian Temptation," *U.S. News and World Report*, December 10, 1990, 39.

## Sources

Craig, Mary. *Lech Walesa and His Poland*. New York: Continuum Press, 1987.

*Current Biography*. Detroit: Gale Research, 1981.

*International Who's Who*. Detroit: Gale Research, 1982.

Lacayo, Richard. "A Stranger Calls," *Time*, December 10, 1990, 48-49.

Lamb, Charles, and Andrew Nagorski. "The Perils of Poland," *Newsweek*, December 10, 1990, 40-42.

Masterman, Sue. "Walesa's Tumultuous Life," *Maclean's*, December 19, 1983, 21-23.

Nemeth, Mary. "A Lesson for Walesa," *Maclean's*, February 24, 1990, 16.

"Poland's Prayers for Freedom Rest in a Man of Faith—and Bold Deeds," *People Weekly*, December 28, 1981, 28-30.

Pope, Victoria, and Christopher Bobinski. "Weimar Poland?: The Authoritarian Temptation," *U.S. News and World Report*, December 10, 1990, 38-39.

Walesa, Lech. *A Way of Hope*. New York: Henry Holt, 1987.

"Walesa Sworn in as President of Poland," *Hickory Daily Record*, December 22, 1990, 6D.

Walsh, James. "Populism on the March," *Time*, December 24, 1990, 44.

# Sarah Breedlove Walker

The most satisfying of late achievements come to those who quell negative voices and scale high obstacles. For Sarah Jane Breedlove Walker, being female was one mountain to cross. Behind that mountain lay an even greater obstacle—race prejudice. With little more than a fresh and practical idea for straightening curly hair, at age forty-four she escaped the white world's economic domination and built a cosmetic empire that touched the lives of nearly every black woman in America and a sizeable number of white women as well.

A century after Sarah Walker's discovery, Sara Spencer Washington's Apex System and Annie M. Turnbo Malone's Poro System follow the same procedures that began the boom years for black cosmetics. Curly-haired white customers continue to patronize Harlem beauty emporia, and Fifth Avenue boutiques offer to "transform the most stubborn locks from difficult snarls and curls to sleek, smooth or slightly wavy hair" with a process invented by a St. Louis washer-woman, the daughter of former slaves.[1]

## Humble Beginnings

Life did not give success to Sarah Walker. She fashioned it from hard work, determination, and native American ingenuity. Born on December 23, 1867—during the Reconstruction era, two years after the end of the Civil War—in the tiny village of Delta, Louisiana, due west and across the Mississippi River from Vicksburg, Mississippi, Sarah was the daughter of Owen and Minerva Breedlove, a poor farm couple who died when she was six years old. Her married sister raised her. Besides the fact that Sarah received little education and spoke poor English, little else is known of her early circumstances.

Sarah grew up to be a striking, well-groomed woman with broad, even features, short hair smoothed and shaped into classic pageboy style, and a stocky frame. She was not a beauty, but she had the skills to utilize her features to advantage and the ambition to make the most of her talents. In 1877, she and her sister moved to Vicksburg to find better jobs. There, at age fourteen, she married a man named McWilliams. Her husband died five years later, leaving her with a young daughter. Sarah moved to St. Louis to work as a hotel washerwoman to support herself and her child A'Lelia, whom she hoped to educate beyond her own level of attainment.

## A Better Mousetrap

In her forties, Sarah discovered a solution to a uniquely black problem: how to straighten tightly curled hair. For generations before her revolutionary process, blacks had spread clean hair on ironing boards and pressed it with hot flatirons. This method was unwieldy, dangerous to the scalp and face, and hard on the hair, which often broke from the heavy irons and excess and uncontrolled heat.

Sarah invested in a better system. Reflecting on the discovery later in her life, she claimed that she abandoned her soapsuds one afternoon, lay down on a wooden bench for a nap, and dreamed of a method that showed her each step of a hair-straightening process. She declared that she applied simple laundry room techniques to the problem and paid her way with "two dollars and a dream."[2] She fashioned a hot iron comb to press each tress and formulated a hair ointment to soften strands and produce sheen. She made up batches of her pomade in a tub, then packed the mixture in jars and sold them to her many customers.

## From Process to Sales

In 1906, Sarah followed her brother to Denver, where she met and married newspaperman Charles Joseph Walker and, because of its Continental connotation, adopted the name Madame C. J. Walker. To increase sales of her facial and hair care products, she began selling door to door, then organized agents in "Walker Clubs" to assist her. Her process worked so well that she opened her own shop and trained a staff of assistants. She awarded her workers with praise and cash bonuses and encouraged them to keep sanitary shops. Later, she increased her outreach through mail-order sales.

Word of Sarah Walker's achievements spread among the black communities of the South, the East, and the Caribbean as a result of her travels, department store demonstrations, and lectures to church groups and women's clubs. At first women ridiculed the idea of straightened hair because it violated the black norm. Then the idea caught on. Soon white women were admiring the smooth hair of their housemaids and inquiring about the process that could deliver snarl-free tresses to any person with untamed natural curl.

The idea of black business success appealed to young girls who hoped to start their own shops. Walker, to meet the demand, opened a beauty school, charged $25, and issued diplomas to hair culturists and scalp specialists who applied the Walker Method of hair straightening and hair growing. After singer Josephine Baker began lending her name to the Walker Process, its popularity spread to Europe.

246 / SARAH BREEDLOVE WALKER

For protegées to follow Sarah Walker's example, they needed the right tools. She began marketing softening pomade, hair-growing tonic and strengtheners, and hot combs to do the straightening. To her line of hair goods she added sixteen toiletries, fragrances, and facial treatments, notably a complexion cream formulated to remove wrinkles. In 1908, she opened a branch office in Pittsburgh and placed A'Lelia in charge. Two years later she moved the operation to Indianapolis and built her first factory to manufacture her products on a large scale. Her company became a mainstay of the Indianapolis economy.

By 1917, Sarah Walker was employing 3,000 workers in America's largest black-owned business and was earning more from sales of equipment and supplies and from her chain of beauty schools than from the original sales operation. The payroll rose to more than $200,000. Her skill with advertising kept her name and products before the public.

## The Black Entrepreneur

Walker's success fit neatly into a pattern of increasing wealth and independence among blacks. After the Civil War brought emancipation to American blacks and Reconstruction began the healing process, two clarion voices impelled blacks to open their own businesses and seek success apart from the white marketplace. Marcus Garvey, who began the Back to Africa movement, and Booker T. Washington, scientist and educator, both encouraged commerce. In 1900, Washington established the National Negro Business League in Boston, where delegates from thirty-four states met to discuss issues.

Detrimental to this surge of black businesses was the lack of capital and credit, which crippled entrepreneurs from the start. To improve this situation, Albon L. Holsey organized black-owned grocery markets into the Colored Merchants Association. Unfortunately, his timing was poor. The Depression ended his hopes for an alliance.

Other blacks were more successful than Holsey. C. C. Spaulding, who owned the North Carolina Mutual Life Insurance Company in Durham, became a multimillionaire. His philosophy was anchored to the Puritan work ethic. In his words: "The most efficient weapon with which to fight segregation and discrimination is success. But you can't drink from the spring high up on the mountain unless you climb for the water. You must not expect the law to hand it down to you."[3]

## First Lady of Harlem

Sarah Walker followed the pattern set by these turn-of-the-century black leaders. Because of her willingness to invest in black pride and to build a clientele among her own race, she became a social leader among *La Bourgeoisie Noire* or black middle class. Establishing herself in Harlem, she began her climb in 1913 by opening Lelia College and a chain of beauty salons.

Three years later Walker tried to buy land on which to build a country house in the Bishop Court section of Flushing, Long Island. When white residents rejected her money, she gave up hopes of living among the white middle class. Instead, she purchased three adjoining lots on an exclusive strip on West 136th Street along Irvington-on-the-Hudson in Harlem.

Walker made a bold move in razing the brownstone tenements that occupied the lots. She hired black architect Vertner W. Tandy to replace them with a modern hair care laboratory alongside an impressive Georgian mansion built out of cream-hued stucco and Indiana limestone. The building cost a quarter of a million dollars. The famed Italian tenor Enrico Caruso gave it its distinctive name, Villa Lewaro.

Inside, Walker splashed profuse evidence of her rise in society: colorful tapestries, French Renaissance and Hepplewhite furniture, wall-sized oil paintings, silver satyrs and cherubs, and lush Persian rugs. In grand style, she bought a twenty-four-carat-gold-plated grand piano with matching phonograph, a pipe organ costing $60,000, and a clock as tall as a telephone pole. Her penchant for luxury and splendor was everywhere—in the impressive sweep of the white marble staircase, the landscaped gardens, the monogrammed linens and silverware, the best in china and glass, and the imported Japanese prayer trees, each costing $10,000. At the door stood a black majordomo, whose demeanor matched the hauteur of his employer. The total spent on interiors came to $400,000. The Walker mansion achieved supreme status as a New York landmark when tour buses began passing the location and giving short descriptions of the splendors inside.

To expunge the stigma of her earlier role as laundress, Sarah employed a tutor, studied elocution, and practiced standard English. Other indications of her success were manifold. She greeted the cream of black society, including both Washington and Garvey, her friend and mentor. Attached to her name was the sobriquet of first black female millionaire in the United States and one of the first of all American women to achieve entrepreneurial success by her own enterprise. To her musicales, balls, and soirées came not only black entertainers, but also European opera stars, actors, musicians, artists, politicians, and statesmen. She became known as the social dictator of black New York.

Sarah Walker also supported black causes. She was a generous contributor to the National Association for the Advancement of Colored People as well as retirement homes and halfway houses for the poor in St. Louis and Indianapolis. She also underwrote scholarships for women at Tuskegee Institute, Bethune-Cookman College, and Palmer Memorial Institute. With liberal amounts of funds, she endowed black YWCA chapters and homes for orphans.

## The End of an Era

Within a short time, Madame C. J. Walker's rise in social and business circles became legend. But the story ended quickly. Deep into plans for a trip to Africa, she ignored warnings of high blood pressure from doctors at the Kellogg Clinic in Battle Creek, Michigan. A short, intense bout with hypertension ended with Sarah's death from nephritis at the age of fifty on May 24, 1919, only two years after the completion of her house. Sarah was eulogized at Mother Zion Church and buried at Woodlawn Cemetery in the Bronx.

To her credit, she established a noteworthy dynasty that continued to influence Harlem affairs, particularly the arts, for a dozen more years. Many black schools and benevolences received bequests from Sarah's will, particularly a girls' academy in West Africa, which she established with the generous sum of $100,000. In all she left two-thirds of her estate to charity. Her daughter, A'Lelia McWilliams Robinson, dubbed the "Mahogany Millionairess," received the rest—an estate worth $2 million.

A'Lelia inherited extravagant tastes from her mother and continued the Walker tradition. A tall, broad-backed, brown-skinned beauty, she decked herself in overdone ball gowns and towering turbans. In 1923, she used her mother's wealth to spotlight her own daughter, who was married in a lavish church ceremony called the "million dollar wedding."

Held at Harlem's swanky St. Philip's Protestant Episcopal Church, the ceremony, actually costing $62,000, was attended by 1,500 guests. It brought 10,000 lookers-on. The sumptuous display blocked downtown traffic as gawkers waited for a glimpse of the pampered bride. As Roi Ottley described the show, Harlemites wanted to see the "granddaughter of the woman who, having pulled herself up by the roots of other people's hair, founded America's first black plutocratic dynasty."[4] The day was complete with an even showier catered wedding breakfast and reception at Villa Lewaro.

Eventually, A'Lelia's nonstop spending topped even her mother's reputation for extravagance. The bizarre costumes and the completion of Dark Tower, her salon for the elite of the art world, brought in the greatest of black literati, particularly James Weldon Johnson, Zora Neale Hurston, Langston Hughes, Countee Cullen, and other notables of the Harlem Renaissance. In 1928, A'Lelia dedicated one floor of her mansion to cultivation of the arts. To regular gatherings came royalty, white socialites, and even the fabled Rothschilds. The *Inter-State Tattler* reported: "All classes and colors met face to face, ultra-aristocrats, bourgeoisie, Communists, Park Avenuers galore, bookers, publishers, Broadway celebs, and Harlemites giving each other the once-over."[5] A'Lelia halted the gaudy parade in 1930, auctioned off the appointments of Villa Lewaro, leased the building to New York City for a health clinic, then, like her mother, died suddenly in August 1931. Because of the Depression, few bidders vied for the splendors of Sarah Walker's empire. Times had changed. Madame Walker's era had passed.

## The Walker Legacy

Today, the wedge-shaped Madame Walker Urban Life Center stands on Indiana Avenue as a landmark of Indianapolis's black community. A monument to Madame Walker, the building honors the daughter of former slaves who made the American dream a reality for non-whites. The four-story building, which A'Lelia built in 1927 for $1 million, features African and Egyptian decor and once housed Sarah Walker's College of Beauty Culture as well as a dance company, theater and casino. At one time the casino drew top jazz and blues performers Ella Fitzgerald, Lena Horne, Louis Armstrong, Duke Ellington, and Cab Calloway. Today the center is a memorial not only to Madame Walker but also to the black entrepreneurial spirit.

Sarah Walker was a powerful and vocal proponent of black pride. She set an example of cleanliness and beauty, a philosophy and practice that undergirded her image. An editorial that appeared in *The Crisis* two months after her death applauded the fact that Walker "revolutionized the personal habits and appearance of millions of human beings."[6] James Weldon Johnson memorialized her for helping black women enhance their beauty. In later years, *Ebony Magazine* selected Madame Walker as its first recipient of the Hall of Fame award given to outstanding black Americans.

Today Madame Walker's example remains strong. Students from the United States and foreign countries still study the Walker Method at beauty colleges, and agents sell her cosmetics worldwide. On October 14, 1988, the Walker Theater, which closed in 1965, reopened following a $3.5 million restoration. Notables such as Gregory Hines, Alex Haley, Roscoe Lee Brown, George Faison and his dance ensemble, and Isaac Hayes attended the gala celebration.

At the opening night ribbon-cutting festivity, Sarah Walker's great-great grandchildren, Mark and A'Lelia Bundles, attended. A'Lelia, a producer for NBC-TV, commented proudly on her famous forebear and her contribution to black history: "This building has been preserved as a center for the black community. The building opened in 1928, but [my grandmother] never saw it. But I'm sure this is what she would have wanted. I'm sure she's smiling down on us now."[7]

## Notes

[1] Roi Ottley and William J. Weatherby, eds. *The Negro in New York.* Dobbs Ferry, New York: Oceana Publications, 1967, 239.

[2] Roi Ottley. *New World A-Coming: Inside Black America.* Boston: Houghton Mifflin, 1943, 247.

[3] Roi Ottley. *Black Odyssey: The Story of the Negro in America.* New York: Charles Scribner's Sons, 1948, 240.

[4] *New World*, 173.

[5] *New World*, 174.

[6] Rayford W. Logan and Michael R. Winston. *Dictionary of American Negro Biography*. New York: W. W. Norton, 1982, 621.

[7] "Rebirth of Walker Theatre Brings Celebs to Indianapolis," *Jet*, October 31, 1988, 62.

## Sources

James, Edward T., et al., eds. *Notable American Women, 1607-1950*. Cambridge, Massachusetts: Belknap Press, 1971.

Logan, Rayford W., and Michael R. Winston. *Dictionary of American Negro Biography*. New York: W. W. Norton, 1982.

Low, W. Augustus, and Virgil A. Clift. *Encyclopedia of Black America*. New York: McGraw-Hill, 1981.

McHenry, Robert, ed. *Liberty's Women*. Springfield, Massachusetts: G. and C. Merriam, 1980.

Ottley, Roi. *Black Odyssey: The Story of the Negro in America*. New York: Charles Scribner's Sons, 1948.

_____. *New World A-Coming: Inside Black America*. Boston: Houghton Mifflin, 1943.

Ottley, Roi, and William J. Weatherby, eds. *The Negro in New York*. Dobbs Ferry, New York: Oceana Publications, 1967.

Ploski, Harry A., and James Williams. *The Negro Almanac, a Reference Work on the Afro-American*. New York: John Wiley and Sons, 1983.

"Rebirth of Walker Theatre Brings Celebs to Indianapolis," *Jet*, October 31, 1988, 53-62.

Sterling, Dorothy. *We Are Your Sisters: Black Women in the Nineteenth Century*. New York: W. W. Norton, 1984.

Toppin, Edgar A. *A Biographical History of Blacks in America Since 1528.* New York: David McKay, n.d.

Van Doren, Charles, and Robert McHenry, eds. *Webster's American Biographies.* Springfield, Massachusetts: G. & C. Merriam, 1974.

# Sam Moore Walton

For the central character in one of America's most noteworthy success stories, a late change in direction required only a minor shift. Sam Moore Walton—rail-thin, silver-haired financial success known affectionately as Mr. Sam and touted as America's richest man—began his career with training in the variety store business. Early on, he demonstrated adaptability by tinkering with contemporary modes of merchandising.

From small changes, he made giant strides into first place. Out of Sam Walton's successful venture in the mass-merchandising Wal-Mart chain came the legend of a small-town boy turned billionaire. As proof of his expertise, his competitors, especially K-Mart, tremble at the mention of his name. And he loves the challenge, beginning each week with his motto, "Thank God it's Monday!"[1]

Known more than anything else for finely tuned management, Sam Walton remains disarmingly folksy. Topped by the ubiquitous ball cap, his outward appearance is unassuming, his style gracious, his habits work-centered. His open and friendly attitude pays off in the motivation and loyalty of his workers. But closer to the pocketbook, he knows the way around a dollar and the best way not to spend one. Growing at an anual rate of 40 percent, his company tops the heap on Wall Street.

## Inauspicious Beginnings

Walton was characterized by a *Fortune* cover story as "rich, homespun, self-made and plain-spoken."[2] Born in Kingfisher, Oklahoma, on March 29, 1918, to a farm-country moneylender, Sam Walton was the oldest of three boys. He grew up in Bentonville (population 9,919), an Ozark Mountain town in the far northwest corner of Arkansas, where it comes together with Oklahoma and Missouri. During the Depression, he worked as a paperboy and dairy hand to augment family finances. Ambitious even during hard times, he entertained notions of becoming president.

In 1940 Walton earned a degree in economics from the University of Missouri. From there he moved to an $85-dollar-per-month trainee position at J. C. Penney's in Des Moines, Iowa. He married Helen Robson and began a family, which came to include one daughter and three sons. One of the sons, attorney S. Robson "Rob" Walton, is the owner of the *Bentonville Daily Democrat* and Wal-Mart's vice chairman. During World War II Walton served a three-year stateside hitch in the Army as an intelligence officer.

After the war, he invested $25,000 in a Ben Franklin variety store franchise in Newport, Arkansas. A workaholic from the outset, he established his pattern of eighteen-hour days. His expertise drew attention from the home office. When the lease expired, he opened Walton's Five & Dime adjacent to the town square in Bentonville in 1950. At the suggestion of his employer, Don Soderquist, president of the Ben Franklin chain, Walton investigated the phenomenon of the mammoth discounters. His method was simple and direct—he visited a K-Mart store, interviewed its personnel, and took notes.

## A Period of Growth

From this simple beginning, Walton expanded the discounting concept in 1962 by moving from urban centers to the country. With brother James L. "Bud" Walton, three years his junior, he opened his first Wal-Mart, an all-purpose general store, in Rogers, Arkansas, a rural town in Benton County about seven miles southeast of his hometown. The second Wal-Mart opened in Harrison, Arkansas, and featured truckloads of watermelons plus donkey rides in the parking lot to entertain customers' children.

By the late 1960s, Sam and brother Bud owned twenty stores, each marked by clean, linoleum-covered aisles and neatly stacked shelves with signs pointing out everyday bargains alongside comparisons to the prices of their competitors. Beleaguered by union organizers at one time, Sam consulted with labor lawyer John Tate and came up with a new twist. Rather than capitulate to union pressures, he opted to prove to his minimum-wage workers that he cared.

By sharing inside information and pulling low-ranking managers into the "we" mentality of his operation, Walton convinced them that cost-management was the way of the future. For added sparkle, he offered his workers incentives to reduce theft and damage as well as profit-sharing and retirement plans. To keep them as customers, he pioneered associate stores where employees receive substantial discounts on company merchandise. For a treat, Walton has been known to fly employees to the opening of a new Wal-Mart in a distant city.

The bonus ploy worked. As Charlie Cate attests, "People who work for him don't mind making him richer, because they know he is going to share it with them. They know it is a two-way street."[3] And Walton himself continued to profit from the system. He augmented his holdings to 1,300 stores selling about $20 billion in merchandise per year in twenty-five states. *Forbes* magazine named him America's richest man; his net worth exceeds that of names like Rockefeller, Getty, and Kennedy.

## Developing an Empire

Known for his ability to inspire workers with straight-from-the-shoulder, forthright pep talks, Sam Walton keeps a close rein on the motivation of his "associates," enabling them to overleap competitors, namely Sears, Zayre, Target, Rose's, and K-Mart. He sparks loyalty in everyone from dockhands to uniformed cashiers by remembering names and taking an interest in individual progress. Walton is even known to greet workers with a box of doughnuts as a reward for their diligence. He brags that well-motivated workers keep the best ideas moving in the right direction—from the bottom toward open ears at the top.

Wal-Mart stores demonstrate the innovative genius of their creator. From the gray-haired retiree greeter at the door to the pinchpenny buyers at the company's warehouses, Wal-Mart keeps a close eye on business deals, which they are famed for cutting to the bone. As one rueful vendor noted, "They talk softly, but they have piranha hearts, and if you aren't totally prepared when you go in there, you'll have your ass handed to you."[4]

Linked by a six-channel satellite system, the company stresses keeping in constant touch with managers in order to move merchandise and solve problems. The system not only oils the company's joints, it also slashes telephone bills. In addition, Sam Walton utilizes it as a training method. To augment the advantage of instant communicators, Wal-Mart executives speed to member stores on the company's eleven turboprops, any one of which could be piloted by Walton himself.

## Good Ideas Lead the Way

One of Walton's entrepreneurial devices is the use of company trucks to deliver goods from the manufacturers to his fourteen warehouses, each within a day's drive of the stores they service. At each warehouse, laser scanners speed orders down a conveyor belt. To keep close tabs on what's in and what's out of stock, the company employs bar codes and a computer-monitored perpetual inventory system. This tactic of keeping close tabs on warehousing helps hold advertising at one-fourth to one-fifth the cost of competitors' outlay.

Walton describes the evolution of his close-to-home warehousing. Because his company lay in the remote realms of the Sun Belt, "We didn't have distributors falling over themselves to serve us like our competitors did in larger towns. Our only alternative was to build our own warehouse so we could buy in volume at attractive prices and store the merchandise."[5]

Another important factor in the Sam Walton success story is his emphasis on humility and frugality. In the early 1980s, store employees of one Wal-Mart pooled their money and had a color portrait made of Walton. To honor their employer, they mounted the picture at the front of the store. Walton, without hurting their feelings, had the manager remove the picture to spare him embarrassment.

The big man himself expects no perks. He waits in line to pay for his purchases, inhabits no palatial office, and stays close to the troops in both class and style. The nerve center at his headquarters, a 70,000 square-foot brick building northwest of Bentonville, across U.S. 71, is paneled in cheap covering and features fanny-shaped plastic seating. Walton's lawyer, Jim Henderson, explained the logic of his client's objectivity: "[He] believes it unhealthy to marinate in your own press clippings, and urges associates ... to remain vigilant toward salespeople who would flatter, con or cajole to land a lucrative Wal-Mart account."[6] A public relations official does stand guard, though, to keep away intruders and pests so that Walton can maximize his workday.

Walton caters to a decidedly proletarian clientele, with which he closely identifies, both at home and on the job. *Fortune*'s 1989 cover story compared him to an amalgam of Jimmy Stewart, P. T. Barnum, Billy Graham, and Henry Ford. Writer John Huey concluded, "Overlaying everything is a lot of the old yard rooster who is tough, loves a good fight and protects his territory."[7] Walton takes no chances with complacency. To remain in first place, he stays on top of every operational detail.

## Commerce American-Style

One of the Walton trademarks is emphasis on American goods as demonstrated by the "Bring It Home to the USA" program. In 1984, he became alarmed by the flight of American manufacturers to Taiwan. In his words, "I felt that we needed to do all we could to buy in the United States, proving that we could be competitive."[8] Beginning with a contract to a maker of flannel shirts, Walton moved on to washcloths, bedding, microwaves, and videotapes.

By March 1985, Walton expanded his cooperative effort to manufacturers across the country. The upshot of the program was an emphasis on jobs for Americans. Part of the idea was to promote sales by building worker and shopper loyalty. Walton himself commented, "We want to get our manufacturers to create a partnership with their workers the way we've tried to do with our people, and share the profits with them."[9]

A second approach that is bringing home the bacon is the Wal-Mart spinoff known as Hypermart USA. From these mammoth malls without walls, such as the prototype in Dallas, come hopeful signs of future frontiers to be blazed in the discounting trade. Another unusual touch is Sam's Wholesale Club. These warehouse stores stock supplies necessary to small businesses. From this service, Walton plans to develop Wal-Mart Supercenters to lure shoppers with all the goods they might have on their lists, from doorknobs to pantyhose to T-bones.

On the other hand, not all of Sam Walton's ideas have paid off. The company has not done well with its drug chain. It also bombed with a line of do-it-yourself building supplies. Aside from these few minor gaffes, though, Wal-Mart continues to dominate the merchandising world.

The company's method of moving into new territory remains the same. After an initial investment at a few locations, the firm then saturates the area with numerous stores. To guide growth, it keeps a master list of potential sites. So long as Wal-Mart remains flexible and concentrates on the working-class customer, it believes it will continue to grow. The company's growth record substantiates the claim: since it went public in 1970, stock prices have made multi-millionaires out of early investors.

## A Private Life

Like his plain-as-shoe-leather merchandising style, Sam Walton is noted for his laid-back unpretentious lifestyle. Not exactly a recluse, he is nonetheless elusive and refuses interviews with reporters, even "60 Minutes." His rejection notes are couched in polite language and inscribed on white stationery with blue letterhead. If, on some rare occasion, Walton chooses to talk, the subject is Wal-Mart, not Sam Walton.

Far from spoiled by fame and excess wealth, Walton prefers the small-town ways of Bentonville, where he employs more than 20 percent of the town's population. He patronizes the same barber and bank that he always has. He is rumored to give generously to local causes, but keeps matters of charity unpublicized. Among the most public of his good works are funds for employees hit by tragedies and a scholarship fund for workers' children. Around Bentonville, Wal-Mart money has subsidized recreation and athletics, a gathering place for aged citizens, day-care, and the public library.

Walton's friends insulate him from intrusion by the outside world. They worry that his ultimate retirement may sap town resources if foreign interests buy out his 38.6 percent share in Wal-Mart. To show their appreciation of his community spirit, they saluted the Waltons in 1983 with a parade, brass band, dignitaries, and the renaming of U.S. 71, which is now Walton Boulevard.

Walton lives in an unassuming brick and wood-shingle ranch house northeast of town on F Street, a cul-de-sac facing the woods. The house, built on earlier foundations around 1975, replaced the first Walton home, which burned. There is a lighted tennis court in the front yard and an undistinguished Chevrolet sedan in the carport. The run-of-the-mill mailbox is marked "Sam and Helen Walton." The neighborhood is unremarkable, even mundane. Across the street is a horse paddock; behind the house stands a birdhouse surrounded by rose bushes. On a normal day, Walton arises at daybreak and eats breakfast before work at the Ramada Inn coffee shop. He drives a seasoned 1979 red and white Ford pickup complete with carrying cages for his champion bloodline quail-hunting dogs, Leroy and Kate, who are famed for lining his steering wheel with teeth marks.

For evenings out, Walton and his wife prefer Fred's Hickory Inn, famed for its barbecued ribs and cheesecake. Sundays find him in the family pew at the First United Presbyterian Church. He is a member of the Rotary Club and at one time served as town alderman. On frequent business forays, he pilots a twin-engine Cessna Navajo but prefers to relax with a good game of tennis. He is apt to take time off and leave his chief executive officer in charge.

## A Go-Getter

While recovering from leukemia and bone cancer, Walton continues leading Saturday satellite pep talks, during which he promises success to people who apply his "customer first" policy of greeting arrivals, looking them in the eye, and offering genuine assistance. He pulls no punches with the public—his game, as always, is brand-name goods at the lowest prices with the most hospitable service. A friend to the people who trust him, Walton is not shy about leading a cheer for his own success.

## Notes

[1] "The Forbes Four Hundred," *Forbes*, October 22, 1990, 124.

[2] John Huey. "Wal-Mart: Will It Take Over the World?" *Fortune*, January 30, 1989, 52.

[3] Timothy Dwyer. "In Search of the Richest Man in America," *Philadelphia Inquirer*, January 22, 1989, n.p.

[4] Huey, 53.

[5] Howard Rudnitsky. "Play It Again, Sam," *Forbes*, August 10, 1987, 48.

[6] Art Harris. "The Richest Man in America," *Reader's Digest*, May 1986, 91.

[7] Huey, 58.

[8] Michael Barrier. "Buy American—the Right Way," *Reader's Digest*, August 1988, 123-124.

[9] Barrier, 125.

## Sources

Barrier, Michael. "Buy American—the Right Way," *Reader's Digest*, August 1988, 122-125.

Cawthon, Reed. "America's Richest Man Just Mr. Sam at Home," *Atlanta Journal*, October 21, 1985.

Dwyer, Timothy. "In Search of the Richest Man in America," *Philadelphia Inquirer*, January 22, 1989, n.p.

"The Forbes Four Hundred," *Forbes*, October 22, 1990, 124.

Harris, Art. "The Richest Man in America," *Reader's Digest*, May 1986, 90-94.

Huey, John. "Wal-Mart: Will It Take Over the World?" *Fortune*, January 30, 1989, 52-61.

"Make That Sale, Mr. Sam," *Time*, May 18, 1987, 54-55.

Rudnitsky, Howard. "Play It Again, Sam," *Forbes*, August 10, 1987, 48.

# Ethel Waters

Some late achievers blossom at a time when they appear to be withering on the vine. Ethel Waters, a well-upholstered black actress who has played numerous roles in radio, television, movies, and theater, began her career in fly-by-night clubs and neighborhood gatherings. Her personal development linked her with the black community's struggle for recognition and dignity.

Not much happened to make her name a household word until she made the movie *Pinky* and caught the nation's eye in the part of the grandmother. She played the stereotypical role of black nanny in numerous subsequent performances, all tinged with her special brand of maternal love, religious faith, and good nature. Then a change of heart brought her to Dr. Billy Graham. As an instrument of his crusades, she continued to sing and witness for God until her death in 1977.

## Ghetto Child

Ethel Waters, vibrant illegitimate daughter of Louisa Tar Anderson and pianist John Wesley Waters, knew poverty and crime from firsthand experience. Conceived as the result of a rape at knifepoint, she was born October 31, 1900, and grew up on Waverly Street in Chester, Pennsylvania, a slum on the fringe of Philadelphia known as the "Bloody Eighth Ward." Amid the squalor of shacks, gutter drunks, pimps, and heroin addicts, she grew up the only way she knew how—wild and tough.

Her mother, little more than a child herself, resented the derision and ignominy that accompanied her unwanted pregnancy, so Ethel relied on her grandmother and aunts for rearing. Soon both her parents married other people, produced legitimate children, and paid her little attention. Because of her family's enmity for John Waters and his uncouth behavior, Ethel never used the name "Waters" during her girlhood. Instead she took "Perry," her grandmother's surname.

Ethel claimed some Indian ancestry on her mother's side; her great-grandmother was a slave. Ethel inherited the gift of song, which surfaced in all the women in her family when the blues struck. From Sarah Harris Perry, her feisty, proud grandmother, she learned to be strong, even when she had to steal food to survive. Later, when money troubles ceased to plague her, she confirmed every hungry child's right to fill its stomach, even with stolen bread.

Ethel's grandmother was obsessed with dirt. As Ethel described her, "Mom never accepted our dismal surroundings or felt they were good enough for her. She was passionate, almost fanatical, on the subject of personal cleanliness."[1] After success brought money and creature comforts, Ethel wished she could have moved her grandmother to California and treated her like royalty, even serving her meals in bed, but it was too late. Sarah had died before Ethel became famous.

Ethel's early life toughened her and enabled her to withstand adversity. Once, she ran away from the seamy, disorganized family conditions in which she lived. She ran into the path of a streetcar and lost two teeth. She was often hard to discipline, took pride in her shoplifting skills, and cut a path through difficulties with belligerent looks and streams of swear words.

Ethel was pragmatic about survival. When she needed spending money, she often ran errands for the prostitutes who populated her neighborhood. Later, in explanation of her ascetic ways, she commented, "Whatever moral qualities I have, come, I'm afraid, from all the sordidness and evil I observed firsthand as a child.... I was tough always and, like all slum kids, was able quickly to adjust myself to any and all situations."[2]

## Finding Religion

Ethel's grandmother enrolled her in an integrated convent school at the corner of North and Pine streets. Classes and prayers delighted her, but mealtime was a trial. Unable to endure taunts from children who carried tasty lunch treats from home, she would find excuses to avoid the dining area or earn meals by running errands for the sisters.

Her budding Catholicism at this time put her at odds with her hard-drinking, squabbling aunts, Vi and Ching, who cared for her while her grandmother worked at a live-in domestic job. Her aunts, more in tune with fundamentalism, forced her to give up the convent school, but the nuns' lessons made her a life-long Christian. When fame brought a ready supply of cash, she contributed heavily to church causes.

Ethel knew little stability in her living arrangements. After her grandmother became too weak to work, she and Ethel moved in with Ethel's mother, whom she called Momweeze, and her husband. When the marriage failed, Sarah and Ethel again had to scramble for new quarters.

Ethel was quite large for her age and took pleasure in giving dancing lessons in a neighborhood dive, for which she earned a few pennies. While shimmying in public, she drew the attention of twenty-three-year-old Merritt "Buddy" Purnsley. Inexperienced with boys, she was not attracted to him, yet she took him seriously because his proposal of marriage was the answer to her need for a home.

## On Her Own

Married to Buddy at thirteen, Ethel took no pleasure in her new maturity. Their relationship, filled with jealousy, accusations, and violence, lasted less than a year. Ethel wised up to his cheating and determined to end the dishonest marriage. She left him and supported herself on $3.40 a week as maid and waitress at the Harrod Apartments. Buddy pursued her and promised to stop beating her if she would return, but their brief reconciliation was short-lived.

An outcast from birth, Ethel learned to get the attention of others by imitating songs and dances from vaudeville acts. In 1913 she sang in public for the first time at a Baltimore night club. Dared by two local boys, she made her way on stage. Within four years she was performing at Baltimore's Lincoln Theatre for $9 per week under the name of Chippie Waters. She lied about her age, adding four years to make her appear more mature. Years later, news reports continued to misstate her age. At her death it was given as eighty-one instead of seventy-seven.

With the arrival of local fame and audience approval, Waters, thin and long-limbed, changed the name of her act to Sweet Mama Stringbean and the Hill Sisters. She added W. C. Handy's "Saint Louis Blues" to her regular lineup of songs and ballads, becoming known as the first woman to sing it onstage. The song became her calling card.

Even though money was no longer such a problem for Waters, she still lacked the goal of her lifetime—a home and stability. Traveling constantly, often in the Jim Crow compartments of trains, she got little satisfaction from living out of suitcases and rooming at second-class hotels. Her love affairs were transient and less than satisfying. Fame was not bringing her the paradise that she had envisioned.

## On the Rise

During World War I, Waters was known for gutsy double entendres in her jazz performances. Men would urge her on by yelling, "Come on, Ethel, get hot."[3] She appeared in rinky-dink clubs, halls, and carnival tents. While touring the South, she was seriously injured in a car wreck and nearly lost a leg because an incompetent and hostile medical staff sewed up her torn flesh around pieces of dirt and gravel. Only the intervention of an observant nurse saved her from permanent crippling.

Waters's first time before a white audience at Harlem's Plantation Club in 1925 left her disappointed with the weak applause. Later she realized that pleasing a white audience was a far cry from appealing to the black audiences in the familiar neighborhood nightclubs of her youth. Never comfortable among white people, she developed a knack for learning their tastes and coexisting.

Waters toured the United States, rejecting an offer to sing in Paris, and produced records on the Black Swan label of her blues classics, including her hit renditions of "Dinah," "Stormy Weather," "Shake That Thing," "Eili, Eili," "Am I Blue?," and "Having a Heat Wave." She performed with the big names of her times, notably Duke Ellington and Benny Goodman; composers, impressed by her vocal quality, intonation, and diction, wrote songs for her.

While working at the Café de Paris in Chicago, Waters met Clyde Edward Matthews, a far cry from Rocky, the abusive junky she was involved with at the time. When her doctor suggested a long rest to ease her throat, she accompanied Clyde to Europe aboard the Ile de France. Safely hidden under the name of Mrs. C. E. Matthews, she enjoyed an eight-month respite from the press and mobs of fans.

In need of an outlet for repressed love, Waters took with her a friend's child, Algretta Holmes, whom she longed to raise as her own. Mindful of her own wayward youth, she brought the girl up with a combination of tenderness and stern discipline. Algretta remained in her care until age twelve, when she returned to her birth mother. Waters replaced Algretta many times in her life with needy children who responded to her mothering.

Ethel enjoyed the adulation of European audiences, some of which were composed entirely of bluebloods and royalty. When her throat condition worsened, she consulted Dr. Cyril Horsford, throat specialist to the elite, and had a large nodule removed from her vocal cords. By the time of her return aboard the Aquitania, Waters could sing for fellow passengers and was pleased to discover her voice clear and devoid of huskiness.

Work in minor revues, including Africana, Blackbirds, and Rhapsody in Black, carried Ethel into the 1930s. In 1933 she starred in As Thousands Cheer, a musical by Irving Berlin, and followed two years later with At Home Abroad. She shared the spotlight with the great names of musical theater, including Cab Calloway, Al Jolson, Will Rogers, Beatrice Lillie, and Fred and Adele Astaire. Among her admirers were Al Capone, Irving Berlin, and the Prince of Wales. In 1938 she performed at Carnegie Hall.

## From Singer to Actress

That same year, at the age of thirty-eight, Ethel Waters made the transition from singer to actress. After a chance meeting with Dorothy Heyward, she began to consider serious theater as a possibility for her talents. In explanation of her previous refusal to act, she wrote in her autobiography: "Those plays never seemed quite true to life to me. The characters in them had been either created by white men or by Negro writers who had stopped thinking colored."[4]

Her first role was at the Empire Theatre as Hagar in DuBose and Heyward's Mamba's Daughters. She identified with the role because it reminded her of her mother's courage. Reviews were weak, but the audience gave her seventeen curtain calls. Supporters Oscar Hammerstein, Burgess Meredith, and Tallulah Bankhead rated her performance superb. Her personal response had the Waters touch: "If I died here and now, it would be all right.... At last I have fulfillment."[5]

By her early forties she was more at home in theater, taking the singing and acting role of Petunia in *Cabin in the Sky*. In 1943, she reprised Petunia in the film version. The proceeds allowed her to buy her first house, a sunny ten-room bungalow in southwest Los Angeles.

Critics found much to praise in her soulful, energetic acting. She appeared in *Tales of Manhattan*, *Cairo*, and *Stage Door Canteen* as well as wartime USO shows. Her success brought her the vice presidency of the Negro Actors Guild and membership on Hollywood's wartime Victory Committee and the executive board of Actors Equity. Her patriotism and congenial spirit netted their own rewards in the form of honorary membership in the California State Militia and the Women's Ambulance Corps. After the war, Waters's critical appraisal wavered with a flawed performance in *Blue Holiday*, then surged upward with stints at New York's Embassy Club.

## Making an Impression

In 1949, Ethel Waters began to make a permanent mark in movies. She played the grandmother in *Pinky*, a part that critics praised for her warmth and appeal. Later she remarked, "It was God that allowed me to play that part."[6] Her reward—a plaque from the Negro Actors Guild—gave some satisfaction, although it appeared that only blacks found her creative work noteworthy.

Perhaps her most memorable role came in 1950 with the Broadway version of Carson McCullers's *The Member of the Wedding*. In this moving part, Waters played Berenice Sadie Brown, the one-eyed maid, governess, and confidante to two southern white children. The opportunity came at a low point when Waters needed the work. At first she rejected the job because she saw Berenice as a hard-drinking, chain-smoking, godless character. When convinced of the role's worthiness, she blended in well with Julie Harris and Brandon de Wilde, the child stars who played the parts of Frankie Addams and John Henry.

A major portion of the play's success was Waters's own interpretation of Berenice. Critics thundered their approval, claiming that her work, more than any other facet, held the play together. In 1953, she again assumed the persona of Berenice for the movie version.

From the gospel hymn that Berenice crooned to Frankie came the title for Waters's autobiography, *His Eye Is on the Sparrow*, written in collaboration with Charles Samuels. The book was published in 1951 and was a featured selection for Book of the Month Club. Her career, firmly established at this point, expanded to include radio and television appearances, a TV series, *Beulah*, and a one-woman show entitled "An Evening with Ethel Waters."

Ethel Waters's belief in prayer and worship produced a major change in the latter portion of her career. Under the direction of music manager Cliff Barrows, she began appearing with Billy Graham's crusades in the late 1950s and traveled to Boston, Charlotte, Honolulu, and Chicago. From her relationship with evangelism she built a new life dedicated to Christian teachings. During the 1960s she recorded gospels and spirituals for Word, Inc. Among these were songs she composed, including "Partners with God." She also reprised *Member of the Wedding* in various playhouses in California, in which she sang "His Eye Is on the Sparrow."

## Lifetime Satisfactions

Ethel Waters subscribed to the Puritan work ethic in that she continued to perform long after she needed the money. In an interview she commented, "There's just no time, no time at all, to rest on your laurels, you've got to make your own social security."[7] In 1972 she published her second personal reflection, *To Me It's Wonderful.*

After fifteen years of appearances with the Billy Graham Crusades, she enjoyed a testimonial dinner in 1972. Among the dignitaries were Tricia Nixon Cox, Bob Hope, Jim Nabors, Hugh Downs, and Paul Lind Hayes. With her typical humor, she chastised Dr. Graham for labeling her "black": "Please, not that word *black*. I'm a Negress and proud of it.... Nobody in our race is jet black. I'm a brown-skinned woman. The term *black* came into being with the militants."[8]

Ethel's career covered six decades, well into her declining years when she suffered from obesity, diabetes, ulcers, heart failure, and partial blindness from cataracts. After illness depleted her strength, she depended on Twila Knaack to run errands and fend off a too-adoring public. Ethel entered a convalescent hospital and received treatment for blood clots, cancer, kidney failure, and heart problems. She died at her home on September 1, 1977, in Chatsworth, California, at the age of seventy-seven, and was buried in Forest Lawn Cemetery. Flowers poured in to honor her, many simply labeled "Mom."

Among the many memorials to her goodness and generosity are a park named for Waters in her hometown. She numbered thousands of friends, great and small. One, Gloria Gaither, captured Waters's special quality: "She was a great soul. And compassion of her heart came through her voice, and her words, and her performances to touch people, soul to soul, intimately, because we who heard her somehow knew that she had hurt where we hurt."[9]

## Notes

[1] Ethel Waters, *His Eye Is on the Sparrow*, Garden City, New York: Doubleday, 1951, 9.

[2] Waters, 19.

[3] *Current Biography.* Detroit: Gale Research, 1951, 645.

[4] Waters, 239.

[5] Waters, 247.

[6] *Current Biography.* Detroit: Gale Research, 1951, 646.

[7] *Current Biography*, 647.

[8] Twila Knaack, *Ethel Waters: I Touched a Sparrow.* Waco, Texas: Word Books, 1978, 74.

[9] Knaack, 100.

## Sources

*Current Biography.* Detroit: Gale Research, 1951.

Knaack, Twila. *Ethel Waters: I Touched a Sparrow.* Waco, Texas: Word Books, 1978.

Waters, Ethel. *His Eye Is on the Sparrow.* Garden City, New York: Doubleday, 1951.

# Dr. Ruth Westheimer

Making a successful transition sometimes requires a feel for what the public wants and is willing to pay for. In the case of Dr. Ruth Westheimer, her private practice expanded into broadcasting and publishing when she tapped into widespread interest in human sexuality. Part of her success, she acknowledges, derives from American openness and opportunity, which have catapulted her to national stardom on radio, television, and videos, in newpapers, books, and magazines, and on the symposium and lecture circuits.

Dr. Ruth Westheimer, the irrepressible spokesperson for "good sex," disseminates her opinions openly in books and on the air. From her New York psychotherapy practice she has branched out to late-night talk shows, a two-hour radio call-in program, and appearances on guest talk shows, all of which encourage people to question her to learn more about their own sexuality. Riding the crest of a pop psychology boom, Dr. Ruth outdistanced her competition and became the best-known and best-loved name in sexual self-help.

## An Early Learner

Born Karola Ruth Siegel in Frankfurt am Main, Germany, June 4, 1928, Dr. Ruth came from middle-class beginnings. Her parents, Irma Hanauer and Julius Siegel, were Orthodox Jews. He was a wholesale dealer in buttons, handkerchiefs, radios, and notions. The family, including Ruth's maternal grandmother, Selma, lived in a cramped four-room apartment in the north part of town. Because her parents were tight-lipped, Ruth was grateful to have her affable grandmother in the house, even if the old woman was a snob. A perky, round-faced, blue-eyed blonde, Ruth, petite at four feet seven, has always been sensitive about her short stature. In her autobiography, *All in a Lifetime*, she recalls the cruelty of other fifth-graders who put her in a garbage can, covered it with a lid, and left her to cry in the darkness for rescue.

Despite difficulties with her stature, Ruth grew up in a loving home atmosphere. An intelligent, irrepressible child, she learned her multiplication tables even before enrolling in school and satisfied her curiosity about sex by reading books from her father's collection. When the menace of Nazi Germany endangered Jewish families, the Siegels planned to move away until better times. Ruth's grandmother altered the family's proposed emigration by refusing to join them. Shortly afterward, Julius Siegel was arrested by the SS. The Siegels opted for a revised plan and sent their daughter to school in Switzerland with 300 other Jewish children in a joint program sponsored by Switzerland, Great Britain, Holland, Belgium, and France to help the offspring of German-Jewish internees in concentration camps.

The war years devastated the Siegel family. After Hitler initiated his plan for a master race, he systematically destroyed Jews, deemed unfit to inhabit his utopia. Ruth, never to reunite with any of her relatives, believes that they met their deaths at Auschwitz, a super-efficient death camp and crematory. She felt guilty that she was unable to save them and yet remained alive herself. Her only outlet during her years in Switzerland was a diary in which she confided her misery.

To add to her discomfiture, Ruth suffered psychological scars even in the free air of Switzerland. The experience of living as a charity case was exacerbated by condescension from the school principal. She insisted that Ruth be trained for menial work, even though the staff recognized the child's bubbly exuberance, energy, intelligence, and volubility. Compounding her difficulties with the school power structure, Ruth spread information about reproduction among the other girls. The principal ordered her to stop.

## A New Life

At sixteen, Ruth made drastic changes. She dropped her first name and gave up her family's religious beliefs, replacing them with a firm commitment to the Zionist movement. In 1945, she and other orphan children were transported to Israel. On an Israeli kubbutz she picked tomatoes and olives and swabbed toilets. Her journals showed the anguish of her teen years, particularly the abrupt separation from family: "Is life never going to be different, only full of sorrow and sleepless nights? I want to be young and happy like the others. Is it only because I'm small and ugly?"[1]

In 1946, Ruth arranged to work in the kitchen at another kibbutz in Haifa to pay for training in the kindergarten seminary. The next year, as tensions mounted between Jews and Arabs, Ruth got involved with the resistance movement. As a member of Haganah, freedom fighters in the Jewish underground, she became a crack shot with a sten gun, but continued to prepare herself to teach. In the confines of the classroom, she narrowly survived an artillery attack, sustaining shrapnel wounds and more serious injuries to her ankles and feet. The hospital she was sent to was so crowded from all the wounded that Ruth had to sleep on a bookshelf. By 1949, she recovered fully, received her degree, and began teaching Yemenite kindergartners in a small town between Jerusalem and Tel Aviv.

At twenty-two, Ruth's horizons began to change after she married David, an Israeli soldier from Romania, and in 1950 settled in Paris. A gifted scholar fluent in German, French, Hebrew, and English, she enrolled at the Sorbonne to study psychology and direct a kindergarten program while David entered medical school. Because of David's discontent with his career, the couple parted. David returned to Israel; Ruth remained in Paris and was divorced at twenty-seven. A dedicated Zionist, she continued to work and send money back to Israel. For a time, she enjoyed the camaraderie of fellow students who shared her poverty.

In 1956, Ruth decided to marry Dan, her French lover, and move to New York, where they settled in Washington Heights, a German Jewish section of Manhattan. She immediately got a scholarship and began work on a master's degree. After giving birth to their daughter Miriam by cesarean section, Ruth felt a definite affinity for motherhood but no real loyalty to Dan. Their marriage ended amicably in divorce in 1958 with Ruth determined to support herself and her child.

Ruth scraped by on minimum wages as a maid. To strengthen her English on a low budget, she bought and studied *True Confessions* magazines, yet maintained her heavily guttural German accent. The Jewish Family Service helped out by providing day-care for Miriam. During these tenuous times, Ruth managed to complete her education in night classes with a master's degree in sociology from the New School for Social Research in 1959 and a doctorate in education two years later from Columbia University, where she served as a graduate assistant and lecturer.

## A Lasting Love and a New Direction

At thirty-three, Ruth encountered a man who met her intellectual and emotional requirements for a life mate. While vacationing in the Catskills she discovered telecommunications engineer Manfred Westheimer, a German Jew whose history paralleled her own. Fred, a nonstop talker like Ruth, helped stabilize her impulsive nature. She gave up dreams of returning to Israel and married Fred on December 10, 1961.

With this third marriage came a satisfying relationship and a second child, son Joel, born in 1964. The following year, Ruth became an American citizen. At 39, she began a career that was to make her a late-in-life success: she served as project director at a Harlem Planned Parenthood clinic. Even though she was a tiny white woman entering a community filled with seething racial unrest, she walked to work and met no opposition to explicit questions about abortion and birth control. As she viewed the task, she wanted to work together with Harlemites to improve their lives.

At first, Westheimer was astounded that people could talk about sex all day. Then the job began to grow on her, setting her on a path toward her eventual career choice as a sex therapist. After three more years of training in family and sex counseling, she wrote a dissertation about her work with Planned Parenthood in Harlem and received her PhD in 1970. She took a teaching job at Lehman College in New York, where she prepared instructors to teach sex education. To ease transportation problems, she bought her first car. This idyllic period was marred by one unpleasant complication: she had to end her third pregnancy. The loss of the fetus was followed by a severe blow—a partial hysterectomy.

## A Chance Success

Serendipity soon renewed Dr. Ruth's flagging spirits. She attended a lecture given by Dr. Helen Singer Kaplan and soon began studying at Cornell with noted sex therapists and observing therapy through a one-way mirror. After certifying as therapist, Ruth began seeing clients and opened an office on East 73rd Street in New York. Her career took another bump when tight funds ended all non-tenured positions. She worked at Brooklyn College for a year but was fired from that position.

Reeling from the double blow to her self-esteem, Westheimer fought the power structure of Brooklyn College; eventually, she gave in to reality. It was at this precarious point in her life that Dr. Ruth met good fortune. While lecturing to broadcasters about the need for sexual literacy, she touched a nerve in Betty Elam of station WYNY-FM. Their association led to a fifteen-minute show, Saturdays at midnight, which developed into a full-time job. "Sexually Speaking" was an instant success.

The show covered a variety of subjects: sex therapy, contraception, case histories, and sexual myths. Dr. Ruth described her technique in her autobiography: "From the beginning I was explicit, not to be titillating, but because it is my strong feeling that in talking about sexual matters you should not use euphemisms or mince words."[2] She asked that people with specific questions send her letters. From letters she went on to taking listeners' calls.

By 1981, Dr. Ruth's fifteen minutes had expanded to an hour, resulting in 4,000 calls per night. Her audience ballooned to 250,000. To explain the phenomenon of interest in basic biology, Dr. Ruth replied, "In America, we take care of our diet and meals first. About the sex life, we don't pay enough attention."[3] She explained that because people are reluctant to teach children the facts about reproduction, they end up with myth and an alarming number of questions. She held to the belief that sexual information should be explicit and factual rather than judgmental.

## Dealing with Success

Open and candid with her fans, Dr. Ruth eased the way to a fruitful exchange of information by her generous outlay of charm coated with a concerned, nonmoralistic attitude. Her outlook on human sexuality accorded respectability to most practices so long as they occur between consenting adults and cause no pain. Not confining herself to either conservative or liberal viewpoints, she championed traditional birth control, the Ten Commandments, monogamy, religion, better sex education, and abortion rights. Dr. Ruth shocked some people by rejecting the confining label of feminist, yet advocating such liberal methods of mutual arousal as X-rated movies, magazines, and sexual aids. Her basic advice boiled down to common sense and respect between partners.

Dr. Ruth refuted critics who accused her of loose morals and claimed instead that her goal was a simple transfer of information, an understanding of body parts and how they function. Without dismissing prudes or religious fanatics out of hand, she encouraged people who disagreed with her frankness to turn the television dial or not read her column in the newspaper. She reminded them that their children, blessed with normal libido, would seek sex education from some source. At least from her program, they would hear fact, not myth. If they listened to her call-in program, they might be bored, but not misinformed.

A conservative at heart, she urged people to look for love and commitment rather than short-term gratification. Commitment to Dr. Ruth included a mature attitude toward birth control and an awareness of sexually transmitted diseases, particularly AIDS, which she considered a serious threat. She railed against a society that absorbs itself with sensual advertising and prurient interests but fails to provide simple biological information. Then, with a twinkle and a giggle, she commented, "I don't treat sex as a solemn business.... We should all learn to be sexual gourmets."[4]

By 1982, Dr. Ruth advanced from talking about sex to writing a column about it each month in *Playgirl*. She became a priority speaker on college campuses and developed a TV version of her radio show without giving up private family counseling. Associated with the New York Hospital-Cornell Medical Center, she also conducted therapy sessions at Bellevue Hospital and taught cadets at West Point.

At fifty-five, Dr. Ruth continued developing outlets for her philosophy in a popular paperback, *Dr. Ruth's Guide to Good Sex*, which sold 169,000 copies. Next she added an agent, a corporation (Karola, Inc.), an NBC radio show, a television program on the Lifetime cable channel, a movie role as a rich American philanthropist in the French farce *One Woman or Two* (starring Gerard Depardieu and Sigourney Weaver), and a *Good Sex* board game and home video. She even conducted a tour of erotic architecture in India. More books followed: *Dr. Ruth's Guide for Married Lovers, First Love, Loving Couples*, and an autobiography. She takes particular pride that her newspaper column runs in fastidious Boston and Catholic Ireland.

## Getting Free

Even with the perks of a limo, hairdresser, honoraria, and more spending money than she ever dreamed of, Dr. Ruth carries emotional baggage of her own, particularly her early beliefs that no one could love anyone so short and ugly as she considered herself. While working with Ben Yagoda on her auto-biography, Dr. Ruth took her own advice: when you need help, get it. To circumvent painful memories, she sought psychoanalysis.

On the bright side, Dr. Ruth found an outlet for her appreciation of American values during the centennial celebration of the Statue of Liberty. She said of her new country: "The statue means something very special to me as an immigrant, an exile. I came to this country with absolutely nothing. I found freedom. You can't know what that means unless you've been denied it."[5]

For relaxation the diminutive Dr. Ruth, who has been called the "Munchkin of the Bedroom" as well as "Grandma Freud," dispenses with regular office hours and outside commitments at regular intervals.[6] She enjoys hiking, skiing (both snow and water), and collecting dolls. She gathers often with her family, including her grown son and daughter, at their weekend home in Peekskill, New York. But most days find Dr. Ruth still pursuing a killer schedule of little sleep, many responsibilities, and an unflagging desire to help people understand themselves.

## Looking to the Future

Dr. Ruth takes pleasure in her stardom. Like a geriatric Shirley Temple, she exults in each day, even enjoying lampoons of her by Johnny Carson and "Saturday Night Live." Also, she is proud of her son and daughter. Miriam teaches English and Joel is a folksinger. On a day-to-day basis, Dr. Ruth pursues a globetrotting schedule, reserving Saturdays for psychotherapy with private patients.

Many critics have characterized Ruth Westheimer's success as a mere flash in the pan, a temporary quirk of the public's taste. Dr. Ruth is quick to counter that society needs her "Jewish mother's" approach to advice. In her words, "If you need help, don't suffer. Go for help. I do sound, to myself, like a broken record. Go see a therapist. Go do something about it."[7]

## Notes

[1] Westheimer, Dr. Ruth. *All in a Lifetime.* New York: Warner Books, 1987, 90.

[2] Westheimer, 165-166.

[3] Mary A. M. Gindhart. "Sex Life: Dr. Ruth Advocates Lasting Education," *Arizona Republic*, Phoenix, Arizona, June 3, 1987, n.p.

[4] Patricia Bosworth. "Talking with Doctor Goodsex," *Ladies' Home Journal*, February 1986, 83.

[5] Bosworth, 167.

[6] Mark Dawidziak. "Dr. Ruth, Sexual Guru," *Akron Beacon Journal*, Akron, Ohio, March 1, 1987, n.p.

[7] Dawidziak, n.p.

## Sources

Bosworth, Patricia. "Talking with Doctor Goodsex," *Ladies' Home Journal*, February 1986, 82, 84, 167.

Burke-Block, Candace. "Hot Flash: Dr. Ruth or Film," *Norfolk Virginian-Pilot*, Norfolk, Virginia, February 13, 1987, n.p.

Connell, Steve. "Dr. Ruth Answers Her Critics," *Sacramento Union*, Sacramento, California, May 13, 1987, n.p.

Dawidziak, Mark. "Dr. Ruth, Sexual Guru," *Akron Beacon Journal*, Akron, Ohio, March 1, 1987, n.p.

Gindhart, Mary A. M. "Sex Life: Dr. Ruth Advocates Lasting Education," *Arizona Republic*, Phoenix, Arizona, June 3, 1987, n.p.

Lichtenstein, Robin. "Dr. Ruth: Sex, Aging Are Compatible," *Trenton Times*, Trenton, New Jersey, November 16, 1989, n.p.

Mano, D. Keith. "Good Sex!," *People*, April 15, 1985, 109-112.

Schaefer, Stephen. "Dr. Ruth Makes Film Debut," *Boston Herald*, April 3, 1987, n.p.

Stricklin, Robert. "Dr. Ruth: Is She Freud or Fraud? Legitimate Teacher or Just Titillator?" *New York Tribune*, June 20, 1988, n.p.

"To Have and Have Not," *Philadelphia Inquirer*, October 1, 1989, n.p.

Vincent, Mal. "Ruth Westheimer: The Doctor Is Still In," *Norfolk Virginian-Pilot*, Norfolk, Virginia, May 7, 1988, n.p.

Westheimer, Dr. Ruth. *All in a Lifetime*. New York: Warner Books, 1987.

# Laura Ingalls Wilder

A few achievers seem forever young, even though they began their careers late in life. One such person is Laura Ingalls Wilder, known to television viewers as a central character in the series based on her early life, *Little House on the Prairie.* On the TV screen, she frolicked once again with Mary and Carrie and enjoyed the outdoors and the freedom common to prairie children. Viewers came to visualize Laura as a symbol of the westward movement in which she took part.

The child of a pioneer family, Laura Ingalls Wilder wrote in her mid-sixties about the adventures she lived from ages five to eighteen. She spoke of cooking along the trail, teaching school in an abandoned shanty, and making hay under the fierce prairie sun. Her books continue to delight readers, including those in foreign lands who read her historical fiction in translation.

The American Library Association created the Laura Ingalls Wilder Award in 1954 to encourage contributions to children's literature. The *New York Herald Tribune* presented Wilder with its Spring Book Festival Prize. Likewise, *Horn Book Magazine* proclaimed her a living heroine. She became so popular that libraries were named for her and people continue to celebrate her birthday.

## Pioneer Roots

Laura Elizabeth Ingalls, born in Pepin, Wisconsin, on February 7, 1867, was the second child of Charles Philip and Caroline Lake Quiner Ingalls, both descendants of families that obeyed the wanderlust for open lands and deep woods. Laura was named for her paternal grandmother, a light-hearted woman of French-Canadian descent who loved to dance a jig at sugaring-off time. Laura's father also shared the winsome, carefree spirit of his French ancestors, even during the trying times.

Laura's daughter, Rose Wilder Lane, remembers her mother as serious, wide-eyed, and girlish. She was five feet tall with small hands and feet, long braids, and violet-blue eyes. Laura often spent long stretches of time without speaking, choosing instead to rely on inner thoughts for company. Two characteristics impressed people—her pleasant voice and her iron will.

The family (including Charles's parents, brother, sister, and their families) moved to Pepin County in the big Wisconsin woods in pioneer style. They lived out of their wagons until they could cut hardwood timber for new homes. Neighbors helped them complete the work before winter made it too cold to sleep on the ground. For entertainment, the family listened, clapped, and sang while Charles played his violin.

Charles and his brother Henry then left their parents behind and located land on which to establish their own families. Mary Amelia, Laura's older sister, was born on January 10, 1865. By the time Laura was born two years later, the Civil War had touched the family's life. Two of Charles' brothers—Hiram and James— had joined up on the Union side and later returned home safely. Of this period, Laura recalls no conflict, only the snug security she enjoyed with a loving family.

## Journeying to Indian Territory

When Laura was one and a half years old, her father, lured by ads for virgin land in Kansas, chose to sell out and move again, this time to Independence, Kansas. Charles' brother and family joined them, but after a discouraging season, the brothers split up. Charles moved further on to the prairie, settling at Walnut Creek near the Verdigris River, many miles west of Springfield in Indian Territory.

In their new house in Montgomery County, Caroline gave birth to her name-sake, Caroline "Carrie" Celestia. Often Laura's mother tended the girls alone while Charles made necessary trips into town to sign legal papers or buy supplies. Sometimes, when they needed cash, he hired out as a carpenter or day laborer. Laura later wrote of this time: "The teachings of those early days have influenced me and the example set by my mother and father has been something I have tried to follow, with failures here and there, with rebellion at times, but always coming back to it as the compass needle to the star."[1]

Laura recalls visits by the Osage Indians, who came infrequently and terrified them with eerie war chants. On one occasion, the warriors, dressed in blankets, calico shirts, flannel leggings, and moccasins, rode up boldly and threatened to scalp them and tear down their home if they didn't vacate Indian Territory. When the situation proved most threatening, the Ingalls withdrew to Independence for safety. Another drawback to life on the prairie were bouts of fever and whooping cough. Fortunately for the Ingalls family, Dr. George Tann lived only a mile away and treated ailments with homeopathic medicine, a method that uses herbs to mimic the symptoms of the disease.

## Return to the Big Woods

After three years on the prairie, the Ingalls family abandoned their little house on Walnut Creek and returned to Wisconsin to take possession of the land that their prospective purchaser had left vacant. Along the way, Charles found work as a carpenter to earn food money. By age four, Laura was again at her home near Lake Pepin. Caroline sent Mary away to the Barry Corner School.

## The House at Plum Creek

In 1873, when land around the Ingalls' home filled up with settlers and game became scarce, Charles moved his wife and three girls again. This time they settled in a dugout house west of Plum Creek, Minnesota, on virgin land bordering the Cottonwood River. Charles hired out to another farmer so that he could earn enough money to buy a cow; later he worked as a miller and butcher. Laura recalls that the family lived close enough to Walnut Grove to attend church, where Charles was elected deacon.

In 1875, by the time that Charles had completed a sturdy house for his family, the town had a school. There Laura met her best friend, eight-year-old Nettie Kennedy. She also met one of the most memorable characters in her books, Nellie Owens, a bossy, showy town girl whose father owned the local store. In the presence of the pretentious Nellie, Laura first learned the pain of being snubbed as "country folk."

In November 1875, Charles Frederick "Freddie" Ingalls was born. During this period, the family lived in town so that Caroline would have an easier winter with the new baby. Back at Plum Creek that spring, Caroline got desperately sick and Laura had to risk drowning in the roiling waters to call to a neighbor on the far bank. Other disasters followed. After a plague of gnawing grasshoppers, Charles gave up on his ruined crops and decided to join family members and return to the eastern part of the state.

## Centennial Year

The Ingalls made their way back through Minnesota to a relative's farm near the Mississippi River. Times were difficult because of the illness of Caroline and Freddie. That August, the family watched helplessly as Freddie died. Laura's journals have little to say of this era except that their next journey, to Burr Oak, Iowa, was cold and miserable. The family lived at the Masters Hotel, which they managed. Later they took rooms above a noisy saloon. Laura's parents feared that this was not the best environment for their daughters. When Caroline was again pregnant, Charles moved the family to a rented brick house.

In May 1877 Caroline bore a fourth girl named Grace Pearl. The family, discontent with town life, worked its way out of debt in order to move back to Plum Creek. Laura, who loved their prairie home, also recalls her joy in school, particularly the regular Friday night spelling bees. For one dreary fortnight, Laura took a job outside of town and had to miss school. She carried her books along so that she wouldn't fall behind in her studies. It was at this point in the family's history that Mary suffered scarlet fever, had a stroke, and lost her vision.

## The Last Journey

Charles, drawn by his brother Hiram's need for a bookkeeper and pay-master, moved his family one last time to be near Hiram's general store. On the train to Tracy, Minnesota, Laura, at age twelve, helped Caroline supervise Mary, Carrie, and Grace. The Ingalls family then traveled by wagon into Dakota Territory. They settled in a railroad camp on the Big Sioux River, where work was plentiful and the family had the use of the surveyor's house on Silver Lake for the winter. Within months, the town of De Smet, South Dakota, began to take shape; Charles, always searching for the feel of the outdoors, moved his family to a shanty on his claim outside of town near the Big Slough.

Everyone took a share of the work. To shade the house, all the Ingalls planted cottonwood seedlings. Laura helped her family by doing adult work, including laundry, cooking, planting, and harvesting. In spite of her efforts, the family had to move back to town for the winter. In 1881, Mary, then sixteen, went east to a school for the blind, paid for with considerable family sacrifice. Laura looked after the two younger girls while Caroline and Charles accompanied Mary on the train.

## Laura and Almanzo

That year Laura had a new teacher, Eliza Jane Wilder. To Laura's surprise, Jane Wilder's brother, Almanzo, a homesteader near Silver Lake, courted Laura, even though she was ten years his junior. About this time, Laura received her teaching certificate and began work at a school 12 miles south of De Smet, where she boarded with the Bouchie family. On weekends, Almanzo drove her home in his cutter pulled by matched Morgans. For three years, she continued seeing Almanzo, whom she called Manly. He called her Bess. Then, not wholly pleased with her new career, she returned to her family.

A week before Christmas in Laura's seventeenth year, Almanzo kissed his best girl in front of her family, thereby demonstrating his intentions to marry her. With her earnings from a school term at the Wilkins School, Laura bought sheep for her future home. She wed Almanzo Wilder on August 25, 1885. The weekly newspaper noted, "Thus two more of our respected young people have united in the journey of life. May their voyage be pleasant, their joys be many, and their sorrows few."[2]

## Laura Wilder, Farm Wife

The good wishes of the newspaper item failed to charm away a depressing series of miseries for the new family. On December 5, 1887, Laura gave birth to a daughter, Rose. She was not at all sure she enjoyed the life of a farm wife, even though she was married to a progressive farmer like Almanzo Wilder who bought the latest machinery for plowing and harvesting. Debts piled up. Their barn burned the summer of 1887.

The troubles of the Wilders became more life-threatening. Laura and Almanzo suffered diphtheria. As a result of the illness, Almanzo had a stroke and never recovered full strength on one side of his body. In 1889, Laura had a second child, a son, who died within twelve days and was buried without a name. Two weeks later, the Wilders' house burned to the ground. Laura managed to save one dish, a glass bread plate etched with the words "Give us this day Our daily bread."[3]

The family sold Laura's sheep to finance a move to Almanzo's parents' house in Spring Valley, Minnesota, and from there by train to Westville, Florida. By 1892, they had returned to the Dakota Territory because of Laura's inability to adjust to the damp swampy climate. They returned to De Smet, where Charles and Caroline had built a frame house and Mary had returned from school. The Wilders bought a house nearby. Laura worked for a dressmaker; Almanzo did odd jobs.

## Home in the Ozark Hills

By 1894, the family had saved enough to leave the dreary Dakota prairie. On the way, Laura continued writing her impressions in her journal. To improve the family's health, they settled on a farm in the Ozark mountains near Mansfield, Missouri. Laura noted that "one of us was not able to stand the severe cold of the North, while another could not live in the low altitude and humid heat of the Southern states."[4] She wrote an account of her journey and mailed it to the *De Smet News*. It was her first publication.

The couple settled a mile east of town on an unpromising ridge surrounded by apple trees. Laura named it Rocky Ridge Farm. Their work was arduous. Laura helped cut wood to be sold in town. In time their homestead grew from 40 acres to 200. They built their dream house out of local materials. Rose, grown by then, moved to Louisiana with her aunt Eliza Jane and became a journalist, well traveled and sophisticated. Laura and Almanzo lived out their days on the farm.

## Laura the Writer

During her farm years, Wilder wrote for local newspapers, including the *Missouri State Farmer*, Saint Louis papers, and the *Missouri Ruralist*. She wrote a column entitled "The Farm Home," which evolved into a more elaborate department called "As a Farm Woman Thinks." Wilder helped organize clubs for farm women to offer them horizons beyond daily drudgery. She also served as secretary/treasurer of the local branch of the Federal Loan Bank. In 1915, Laura visited Rose in San Francisco and took in the Panama-Pacific International Exposition, but she was eager to return home to describe the sights to Almanzo, who stayed behind to tend the farm.

At age sixty-three, when the Depression robbed people of their hopes and dreams, Wilder, at Rose's insistence, began writing in pencil at her corner study, filling *Little House in the Big Woods* (1932) with details of her pioneer life in Pepin, Wisconsin. Of that first effort she noted, "That book was a labor of love and is really a memorial to my father."[5] Her publisher and readers immediately demanded more of her memories.

From there she followed with *Farmer Boy* (1933), which tells of her husband's childhood. The third book, her most famous, *Little House on the Prairie* (1935), catches up her family's experiences as they move to Kansas. Then follow the remaining five works: *On the Banks of Plum Creek* (1937), concerning the Wilders in the Minnesota wheatlands; *By the Shores of Silver Lake* (1939), detailing Laura's early teens in the Dakota territory; *The Long Winter* (1940), more about her life in the Dakotas; and *These Happy Golden Years* (1943), which describes Laura's classroom experiences at the age of fifteen and her marriage three years later.

Looking over the series near the end of her life, Wilder found a thread of truth that bound them together—the character traits that made her family strong. She enumerated her pioneer values: "They were courage, self-reliance, independence, integrity, and helpfulness. Cheerfulness and humor were handmaids to courage."[6]

## Later Life

Laura and Almanzo returned to De Smet in 1939 for the Old Settlers Day Celebration. Laura wrote of her visit with her sisters and old schoolmates in the *Christian Science Monitor*. Settled back into the routine of Rocky Ridge, the Wilders lived out their days doing chores, playing cribbage, raising goats, reading newspapers, and enjoying each other's company. In the 1940s both Carrie and Grace died, followed by Almanzo in 1946.

Wilder lived on in her farmhouse and continued in her role of local story-teller, buoyed in spirit by neighbors and fan letters, which numbered as many as fifty per day. She even journeyed to Danbury, Connecticut, by airplane to visit Rose. Laura spent part of her last winter in the hospital, lost in memories of the past and awaiting her ninetieth birthday. In January she was allowed to return to Rocky Ridge. She died three days after her birthday, on February 10, 1957, and was buried beside her husband in Mansfield Cemetery.

To the clamor of readers who wanted to know more about Wilder's pioneer adventures, Rose provided a reply. She took her mother's memo pad that served as a journal of the trek from De Smet to Rocky Ridge and transformed it into *On the Way Home* (1962). It left readers with a happy portrait of Laura whistling over her pots as she cooked supper in the windowless cabin.

# Notes

[1]Donald Zochert, *Laura: The Life of Laura Ingalls Wilder.* Chicago: Henry Regnery, 1976, 210.

[2] Zochert, 207.

[3] Zochert, 214.

[4] Zochert, 217.

[5] Zochert, 233.

[6] Zochert, 239.

# Sources

Ehrlich, Eugene, and Gorton Carruth. *The Oxford Illustrated Literary Guide to the United States.* New York: Oxford University Press, 1982.

Wilder, Laura Ingalls, and Rose Wilder Lane. *A Little House Sampler.* Lincoln, Nebraska: University of Nebraska Press, 1988.

Zochert, Donald. *Laura: The Life of Laura Ingalls Wilder.* Chicago: Henry Regnery, 1976.

# William Griffin Wilson

A very few late achievers earn the kind of acclaim that approaches sainthood. One of the most beloved of achievers, known to millions as Bill W., ironically succumbed to alcohol in the period from 1920 to 1933 known as Prohibition, America's doomed experiment with universal temperance. In 1934, he joined with Dr. Bob, a fellow alcoholic, to create Alcoholics Anonymous, the most famous self-help organization in the world.

The birth of their group in 1934, along with the rise of a new philosophy that viewed alcohol as a disease, did more to help recovering alcoholics than all the sanitariums and psychiatric clinics of the past. By sharing experiences, committing themselves to God, and offering strength one on one, Bill Wilson and Bob Smith enabled AA to thrive. Soon there were fledgling groups springing up in communities nationwide.

Through his writings, Bill helped other alcoholics follow twelve steps toward reshaping behavior. In the introduction, he kept a low profile while offering the hope that saved many from early death. The foreword began: "We, of Alcoholics Anonymous, are more than one hundred men and women who have recovered from a seemingly hopeless state of mind and body."[1] Then he explained exactly how a willing candidate could make the transformation from drunk to worthy human being.

Bill continued his work until his death. The *New York Times* placed his obituary on the front page, revealing his identity as the founder of AA. In 1990, *Life* magazine honored Bill by naming him one of the 100 outstanding people in America in the twentieth century.

## A Drinking Family

William Griffin Wilson was born of Scotch-Irish stock in East Dorset, Vermont, on November 26, 1895. From childhood, Bill, son of Emily and Gilman "Gilly" Wilson, accepted his father's heavy drinking as a normal pattern. Bill's father, the foreman of a marble quarry, cultivated his winning ways and entertained company with witty stories and comic antics. Bill and younger sister Dorothy found more substance in their mother, a bright, cheerful, purposeful woman, who held the family together as her husband slid deeply into alcoholism.

By 1904, however, the family unit was shattered by divorce, brought on, as Bill recalls, by Gilly's drinking. Bill and his sister settled in with their maternal grandparents while Gilly moved to Canada to establish a new life and eventually remarry. Emily, their mother, moved to Boston and enrolled in osteopathy training. Bill never thought of himself as deprived. On the contrary, his doting grandparents bought him a horse, radio, motorcycle, and violin. He played first chair in the school orchestra. Even though he never became adept at music, he depended on it to soothe his emotional problems.

Like his experience with music, many of the challenges Bill faced he failed to master. Yet his drive, ambition, and competitive spirit assured him that he had the capacity to do almost anything he desired, For example, he was a mediocre athlete, yet drove himself to be captain of the school baseball team.

While boarding at Burr and Burton Seminary in Manchester, Vermont, in 1909, Bill faced ups and downs in his personal life. He formed a lasting friendship with Ebby Thatcher, who returned to his life when Bill needed him most. Bill's first romance ended badly when his girlfriend died in 1912. This period brought on deep depression, which set him on the path to alcoholism. Troubled by manic-depressive mood swings, Bill studied at Norwich University, where he moved from depression into fantasy to compensate for low self-esteem.

## A Career in Alcohol

About this time, Wilson began to show signs of hypochondria. Underweight and immature in many respects, he suffered trembling, heart palpitations, exaggerated fears, and other symptoms connected with anxiety attacks. At one point he dropped out of school and returned to his grandparents' care before re-enrolling.

In addition to health problems, Bill was diffident and felt rejected by his peers. He was moderately handsome at six feet two inches with slender face and features and blue eyes. But he lacked the graces that would bring him social acclaim—skill in sports and music—and received no bids from fraternities. At the age of eighteen, he began dating dark-haired socialite Lois Burnham, who was four years his senior and a graduate of Packer Collegiate Institute. Lois was sophisticated, yet devoted to Bill. Their relationship was rocky from the start, owing in part to Bill's resentment of Lois's maternal treatment and possessiveness. After a three-year engagement, they married in 1918, one year after Bill began drinking.

His first experience with alcohol had come during a party for Army officers shortly before Bill entered World War I. A second lieutenant, he was stationed at Fort Rodman, New Bedford, Massachusetts. To steady himself in the social setting, he took a drink. Bill recalls the beginning: "That barrier that had always stood between me and other people came down. I felt I belonged, that I was part of life. What magic there was in those drinks! I could talk and be clever."[2]

Of this time, Lois, from another perspective, penned in her memoirs: "Bill had been warned since childhood not to touch alcohol. His mother had divorced his father largely because of drink, he thought."[3] The signs were immediately bad for the Wilsons' marriage and Bill's future. From the first episode, he could not control his drinking and never stopped until he passed out.

Finding a job presented an additional set of difficulties to the newlyweds. Bill served in Europe in the Coast Artillery during World War I, returned in 1919, and settled in New York. Without professional training, he had difficulty finding meaningful, steady work. He worked as a clerk, a dockhand, and an insurance fraud investigator. He quit one post because he refused to be pressured into joining a union. In an attempt to set himself up in a profession, he enrolled in a Brooklyn night school to study law, but was never sober long enough to pass the bar exam.

In 1922, Lois, after suffering an ectopic pregnancy, tried two more times to conceive. Each attempt ended the same way—with the egg attaching to the fallopian tube rather than inside the uterus. She and Bill had to accept a bitter truth, that they could not have children. They both wanted a family, so they put their hopes in adoption. Because Bill continued to behave badly in public during drinking bouts, adoption agencies rejected the Wilsons as worthy parents.

## Making It in Business

In the late 1920s, Bill and Lois undertook a new venture. Aboard a Harley-Davidson motorcycle, they traveled for a year to various factories and businesses along the eastern seaboard as far south as Florida. Bill hoped to provide stock market investors with an analysis of each company's prospects. Living from the tent they kept in the sidecar, the Wilsons cooked over a fire and studied stock manuals. Lois, less concerned with business than Bill, encouraged their gypsy existence to keep her husband out of bars.

The upshot of their experiment was a full-time job for Bill as a securities analyst with a New York financier, an old friend of Lois. The Wilsons, riding high at country club affairs and living in luxury, ignored ominous signs that pointed to Bill's growing dependency. The mix of New York night spots and Bill's urge for booze led to bad times. Reflecting over his collapse into full-blown alcoholism, Bill recalls that daily drinking and his resulting testy personality cost him friends. He began to drink alone. His marriage faltered, yet Lois stuck by him.

When the stock market crashed in October 1929, Wilson rejected the easy out of suicide. He found his solace in bars and increased his intake to three bottles of gin a day. The couple, instantly broke with the toppling of the market, had to move in with Lois's newly widowed father in Brooklyn Heights. While Bill drowned himself in drink, Lois took a low-paying job as a counter girl at Macy's department store.

## The Beginning of the End

With the nation suffering a severe depression, Bill skidded to the bottom. He tried to keep up appearances among his brokerage contacts. Bedeviled by hangovers and hallucinations, he begged money on street corners or pilfered from Lois's purse. The couple confronted each other with a host of frustrations, the worst of which were bouts of violence in which Bill vented his drunken rages at Lois's expense, once throwing a sewing machine at her. He lost control and wandered the subways while downing more booze. Back home, he smashed walls and kicked in doors.

The binges took their toll. Bill ate sparingly, lost weight, and demonstrated signs of brain damage. His mood swings carried him from starry-eyed highs to abysmal lows. Like many drunks, he maintained a secret cache of bottles around the house and continued to act the fool in public. To save himself from jumping out a window, he moved his mattress to the first floor. Lois, in exasperation, called him a sot.

In 1933, Dr. Leonard Strong, husband of Bill's sister Dorothy, convinced Bill to seek help. He entered Charles B. Towns Hospital in Manhattan. The facility, a favorite drying-out spot for elite alcoholics, dosed Bill with narcotics and laxatives. Even with the understanding of Dr. William Duncan Silkworth, a pioneer in the philosophy that alcoholism was a physical inability to tolerate drink rather than moral depravity, Bill failed to make the most of his opportunity to gain control, although he did remain dry for several months.

Back on the streets, he drank harder than ever. His drunken stupors resulted in abuse of Lois as well as frequent falls and accidents. In 1934, Ebby, his old schoolmate and former drinking pal, showed up and demonstrated his newfound strength by refusing to join Wilson in a drink. Wilson tittered at the notion of Ebby's finding religion, but he heeded the story of the Oxford Group, a spiritual foundation that promised hope for alcoholics.

## Finding a Cure

Once again admitting himself to Dr. Silkworth's care after three failed attempts to dry out, Wilson committed himself to the plan that had saved Ebby. He established a strong relationship with God, examined his shortcomings, and sought the pardon of those he had wronged. The change was not instantaneous. Bleak moods pushed Wilson toward deeper prayer. While exploring a stronger spirituality, he experienced conversion. In his own words, "I felt lifted up, as though the great clean wind of a mountain top blew through and through."[4] He remained sober from December 18, 1934, to the end of his life.

Not completely sure of his path, Wilson approached his new sobriety from many spiritual directions over the years, including worship, LSD, and seances. With Lois's help, he attended meetings of the Oxford Group, which were held in homes and hotels. Still unemployed, he turned from sodden escapes into gin to missionary zeal toward rescuing others. Although he made no converts in these crude attempts, he found salvation in association with others traveling the path he had abandoned.

## Finding a Partner

Although he was moving in the right direction, Bill still needed shoring up when his confidence flagged. He admitted that his evangelical approach toward curing other alcoholics was ineffective. An optimistic try at re-entering the business world proved fruitless. In the spring of 1935, overcome with the urge for a drink, he made a call from the lobby of the Mayflower Hotel in Akron, Ohio, that led to his meeting Dr. Robert Smith, a surgeon and fellow drunk.

Bob, himself reaching the pits of alcoholic despair, had jeopardized his medical practice and abused his family with a barrage of drunken binges. He learned of the Oxford Group and admired its spiritual calm. Still, he found it difficult to give up his secretive drinking habits and steady himself along the way to sobriety.

In June, Bill Wilson moved in with the Smiths. Following a lost weekend at an AMA convention, Bob took his last drink on June 10, 1935, and then committed himself to Bill's program of helping other alcoholics. Joining a third drinker, a lawyer known as Bill D., Bill W. and Dr. Bob launched a formal association that remained unnamed until 1939. From that time on, the organization helped all comers who were willing to accept God's help in controlling their craving for drink.

After months of work with Bob in Akron, Bill returned home in August 1935. He had to acclimate Lois to his new self. At first, she resented his fellowship with other alcoholics. Then she and Bill opened their door to needy drunks.

## A Neophyte Association

At first, the group met at the Wilson home in New York before moving to West 23rd Street. To solidify the members' intent, in 1938 Bill wrote a 164-page description of the group's method and titled it *Alcoholics Anonymous*. The name stuck. Word spread among people desperate for salvation from drink. More joined the group; some bought Bill's book. Publicity in *Liberty* magazine and *The Saturday Evening Post* supported the idea of a self-help group for alcoholics. By 1941, the prototype group in Brooklyn was emulated throughout the United States.

As Bill evolved the steps to help alcoholics accept themselves and overcome their crutch, he added concepts gleaned from the writings of psychologist William James. Crucial to alcoholic control was the idea that the alcoholic had to reach the extreme of despair. Then came a genuine admission of loss of control. Third in order was hardest for Bill himself to accept—dependence on a higher power.

The group appealed mainly to older men who had "been around" and were ready for a change. Younger alcoholics and all women were excluded in the early days. Most converts submitted to hospitalization and received one-on-one visits from Bob, Bill, or others in the group. During these consultations, they shared stories of their mutual addiction and degradation from alcohol. Those who stayed with the program accepted the assistance of a higher power, inventoried their character flaws, and made amends to the people they had hurt during their addiction.

The meetings, usually held in homes, were quiet times of meditation, Bible reading, and moral support. All members kept their homes open to each other. Because recovering alcoholics were poor, they shared humble meals and kept the coffee pot ready. Spouses were supportive but barred from the actual meetings.

## Returning to Normal Life

Wilson made sporadic attempts to work. In 1937, he was offered a job as lay counselor at the Towns Hospital. But his fellow group members opposed professionalizing the AA concept and Wilson changed his mind about accepting the job and about seeking funds from the Rockefeller Foundation. Instead, he rejected outside funding, receiving money only from book royalties.

Not all medical experts agreed with Wilson's approach to helping recovering alcoholics. In 1939, the American Medical Association ridiculed AA's approach. In contrast, however, the *New York Times* and Harry Emerson Fosdick, noted minister at the Riverside Church in New York, openly agreed with Wilson and his group psychology. By the mid-1940s, Wilson was spreading the word about AA through a monthly magazine, *The Grapevine.*

Following Dr. Bob's death in 1950, Wilson continued to head AA alone. He crossed the country, speaking to groups and offering his literature for their support. He received a Lasker Group Award and an honorary doctorate from Yale. *Time* magazine offered to feature him in a cover story, which he refused. Members of AA bestowed a form of unofficial sainthood on him, which caused him much discomfort.

Money from his publications began to compensate the Wilsons for their years of poverty. Even though Wilson spent his last years with numerous lovers, he and Lois continued their teamwork. His dedication to AA remained unquestioned. A heavy smoker, he developed emphysema in the late 1960s, delivered a final address to an AA convention from a wheelchair in 1970, and died in Miami on January 24, 1971. At his funeral, fellow AA members read from St. Francis's prayer: "That where there is despair, I may bring hope ... That where there is sadness, I may bring joy."[5]

# Notes

[1] Nan Robertson. *Getting Better: Inside Alcoholics Anonymous.* New York: William Morrow, 1988, 71.

[2] Bob P. "Unforgettable Bill W.," *Reader's Digest*, April 1986, 68.

[3] Robertson, 40.

[4] Robertson, 45.

[5] Robert Thomsen. *Bill W.* New York: Harper & Row, 1975, 369.

# Sources

"The 100 Most Important Americans of the Twentieth Century," *Life*, Fall 1990, 66.

P., Bob. "Unforgettable Bill W.," *Reader's Digest*, April 1986, 65-71.

Robertson, Nan. *Getting Better: Inside Alcoholics Anonymous.* New York: William Morrow, 1988.

Thomsen, Robert. *Bill W.* New York: Harper & Row, 1975.

920
S

Snodgrass, Mary
Ellen.

Late achievers.

$24.95